Counselling Skills in Action

SAGE Counselling in Action

is a bestselling series of short, practical introductions designed for students and trainees. Covering theory and practice, the books are core texts for many courses, both in counselling and other professions such as nursing, social work and teaching.

Books in the series include:

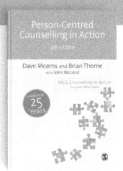

| 978-1-4462-5253-6 | 978-1-4739-1397-4 | 978-1-4739-9816-2 | 978-1-4462-1128-1 |

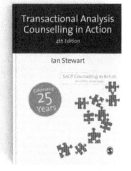

| 978-1-4462-5328-1 | 978-1-4739-1369-1 | 978-1-4462-5293-2 | 978-1-4129-0213-7 |

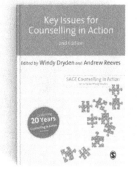
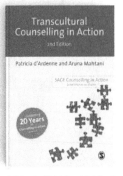
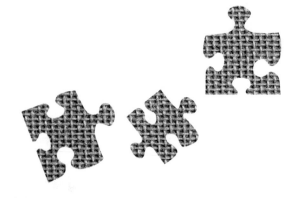

| 978-1-4129-4699-5 | 978-0-7619-6315-8 |

Counselling Skills in Action

4th Edition

Megan R. Stafford and Tim Bond

SAGE Counselling in Action
Series Editor Windy Dryden

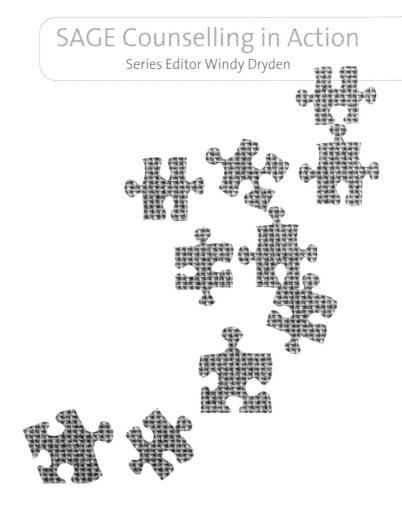

Los Angeles | London | New Delhi
Singapore | Washington DC | Melbourne

Los Angeles | London | New Delhi
Singapore | Washington DC | Melbourne

SAGE Publications Ltd
1 Oliver's Yard
55 City Road
London EC1Y 1SP

SAGE Publications Inc.
2455 Teller Road
Thousand Oaks, California 91320

SAGE Publications India Pvt Ltd
B 1/I 1 Mohan Cooperative Industrial Area
Mathura Road
New Delhi 110 044

SAGE Publications Asia-Pacific Pte Ltd
3 Church Street
#10-04 Samsung Hub
Singapore 049483

Editor: Susannah Trefgarne
Editorial assistant: Ruth Lilly
Production editor: Rachel Burrows
Marketing manager: Dilhara Attygalle
Cover design: Naomi Robinson
Typeset by: C&M Digitals (P) Ltd, Chennai, India

Library of Congress Control Number: 2019949838

British Library Cataloguing in Publication data

A catalogue record for this book is available from the British Library

ISBN 978-1-4739-9817-9
ISBN 978-1-4739-9818-6 (pbk)

For my mum and dad, Lona Samuel and Christopher Stafford, with love always.

Contents

List of Online Resources

Counselling Skills in Action, Fourth Edition comes with over 30 videos. Visit https://study.sagepub.com/staffordandbond4e to gain access to the videos below.

Chapter 1

Video 1.1   The Aims of Counselling Skills

Video 1.2   The Therapeutic Relationship – Relationship vs. Friendship

Video 1.3   The Therapeutic Relationship – Key Points

Video 1.4   Crossing Boundaries – Scenario

Video 1.5   Crossing Boundaries – Discussion

Video 1.6   Avoiding Exploitation of Clients – Scenario

Video 1.7   Avoiding Exploitation of Clients – Discussion

Chapter 3

Video 3.1   Expressing Warmth and Care

Video 3.2   Active Listening

Video 3.3   Reflecting, Paraphrasing, Summarizing

Video 3.4   Asking Open-Ended Questions

Chapter 4

Video 4.1   Can You Help Me? – Scenario

Video 4.2   Can You Help Me? – Discussion

Video 4.3   Contracting – Scenario

Video 4.4   Contracting – Discussion

Video 4.5   Being Non-Judgemental

The videos are also listed at the end of each chapter so you can decide where you want to take your learning journey.

For instructors: The videos come with a 'Guide to Teaching' that includes the video URLs and potential discussion questions, and can be accessed on the online resource site landing page.

About the Authors

Megan R. Stafford is a UKCP (United Kingdom Council for Psychotherapy) registered psychotherapist in private practice, a lecturer at the University of Roehampton and a module leader at Metanoia Institute where she teaches on integrative, relational counselling and psychotherapy training programs. She has worked for many years as a researcher, including work in mental health and wellbeing, developing guidelines for the National Institute for Health and Care Excellence (NICE) at the National Collaborating Centre for Mental Health, and most recently evaluating humanistic therapy for young people at the University of Roehampton. Megan integrates a developmental, relational and transpersonal approach in her practice to consider working therapeutically with her clients' developmental traumas, current relational difficulties and future aspirations. She lives in West London, where she is about to embark on a loving renovation of her flat and perfecting her pastry skills now that she has a little more time on her hands.

Tim Bond is an Emeritus Professor at the University of Bristol and Visiting Professor to the University of Malta. He has used, researched and taught counselling skills in a wide range of settings. He has also written about professional ethics for counselling and the talking therapies. He is a consultant to the British Association for Counselling and Psychotherapy (BACP) on professional ethics and standards, and a member of the Ethics Committee for the British Psychological Society (BPS) and the Executive Council of the International Association for Counselling (IAC). He is a registered member of the BACP and provides counselling supervision and training workshops.

Preface

I am pleased to recommend this new edition to all users of counselling skills, especially trainees in counselling and the talking therapies. Counselling skills are an essential component of being a competent counsellor or therapist that change over time as our profession develops. This edition captures the latest developments by giving priority to the quality of the relationship between practitioner and client as the foundation of how we work with our clients. Every aspect of counselling skills has been reconsidered from this viewpoint.

As I move into retirement, I wanted to find someone from a younger generation who can take this widely used book forward and ensure that it remains relevant to current practice. I was looking for someone who is rooted in practice to ensure that this book communicates well to practitioners by understanding their concerns and challenges. My ideal person is someone who is also involved in training in order to be skilled in communicating ideas and practice in ways that meet the needs of trainees. I was also looking for someone who is actively researching counselling practice so that they are working at the cutting edge of new ideas and developments in practice.

I am delighted to introduce Megan Stafford as the leading author of this edition. She is an experienced practitioner, trainer and researcher. When we met for the first time in the University of Roehampton and I heard her ideas for this edition I was excited. My initial positive impressions have been confirmed as this edition developed. She has cut through the potential complexity of counselling skills to produce a book that is clear, practical and up to date.

I hope that I have been as helpful to Megan as Sue Culley[1] was to me when she was looking for someone to continue writing new editions of the book she started. She used her considerable expertise to write the early editions that helped to establish counselling skills as essential to all good counselling practice. I am fortunate to have carried the baton for counselling skills between two such able people.

One of the delights of learning counselling skills is their dynamic quality and capacity to support life-enhancing changes. They challenge us to relate and communicate better. In doing so they change us, by expanding our awareness of who we are, and how we relate to others. We may set out learning them to help others but, in doing so, we are also helped. I am at that stage of life when I am handing on professional roles and responsibilities to others, but I won't be giving up my practice of counselling skills. I am continuing to use them in new roles as a volunteer.

Tim Bond

---

[1]Sue Culley – the author of the early editions of this book whose expertise helped to establish counselling skills as an essential component of all good counselling practice.

Acknowledgements

I would like to thank Tim Bond and Mick Cooper for their encouragement, belief and this opportunity. Thanks also to Susannah Trefgarne, Talulah Hall and Ruth Lilly at SAGE for their work on this book, and their professional support and patience. I am enormously grateful to the various colleagues at Metanoia Institute and the University of Roehampton who I have worked with over the years, and have been integral to my development as a therapist, trainer and writer. In particular I would like to acknowledge the special support of Steven and Anne Smith, Paula McMahon, Lynette Harbourne and Paul Hitchings who have all in some way shaped and supported my career endeavours. Thanks also to Chris Elliot and Lucy Owen who I worked and learned with in a peer group through some of the writing of this book. In addition, a very special thanks to all the clients and students I have worked with who have taught me so much about the therapeutic relationship.

With personal thanks to my loving family and friends who I feel so blessed to have alongside me in life. In particular, those who have been such a support to me while I have been writing this book, always asking how I'm doing with care and kindness and offering pearls of wisdom and fire under my toes when I've needed it the most: my mum and dad, my Syndicate Girls (Kate McLarnon, Ellie Urban-Large, Bea Brennan and Samantha Thomas), Elaine Shelabarger, Geoffrey Samuel, John McCann, my sister Issy Stafford and brother Rory Stafford, Josh Darling and Caz Coronel. Your interest in what I have been writing about has always meant a lot to me.

Tim Bond would like to thank Sue Culley, the author of the early editions of this book, whose expertise helped to establish counselling skills as an essential component of all good counselling practice.

1

Learning Skills in Counselling and Psychotherapy

Chapter contents

This chapter covers:

- The differences between counselling and psychotherapy and other ways of helping
- What is distinctive about counselling and psychotherapy
- The learning process
- Ethics
- Further resources

Introduction

This book is about the art of communication. Specifically, it is about learning to listen, to share and to articulate thoughts and feelings with the express intention of facilitating another person to change and heal. It has been written for trainees learning counselling and psychotherapy skills for the first time; and qualified therapists who are looking to return to the core skills needed in their counselling and psychotherapy practice.

Within this book, you will find a skills-based 'stage model' of counselling and psychotherapy. Skills training is a required component of most training in counselling and psychotherapy and applied psychology. Skills training speaks to the idea that in order to be a competent counsellor or psychotherapist, you will require more than emotional insight and a relevant pool of theoretical knowledge – you will also need to be able to communicate effectively. Feelings, insight and knowledge have little impact if they cannot be articulated and shared. This expands our attention beyond knowledge and insight and out towards an understanding that counselling and psychotherapy is about far more than dialogical content. Rather, it is also about – or perhaps we might even say it is defined by – process. That is, it is not simply about what you communicate, but about how you communicate.

There is an ongoing debate within the profession about the differences between 'counselling' and 'psychotherapy', and indeed, whether any differences really exist in practice. To enter into this debate is beyond the scope of the current text; however, the reader may be interested to look at The Scope of Practice and Education (SCoPEd) project for the counselling and psychotherapy professions (SCoPEd, 2019), in which the British Association for Counselling and Psychotherapy (BACP), the British Psychoanalytic Council (BPC) and the United Kingdom Council for Psychotherapy (UKCP) have collaborated. The aim is to agree a shared, evidence-based competence framework to inform the core training requirements, competences and practice standards for counsellors and psychotherapists. In the current book, we have felt it unnecessary to attempt a differentiation between counselling and psychotherapy as our aim is to provide a key text for the development (and/or improvement) of core skills relevant across these professional roles. We therefore use the terms 'counselling and psychotherapy', 'psychotherapeutic skills [or practice]', 'therapy' or 'therapist' when referring to the profession, professional activity or professional role. In addition, we use the term 'client' for the recipient of psychotherapeutic skills. Some readers may wish to substitute a term that is more appropriate to the context in which they are learning and practising.

This book is structured around a straightforward conceptual framework that provides a 'template' for guiding and shaping the therapy process from initiation to closure. This template is called 'The Stage Model', an overview of which is provided in Chapter 2. The Stage Model rests on a set of values or guiding principles we have called the 'Ten Principles for Practice' (also provided in Chapter 2), and a set of core communication skills referred to as 'foundation skills' (discussed in Chapter 3). Chapters 4, 5 and 6 provide details for each stage of the model: the Beginning Stage, Middle Stage and Ending Stage respectively. We also offer an example of using The Stage Model in practice, drawing on a clinical case example (Chapter 8). In our experience, the idea of discrete stages is beneficial to learning and applying psychotherapeutic skills as they provide a kind of navigation aid for the therapist to identify aims, plans and skills to employ during different phases of the work. The actual practice of using psychotherapeutic skills is invariably not so well ordered. The client is neither required to read about counselling and psychotherapy nor have trained in these disciplines. Furthermore, they are not required to fit the text book and may present their story in any way they like, even if this complicates the sequence of stages. We therefore hope to respond to the potential complexity of using the skills proffered in this book by offering our thoughts on moving between stages, as well as providing a chapter on 'challenging situations' (Chapter 7). In Chapter 9, we consider achieving success in your practice by applying your learning. As a skills-based resource, this book does not attempt to provide the reader with theory and knowledge derived from any one school, or modality, within counselling and psychotherapy. You may therefore wish to refer to the SAGE Skills in Counselling and Psychotherapy series for details on working from a particular theoretical orientation.

We begin this book with a brief overview of the counselling and psychotherapy relationship, the learning process in acquiring counselling and psychotherapy skills, and the importance of using an ethical framework to inform psychotherapeutic work.

What is the difference between counselling and psychotherapy relationships, and other ways of helping?

Psychotherapy is not a modern intervention, but a relationship-based learning environment grounded in the history of our social brains. (Cozolino, 2016: 17)

We are social creatures. We are born ready to relate to one another, with inbuilt systems that help us attach, engage and manage our relationships through the lifespan. For example, human babies are born with a preference for human voices and a fascination with the human face. Babies have an innate capacity to be soothed by relational activities, such as hearing a familiar voice, being touched and being rocked to sleep (Gerhardt, 2015). Being social improves our chances of survival because relationships offer important psychological, neurological and physiological functions. Numerous research studies within the field of neuroscience have shown that the development of the human brain is 'experience dependent' and without consistent and caring social experiences our neurological development can be significantly and negatively impacted. For example, in 2001, Chughani and colleagues conducted a study of Romanian orphans and found that these babies, neglected for long periods and cut off from forming relationships with an adult caregiver, had significantly impaired neuroanatomical structures in areas responsible for processing emotions, long-term memory, moderating social behaviour, complex cognitive activity and personality expression. Equally striking are research studies looking at the effects of loneliness and social isolation in adulthood. These studies show that these experiences are correlated with a range of health problems – for example, increased mortality (Holt-Lunstad, 2015), coronary heart disease and stroke (Valtorta et al., 2016), cognitive decline (James et al., 2011) and an increased chance of experiencing depression (Cacioppo et al., 2006).

So, we need one another. Our relationships with others not only hold the potential to provide us with essential psychological and physiological regulatory capacities, but also a sense of meaning, of belonging and of being loved. Through interactions with our fellow human beings we learn, grow and find nourishment and healing. Through our conversations with friends and loved ones, our shared construction of narrative and implicit communications provide comfort, support and perspective.

Contemporary thinking within the fields of counselling and psychotherapy focuses on this very idea and acknowledges the centrality of relationship in human suffering and human healing. The 'relational turn' marks a shift away from previous ideas about human beings as individual, separate and entirely autonomous entities, and instead recognizes human beings as fundamentally linked, embedded in a web of co-created relatedness. This is known as a '2-person philosophy'. That is, every act of relating and every interpersonal interaction happens within the context of an 'intersubjective matrix'. This matrix contains the subjective experiences of all parties, and these different subjectivities influence, shape and determine the interpersonal experience between individuals. At one level, the 'talking therapies' are all rooted in this seemingly simple interpersonal capacity. So, what is the difference between talking to a good friend, or an understanding work colleague, and talking to a therapist?

Many of our everyday relationships, like those with friends, mentors, teachers or nurses, have the potential to provide many of the qualities outlined above. However, there are some key differences between these relationships and working with a counsellor or psychotherapist. Bond (2015) also draws our attention to the differences between using counselling skills and 'embedded counselling'. Counselling skills may be evident in some social skills and interpersonal skills, or utilized in other professions such as nursing, personnel management or teaching. However, embedded counselling (and psychotherapy) is exemplified by a particular pattern of communication, the agenda the individuals involved engage with and the explicit contracting that takes place between the individuals.

In counselling and psychotherapy relationships all of the following features are present. This is unlike other kinds of relationships and dialogues wherein these features may sometimes be present and at other times not:

- **Purpose and agenda.** The purpose of the encounter is predetermined and explicit: the intention is to effect some kind of change in, or for, the client. The therapist's role is to provide support for the client to do so. It may be that both parties are changed in this process, but the purpose of the work relates specifically to the client's level of change. Therefore, in counselling and psychotherapy, the client's agenda will be at the heart of the work. That is, whatever the particular approach taken, the purpose of therapy will always be centred around the material the client has brought.
- **Boundaries**. In effective and ethical counselling and psychotherapy, boundaries too are clear and explicit. This helps establish the 'therapeutic frame'. Boundary setting involves a conversation between client and therapist regarding expectations, hopes, fears and limitations of working in a counselling or psychotherapy relationship. A written or verbal contract between client and therapist will also be established as part of that conversation. Boundaries that speak to this therapeutic frame include:
  - creating a confidential space
  - providing a regular, protected meeting time
  - taking an active approach to avoid or minimize role duality and conflicts of interest
  - an appreciation for the issue of time.
- **Role specification**. The role of the counsellor or psychotherapist is to draw on an appropriate set of qualities and apply a particular set of skills. For example, the therapist attempts to take a non-judgemental attitude to their client's issues, actively and empathically listening to what the client brings. Therapists are trained to notice when their own preferences, biases and opinions are preventing or obscuring their ability to stay with the client's agenda, and how to manage this such that the integrity of the work can be maintained. The role of the client is to simply be themselves. In counselling and psychotherapy, there is an active attempt to avoid any ambiguity as to whose job it is to do what.

- **Professional regulation and ethical frameworks**. Counsellors and psycho-therapists who are committed to providing a good standard of care hold member-ship with a regulatory and professional organization. Such organizations clearly stipulate adherence to an ethical framework within which counsellors and psycho-therapists work (see further resources) and maintain standards for training and professional issues in practice. In the UK, two such key organizations are the BACP and the UKCP.

The learning process

Understanding how you learn, and what your personal as well as external resources for learning are, will aid you enormously in the journey of acquiring counselling and psychotherapy skills. This journey is potentially a challenging one. Such skills cannot be learnt as impersonal techniques, and as such the development of these skills can demand a great deal of you emotionally and personally. You may find, for example, that in build-ing these skills your relationships with family members, partners, friends or colleagues are impacted. Good counselling skills can be helpful in your personal relationships, though you may need to be careful about holding space for relating in other ways too. You might also find that you become more acutely aware of when such skills and quali-ties have helped deepen your bonds with others. Conversely, you may become more keenly aware of when they are (and/or have been) lacking in your relationships with people around you.

The stages of learning

Real knowledge is to know the extent of one's ignorance. (Confucius, 551BC–479BC)

The development of counselling and psychotherapeutic skills can be captured as stages, known as the 'conscious competence model' developed by Noel Burch in the 1970s (see Adams, n.d.):

Stage 1: Unconscious incompetence

We start in a place of blissful ignorance. We are not actively or consciously aware of how we communicate, respond and contribute to our interpersonal experiences or our reactions to other people's problems. We take listening and responding for granted. The potential for change and healing through our relationships with our clients sits outside of, or at the edge of, our awareness.

Stage 2: Conscious incompetence

In this stage we start to become aware of the typical ways in which we communicate and relate to our clients. In doing so we become cognizant of our limitations, and how and when we may be responding in unhelpful ways. Equally, we may be unable to recognize when what we are doing is helpful, or why it is helpful. This can be uncomfortable and challenging and as a result we may experience confusion and self-doubt. We may question our own value and the qualities we bring to the work as we recognize that our familiar communication style, that we previously perceived as normal and straightforward, may need to be examined and modified. Nevertheless, this is a vital turning point in our learning as it marks the beginning of a new and deeper sense of self-awareness. Possibilities for new ways of being, communicating and relating appear on the horizon, and with them the potential for acquiring new skills.

Stage 3: Conscious competence

As we acquire and begin to apply counselling the psychotherapeutic skills, and observe and experience the effect they have in our work with clients, we become more consciously aware of the competencies we are building. Conscious competence means that not only are we aware of how we can help, and what we need to do and be in order to provide this help, but also that we are in the driving seat of our own learning and practice. The self-awareness that began to emerge in stage 2 enables us to work with our 'learning edges' as well as our strengths. That is, we are active participants in the work, moving, relating and communicating with purpose and intent.

Stage 4: Unconscious competence

In the final stage we become sufficiently confident in our competence that the newly acquired skills form part of our natural repertoire. That is, the new skills are used responsively and almost instinctively without conscious action. Furthermore, these new skills are incorporated quite organically into our own, personal styles of communicating and relating.

The work of a counsellor or psychotherapist is a constant process of learning. Working with and attempting to help people is a complex task. Each one of us is unique, and we bring our uniqueness to every encounter. This means that every new client, relationship and even every conversation can present us with challenges, rewards and uncertainty. For this reason, these stages of learning are best viewed as a cycle (see Figure 1.1). As a psychotherapist in training I (Megan) acquired a basic set of therapeutic skills. As I look back and reflect on my own training, I can see how I moved through each of the stages outlined above as I built up my clinical hours with clients, attended my lectures, participated in experiential process groups and engaged in personal therapy. That being said, as a qualified psychotherapist and trainer I do not languish happily in a state of unconscious competence! New clients, and new life experiences, draw my attention to the things I am still learning and my blind spots continue to regularly, but gradually, nudge themselves into my line of vision.

Equally, skills develop at different rates for different people. This means that we may feel consciously competent in some areas, and consciously incompetent in others. For example, one of my students has found that they have developed their ability to actively listen relatively well; however, they struggle to constructively challenge their clients without feeling they are being unduly critical. Another student has a naturally sharp analytic mind and has learnt to spot themes and patterns as they emerge in their work with their clients; however, they can struggle to hold back from jumping to interpretations, and to move at their clients' pace.

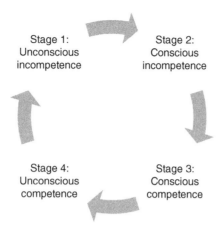

FIGURE 1.1   *The learning cycle*

Experiential learning and learning from experience

Carroll and Gilbert (2011) distinguish between experiential learning and learning from experience. When we are learning experientially, our experience is teaching us unconsciously. We are picking things up implicitly ('Don't touch that, it's hot …'). When we are learning from experience we are deliberately and consciously setting out to learn. Both types of learning – experiential and learning from experience – can aid the development of counselling and psychotherapy skills because together they speak to both the implicit and explicit ways in which we engage with and sense new material and experiences. Kolb (1984) deconstructed learning from experience into a four-stage process:

1.   Experiencing, or 'doing'
2.   Reviewing and reflecting
3.   Learning and drawing conclusions
4.   Applying and experimenting with what has been learnt

Importantly, we can get stuck at any point in this process:

- **We find we are not able to engage in the 'doing'**. For example, in trying to have a conversation with my boss about the amount of overtime I'm doing, and my related stress and sense of dissatisfaction, I find I can't verbalize all the things I planned to say. My heart rate increases, I feel hot and bothered and I can't find my words.
- **We find we cannot draw on our reflective capacity**. Later, when I am reflecting on the conversation with my boss and why I found I couldn't speak, my mind goes blank. I keep thinking, 'I just don't know what happened' and I feel overwhelmed.
- **We find we are confused about what we are learning, or not able to articulate our learning**. I know there is something to be learnt from the

experience, but what is it? Was I under-prepared? Did I choose the wrong time for a meeting? Was his bad mood off-putting? Is this related to my familiar struggle to assert myself?

• **We find we cannot seem to apply what we learn.** When I finally identify that my lack of assertiveness may be the key reason why I struggled to say what I needed to, I find I cannot seem to do things any differently. Back in the office the following Monday I find myself just as tongue-tied and overwhelmed as before.

Reflection point

What impedes your learning?

Think about a time when you struggled to learn from experience – for example, through a conversation with a colleague, or during an experiential exercise in your counselling training.

1. At which point in the four-stage process do you think you became stuck?
2. What got in the way of your ability to learn from experience?
    o   Feeling stressed and overwhelmed
    o   Being driven towards an idea of perfection
    o   Fear
    o   Feeling vulnerable
    o   Wanting to impress someone
    o   Shame
    o   Fatigue
    o   Getting defensive
    o   Overthinking
    o   Something else?

Resources for learning

We all have personal and external resources to draw on in our learning. These resources may also help us to climb out of the hole we can sometimes find ourselves in when we are stuck in any one of the stages outlined above because of fear, or stress or our own defensiveness, etc.

Personal resources

Reflective and reflexive practice

> Reflection is the ability to think about the past, in the present, for the future.
> (Carroll and Gilbert, 2011: 85)

Reflective practice involves using a metaphorical microscope to examine our experience and its component parts. Through this microscope we might notice familiar patterns and identify our strengths and the things that particularly interest us within a given experience. Reflective practice also involves an honest appreciation of our mistakes – that is, understanding, using and building on our mistakes, rather than ignoring or dismissing them. As the Irish novelist James Joyce (1882–1941) once said, 'Mistakes are the portals of discovery.' Reflective practice is therefore an essential component of learning. In fact, Bager-Charleson (2010) describes reflective practice as guiding us to a place of 'transformative learning'. Reflection involves 'Becoming students of our own experience … sitting at the feet of our work' (Zachary, 2002: xv). Therefore, developing the capacity to work in this way will provide you with a great deal of support as you develop and acquire counselling and psychotherapy skills.

Donald Schon (1930–1997) is a key figure in the theory and practice of reflective professional learning. Two of Schon's fundamental theoretical constructs included 'reflection-on-action' and 'reflection-in-action'. These distinguish the acts of looking back on an experience, such as our work with a client, and thinking about what happened with time, space and safety (reflection-on-action), and 'on the spot' observation and reflection occurring in real time (reflection-in-action). Reflecting on and within an experience helps us to make sense of what has happened and to derive meanings and insights which we can hopefully then apply to future practice. In order to facilitate this process, we must engage in both reflective practice and reflexive practice (reflexivity).

When we are reflecting, we are looking back and describing what we noticed. We are asking ourselves things like: What happened? What was said? How would I describe the interpersonal process? What was going on before and after? When we are working reflexively, we deepen our practice further still by appreciating that what we perceive, how and when we interact with what we perceive and what meanings we draw out of a given experience are all influenced by our subjectivity – that is, our particular, unique standpoint. In the moment, we may or may not be conscious of our influence, or that our standpoint is subjective and unique. However, reflexive practice involves recognizing the powerful effect that the 'me' in the experience has. The 'me' includes the influence of such things as race, sex, gender, culture and age, as well as personal histories, values, emotions and beliefs to name but a few. I like to think of reflective practice as involving the ability to watch yourself work, and then respond to what you see. Reflexive practice takes this to another level wherein you watch yourself watching yourself. At this level of deep engagement, you are able to notice what it is about you that shapes the experience and the way you perceive it.

Reflective practice is an essential component of learning and of working as a counsellor and psychotherapist. It can be supported enormously through supervision and personal therapy, which is why accredited training courses emphasize the importance of each throughout the training process. Reflective practice can also be enhanced and supported in other ways – for example, keeping a reflective journal. Throughout this book you will find exercises ('reflection points') that are intended to encourage you to pause and reflect on the material you are encountering. You may wish to record some of your responses to these as you go along.

Reflection point

Your life journey

Reflect on your own life story. Map out your journey to this point, identifying what influenced your choice to train in counselling or psychotherapy (an example is shown in Figure 1.2). Consider the following questions:

- When did you first become interested in the field of counselling and psychotherapy?
- Have you ever been a client in counselling or psychotherapy? What was this experience like?
- What were the significant events, or moments, in your life that might have influenced your interest in counselling and psychotherapy?
- How have your relationships played a role in choosing to train in counselling and psychotherapy?

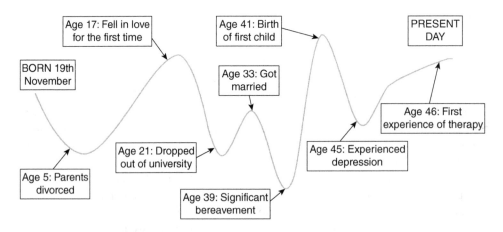

FIGURE 1.2   *Example time line: Personal events of significance to me*

Strengths, limitations, blind spots and learning edges

Understanding our strengths and limitations is an important task in developing counselling and psychotherapy skills. This understanding can be built up through reflective practice and helps us spot where we currently sit in the learning cycle. Most of us are able to name some of our strengths and limitations (though from experience it seems that, sadly, many of us do better at naming our limitations) and it is likely that some of these strengths and limitations that are known to us are also known to others – our friends, family and colleagues. However, there are also aspects of ourselves that sit 'out of awareness', things about ourselves that others know about us, but we do not – for example, a habit we haven't noticed, a facial expression we often pull, a skill we are not conscious of, a tendency or preference we haven't spotted. Joseph Luft (1916–2014) and Harrington Ingham (1916–1995) described this unawareness of self as a 'blind spot' and developed a model to depict what is known and unknown about us in relation to others. They named this model the 'Johari window' (Luft and Ingham, 1955; see Tables 1.1 and 1.2). The Johari window also includes those aspects of ourselves that we know well but keep deliberately and successfully private, as well as those things that neither we or others know about us (e.g. a dormant medical condition). You may like to consider what your own Johari Window might look like, using Table 1.2.

Case example: Zainab

Zainab and her peers recognize that she has a warm, cheerful and confident interpersonal style. What is also known to Zainab and her peers is that sometimes she talks so quickly other people struggle to keep up with her. What her peers have noticed, but Zainab is not aware of, is that sometimes this conversational style can feel overbearing and it can seem as though she hasn't really heard what has been said to her. They also see how knowledgeable she can be and admire her assertiveness – these are qualities Zainab doesn't recognize in herself. What her peers don't know, but Zainab is very aware of, is how insecure and tense she can feel around others and how much she wants others to like her.

TABLE 1.1   *Zainab's Johari window*

	Known to Zainab	**Not known to Zainab**
Known to Zainab's peers	'Open' quadrant • Warm • Cheerful • Confident • Talks quickly	'Blind spot' • Overbearing conversationalist • Doesn't always listen • Admired by others • Knowledgeable
Not known to Zainab's peers	'Hidden quadrant' • Insecure • Tense • Longs to be liked	'Unknown'?

TABLE 1.2 *Your Johari window*

	Known to Self	Not known to Self
Known to others	'Open' quadrant	'Blind spot'
Not known to others	'Hidden quadrant'	'Unknown'

Learning edges can be thought of as the boundary lines that surround our comfort zone. Remember that well known saying, 'Life begins at the edge of your comfort zone'? Well, you might apply this to your learning: 'Learning begins at the edge of your comfort zone.' This learning edge might be also be thought of as the lines dividing the different quadrants of the Johari window. They will be unique to each of us, as well as subject to change as we move iteratively through the learning cycle. The greater awareness we have of what these might be, the better we set ourselves up for learning what our strengths and limitations are.

Practice, practice, deliberate practice

> Just because you've been walking for 50 years doesn't mean you're getting better at it. (Ericcson et al., 2006)

Ensuring the development of your learning through practice may seem like an obvious suggestion. However, we include it here to bring attention to the approach and manner through which you undertake practising. What we want to emphasize is the act of working intentionally to build on your skill set. This isn't just about doing but about a deliberate act of engaging and links to the idea of learning from experience (see above). Deliberate practice includes an appreciation of counselling and psychotherapy skills as evolving and iterative, rather than static, or like a tick box that once ticked no longer needs attention. Ways you might engage in deliberate practice include:

- setting up a time with a peer to specifically practise some of the skills set out in this book
- volunteering for a help-line organization or peer support scheme
- reflecting on how you engage in your everyday conversations with people
- seeking feedback from a trusted peer or colleague on your interpersonal style.

External resources for learning

Supervision

Supervision is a regular and protected space for trainees and qualified therapists alike to reflect on their work with their clients. It is a reflective space which can provide support and facilitate in-depth learning such that the supervisee can develop skills and competencies, grow in confidence and acquire the capacity for creative and ethical work.

The intention of supervision is ultimately to ensure the welfare and best service of the client. Supervision also offers a forum for accountability (Carroll and Gilbert, 2011) as the supervisee is monitored in their work by an experienced and more senior professional. In the UK, two of the key professional bodies for counsellors and psychotherapists – the BACP the UKCP – both stipulate clearly what is expected of trainees and qualified therapists in terms of the amount and frequency of supervision they receive. This can be found on their respective websites (see 'Resources' below).

Working with feedback

> To get where you want to go, you first have to know where you are. (Miller, Hubble and Duncan, 2005)

Learning to give and receive feedback is an art. It is considered one of the most sophisticated skills in the learning process. This may be because feedback can seem so risky: What if I hurt someone's feelings? What if I am humiliated in the process? What if I get stuck? However, feedback is one of the most valuable sources of learning. For example, a research study found that providing therapists with real-time feedback improved outcomes for their clients by 65 per cent (Miller et al., 2006). Think back to those blind spots – there is so much about ourselves that we don't know and other people may be brilliantly placed to help us see. Giving and receiving feedback can be emotionally demanding and requires a lot of courage; however, when it is given and received well it is enormously facilitative.

Tips for giving and receiving feedback effectively

Giving feedback:

- **Be goal-orientated**. Keep in mind what the goal behind what you want to say is – for example, your goal is to be helpful, constructive or facilitative.
- **Be specific**. Focus on a single piece of feedback at a time and avoid overwhelming the recipient with a lot of information at once.
- **Give feedback in the spirit of mutual respect**. Think about feedback as a collaborative form of learning.
- **Give consideration to where and when you give feedback**. You may need privacy and time to discuss what is being shared.
- **Don't be afraid to answer questions**. This may help provide the recipient with the detail they need to really learn from what you are sharing.
- **Own your feedback**. Recognize that there is a difference between your opinions and experiences, and facts. Start with phrases such as, 'I have experienced you as ...', rather than, 'This is who you are ...'.

Receiving feedback:

- **Take an open, non-defensive stance**. Remember that the person providing you with feedback is aiming to help you to develop and learn about yourself.
- **Be curious**. All of us have 'blind spots' – receiving feedback can potentially teach us something completely new about ourselves.
- **Don't be afraid to ask questions**. You may need clarity or want to explore something in greater depth. Questions may lead to an even richer process of self-inquiry.
- **Observe your emotional and thought processes as you hear what is being fed back**. If you find yourself feeling criticized, getting defensive or feeling embarrassed, it may be important to pause the process and try to articulate how you are feeling. We don't learn when we are anxious or feeling ashamed.
- **Commit to reflecting on what you have heard**. This will give you space to consider what is being said and demonstrate to the other that you are prepared to listen to their views.

Drawing on research

Research is an essential ingredient to learning and developing counselling and psychotherapy skills. Research can advance our knowledge base, help us enhance and hone our skill set and evaluate what is helpful and unhelpful practice. Engaging in research to support your learning may involve keeping up to date with the latest projects and findings in the counselling and psychotherapy profession, or conducting research yourself – for example, by using a validated 'outcome measure' or questionnaire with your clients at regular intervals to help you both assess your client's progress. Both the BACP and UKCP consider research a vital aspect of counselling and psychotherapy practice. Further information about this, and how these organizations support counsellors and psychotherapists to engage with research in the field, can be found on their respective websites.

Being ethical

Counselling skills can be extremely powerful and using them can elicit information from people that might not otherwise have been disclosed. Using these skills also places the therapist in a very powerful and influential position.

Deciding what is ethical can be very problematic and will depend on the context, the circumstances and the interpretation of those circumstances. Our willingness to grapple with the ethical dimensions of using counselling and psychotherapy skills will influence both our clients' and colleagues' opinions about our suitability for this work.

Clients' views of what is ethical are usually a good starting point. The bare bones of clients' ethical expectations are often very simple and eminently reasonable. When we have asked clients about their ethical expectations of therapists, they have usually replied that the therapist should be:

- trustworthy
- respectful
- competent
- accountable.

Trustworthiness requires taking account of the risk that the client is taking in seeking help. It also requires protecting personally sensitive information disclosed by clients from being used for purposes other than for which it was originally disclosed. The General Data Protection Regulation (GDPR, 2018) is a significant and important change in data privacy regulation. It is important for therapists to work with and understand GDPR policies. Being trustworthy also ensures the integrity of the therapeutic relationship, such as checking whether you and your client share the same aims in working together.

Respectfulness requires a willingness to accept and value differences between people and to act in ways that affirm the client as a person worthy of respect. The challenge for the therapist is striving to understand and accept difference between people rather than rejecting difference too readily or judging what may seem strange, as wrong or unacceptable. The Power Threat Meaning Framework (Johnstone and Boyle, 2018) funded by the British Psychological Society provides an excellent resource to better understand the importance of anti-oppressive practice.

Competence presents a considerable challenge in counselling and psychotherapy skills. The appropriate and constructive use of these skills is reasonably easily evaluated. However, the use of the therapist's sense of her/himself as a person, the emotional robustness and the depth of knowledge required to assist clients about specific issues can also be essential aspects of competence. There is clearly an expectation that therapists will avoid acting beyond their competence or using skills primarily as an opportunity to resolve their own problems or pursue their own interests. Conflicts of interest can be fatal to trust and bring services of any kind into disrepute. Supervision provides regular evaluation and support in the assessment of competence and its development.

Accountability to the client involves a willingness to explain how you are working and the reasons for the decisions you are making. In some situations, accountability may extend to colleagues, the funders of services and sometimes other members of the client's family or social network. It is not unusual for accountability to exist in tension with being trustworthy, especially when it involves responsibility beyond the client and raises questions of how to honour the client's confidences. Respect may require that differences in culture are considered in how to be accountable. Some cultures require greater formality or deference by the therapist than others. To be accountable when you consider that you have been incompetent is a test of courage and humility. The use of apology and expression of regret has its place in accountability, especially if accompanied by changes to prevent future errors.

Summary

This chapter has provided an overview of the counselling and psychotherapy relationship, a relationship that is born out of our innate social capacities. Within this overview we provided an introduction to the concept of a 2-person philosophy – a theory of the inseparable nature of interpersonal relating, and of individuals as participating in a matrix of subjective experiences which shape and co-create our interactions with others. We also considered the differences between counselling and psychotherapy relationships, and other ways of helping. In addition, we looked at the process of learning, including the learning cycle, and suggested ways in which your learning can be supported through the process of acquiring counselling and psychotherapy skills through personal and external resources. Finally, we outlined the importance of using an ethical framework to inform psychotherapeutic work, and looked at the concepts of trustworthiness, respect, competency and accountability. The next chapter provides an overview to the Stage Model.

Further resources

- The BACP and UKCP have both developed frameworks for ethical practice, as well as supervision requirements. In addition, both organizations provide information about the importance of research to counselling and psychotherapy. All this information can be viewed, for free, online.

  - BACP: www.bacp.co.uk
  - UKCP: www.psychotherapy.org

- Bond, T. (2015) *Standards and Ethics for Counselling in Action* (4th edition). London: SAGE.
- European Union General Data Protection Regulation 2018: https://ec.europa.eu/commission/priorities/justice-and-fundamental-rights/data-protection/2018-reform-eu-data-protection-rules_en

Online resources

Visit https://study.sagepub.com/staffordandbond4e to watch:

Video 1.1   The Aims of Counselling Skills

Video 1.2   The Therapeutic Relationship – Relationship vs. Friendship

Video 1.3   The Therapeutic Relationship – Key Points

Video 1.4   Crossing Boundaries – Scenario

Video 1.5   Crossing Boundaries – Discussion

Video 1.6   Avoiding Exploitation of Clients – Scenario

Video 1.7   Avoiding Exploitation of Clients – Discussion

2

Overview of the Skills-Based Model

Chapter contents

This chapter covers:

- Ten principles for practice
- The Stage Model
- Moving between the Stages
- Summary
- Further resources

Introduction

Learning counselling and psychotherapy skills is a complex activity. For many of us, there will be aspects of the process that feel like natural extensions of who we are and how we relate interpersonally. This will often link to our motivation towards learning these skills in the first place – there may be something quite familiar about a helping role, or often being an emotional support to others, perhaps extending as far back as childhood. However, it is likely that for all of us there will also be significant components of the process that are completely new, challenging and demanding at multiple levels. As with most intricate processes, one way to learn is to break down the operation into its constituent parts. A bit like learning to play a musical instrument, you begin with a specific starting point – for example, when learning the piano, you first learn where middle C is. You then move up the white keys to make a scale. From there you learn a chord, then how to bring in your left hand, then chord progressions. You learn to integrate the language of music – pitch, speed, rhythm, all represented by symbols such as the staff, the clefs and the notes – with what you hear when you press the keys. Your first scale is likely to be laboured and clumsy and require a lot of conscious effort. However, you gradually build your skills and start to master whole pieces of music.

As you become 'unconsciously competent', your playing no longer sounds like different component parts of a piece of music stuck together. Instead, it is coherent, fluid and recognizable. In the same way that aspects of the counselling and psychotherapy process might be familiar to you, you begin to learn to play a piece of music with an idea of how it might sound. Gradually, as you learn counselling skills you add layer upon layer to your knowledge and understanding, just as a piano player moves from a simple scale to a more complex sonata.

Using counselling and psychotherapy skills effectively is more intricate than drawing on a collection of skills. However, developing competency in counselling and psychotherapy may be approached by breaking the process down into its essential parts, identifying and practising some key communication skills and then learning to integrate these into a coherent approach.

This chapter provides an overview and basic introduction for the counselling and psychotherapy skills model described in this book. Fundamentally, this model is a *skills*-based one. It is based on a set of core communication skills, which are rooted in a set of guiding principles we call the 'Ten Principles for Practice'. As described in Chapter 1, what we hope to provide you with are the basic skills needed as you begin your training journey, and to start to work effectively with clients whatever your theoretical orientation. The current model provides a map of the counselling and psychotherapy process, by structuring it according to stages. As the model is underpinned by the Ten Principles for Practice, we present these first, followed by a description of the model's structure (the 'Stage Model'). Finally, we discuss some considerations for moving between stages.

Ten Principles for Practice

Each of us has principles that guide and inform how we move around in the world, how we relate to others and how we relate to ourselves. Similarly, the way that you choose to work therapeutically (the interventions and skills you employ, your presence in the room with your clients, your attitude and the theories and frameworks you draw on to support your work) can all be seen as a reflection of your values and assumptions about people. Equally, how you work therapeutically reflects what you believe facilitates a good learning environment, what needs to happen for people to be able to make personal changes, what is helpful, unhelpful and what is healing. For example, if you believe that we all have the potential to change and for psychological growth to occur if we feel accepted and loved by others, then your therapeutic approach will include an attitude of positive, warm regard for your clients wherein you strive to demonstrate your acceptance of who they are, where they find themselves and what they are struggling with.

Being clear and as explicit as you can about your beliefs and principles means that they are available as anchors in your learning journey and subsequently in your work as a therapist. An awareness of your guiding values also means they are open to examination, challenge and modification as a result of your experiences with clients. Being open in this way strengthens your ethical stance too, as these values and beliefs relate to your sense of responsibility and accountability.

Reflection point

Your personal values and their roots

Consider Figure 2.1. Think about the beliefs and principles you hold dear. How did they develop? Where do you think they are rooted? Do you remember when you first became aware of them as guiding your approach to life? Are you able to specify which are the most important top three or four?

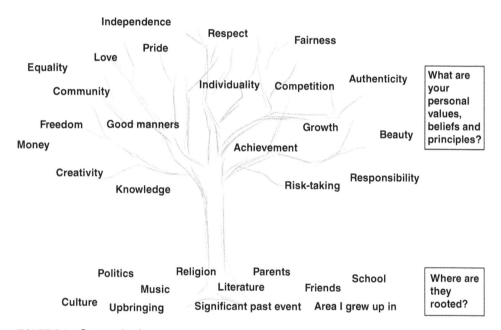

FIGURE 2.1 *Personal value tree*

Here we present the **Ten Principles for Practice** that underpin the model presented in this book:

1. **All people are equally valuable and equally unique**. This expresses the belief that all people deserve to be treated equally and with dignity, while simultaneously prizing our individuality and our differences. This assumption appreciates the variety of human experience and promotes a commitment towards equality, anti-oppressive practice and parity. In practice this means offering our clients choices and creating a therapeutic space which feels safe and free for them to be fully themselves.

2. **Everyone deserves acceptance and understanding because they are human**. Even if we do not at first understand our clients, we have a responsibility to find ways to demonstrate our acceptance and respect for them as fellow human beings, and to strive towards understanding them. This is about seeking to unconditionally value our clients just as they are, with struggles, hang-ups and blind spots. This is not

the same as colluding, condoning or agreeing with all of our clients' choices or behaviours. Rather it is an acknowledgement of, and an act of honouring, where and who they find themselves to be in the present time.

3. **Human beings are relationship-seeking creatures**. This principle is twofold. Firstly, it expresses the view that we are inseparable from, and co-created by, our relational contexts; and secondly, it acknowledges the potential for healing, growth and personal change that can be found in relationships. This requires us to understand how and why relationships hold such potential. We must be willing to work with what emerges from that potential. This includes our clients' vulnerability, as well as our own; inviting our clients into contact and being available for that contact ourselves; encouraging our clients to express themselves authentically and committing to working authentically as therapists. This demands that we work reflexively and with a willingness to develop our self-awareness.

4. **All people are capable of change and are courageous in seeking it**. This assumption is really at the heart of any psychotherapeutic endeavour. It means we understand that clients have discovered and learned ways of being (cognitively, emotionally, behaviourally and interpersonally) that do not serve them well, but that they are creative and capable of identifying and developing different ways of responding to the world. It takes courage to be a client. Change can feel like a risky business. Given a supportive environment and a relationship which is marked by acceptance and respect, clients are better able to own their vulnerability, consider different possibilities and try out new ideas.

5. **Human beings have an innate desire to realize their potential**. Clients are often clients because they want to become more self-directing and more self-empowered. At some level (sometimes clear to us and sometimes hidden) they are motivated to move forward in the direction of growth and change. Within them is the potential and psychic energy needed to expand, negotiate the hurdles of self-sabotage and discover what is right for them. If we miss this desire and this potential, we run the risk of inadvertently disempowering our clients. Clients are thinkers. Clients are psychologically resourceful. Clients are visionaries.

6. **We create our own meanings and our perspectives are subjective**. The way we make meaning of the world around us and the perspectives we hold are developed through a subjective lens and are open to change – that is, our personal narratives contribute significantly to our understanding of reality and what is going on around us and within us. This is in contrast to a view of assumptive certainty and the idea of truth as a static and inflexible concept. What this means in practice is that our clients will arrive with ideas about what their issues and behaviours mean, which may fluctuate over time; and we, as therapists, will also arrive with ideas about our clients which may contrast with their understanding. The challenge is to hold these sometimes divergent subjectivities as two valid ways of looking at a problem, and be open and non-defensive in our approach to the shifting nature of our clients' perspectives as well as our own.

7. **All people have an 'inner me' expertise**. As far as it is possible for us to fully know ourselves, we carry an extensive inner knowledge about ourselves which is unparalleled. Client and therapist are knowledgeable in their own right, both bringing experiences, ideas and areas of expertise that they are ready to draw on in the therapeutic space. However, it is only the client who can tell what their pain, disappointments and fears are like for them and what they most want for themselves. In this sense, the client

brings an exceptional set of expertise and experiences to the encounter. What this also means is that clients are more likely to marshal their resources and struggle for outcomes that they want, rather than goals that have been imposed on them.

8. **Everyone's behaviour is purposeful.** What may seem like chaotic or unhelpful behaviour to us will have some purpose for the client. It will have some rationale and be directed towards some particular outcome. It may be that a behaviour was once effective in a different context, and so developed into an automatic way of being but has now become outdated and limiting. Equally, it may be that it continues to fulfil the client's needs at some level, but is simultaneously unhelpful, undermining or destructive to them at another. Holding this in mind is a valuable starting point in helping you and your client gain insight into their actions.

9. **Human experience is holistic.** We are made up of emotions, cognitions and physiological experiences which are interrelated and we can be conscious or unconscious of. Our ways of communicating these experiences can be both implicit and explicit. For example, a client's negative emotions may be expressed through physical pain. They may be fully aware of their physical pain, but less in touch with their affective experience. This may be communicated explicitly by a client who describes the physical pain, and implicitly in their physical tension or rigidity. We must observe, inquire, listen and help our clients to untangle these experiences, attending to their particular tendencies, familiarities or preferences for different styles of communicating these.

10. **Human experience must be understood within a social, economic, political and cultural context.** As fundamentally social beings, we are not only influenced and shaped by our intra-psychic and interpersonal relational worlds. We also exist, relate, embody and are affected by the social, economic, political and cultural contexts within which we live. We must pay careful attention to the very real ways in which these contexts enable clients to thrive, or conversely serve to constrain and oppress them. Equally, we need to consider the meaning these contexts hold for the client sitting in front of us, and how they have contributed to what is emerging for the client in terms of their current issues and the way they make sense of their current issues. This requires us to reflect systemically, such that we appreciate how our own social, economic, political and cultural influences have informed our outlook, how our clients may see us and the landscape we stand in together.

Reflection point

Reviewing the Ten Principles for Practice

Take some time to review each of the principles described above and consider the following questions:

- How do the Principles resonate with your own beliefs and principles?
- How do the Principles conflict with your own beliefs and principles?
- In what circumstances do you believe these Principles might be challenging for you to work with?

The Stage Model

Viewing counselling and therapy as unfolding like a series of incremental stages or defined points is common to many approaches. It is a way of imposing a conceptual structure on what otherwise might seem to be a random or chaotic activity. The current model is divided simply into three stages: Beginning, Middle and Ending, because all encounters, whatever their length, comprise these three elements.

Within each stage, we have identified the aims, plans and skills required to work with and move successfully through the process of counselling.

- **Aims**. When we are thinking about the aims of a particular stage of the process, we are considering what we want to achieve at a given point in time. Is there a particular outcome we would like to see – for example, to notice a shift in our client's perspective, or an improved score on a measure of depression? Are we looking to achieve a shared understanding of what is at the root of our client's problem? Do we simply want to agree on the practical arrangements of working together, such as the time, place and fee? As well as carefully identifying the aims within each stage of the process, we need also to have some idea of what things will look like when these aims have been met. What will it all look like once the goal has been reached? Working collaboratively with your client will mean developing a shared understanding or agreed definition of this, however tentative.
- **Plans**. How you will realize your aims constitutes the plan. Using counselling skills ought to be a purposeful activity and you will need to be clear about what you are attempting to do at each stage of the process, and why you are attempting to achieve it. A plan might be a concrete activity, such as asking your client to complete a specific questionnaire in order to obtain a quantitative measure of their baseline level of depression; or it may be more process orientated – for example, to demonstrate a particular attitude, such as an attitude of anti-oppressive and non-judgemental practice.
- **Skills**. Counselling and psychotherapy skills refer to a range of different communication skills that can be used to support, help and heal. The skills outlined in this model are the basic tools by which you put your plans into action and fulfil the aims of each stage. Examples of counselling and psychotherapy skills include active listening, empathic inquiry, challenge and open questioning techniques.

Stage model in practice

Let's look at an example of how this works in practice, using an aim inherent to the Beginning Stage of your work with a client: to build a good rapport and establish a therapeutic alliance with them. How will you achieve that aim? Your plan may consist of demonstrating your acceptance and respect for them as a person, by communicating to them that you have heard and understood what they have said. One of the skills you employ to do this might include the skill of paraphrasing, a core technique which communicates empathic understanding and helps to build relationships. One way in which you will know you have achieved this aim will be in the 'degree of fit' you and your client experience in relation to one another. You may also be given an explicit sense of this by your client who expresses their interest in working with you, someone they view as a trustworthy. This aim may be one that you re-visit, and you may suggest that you and your client offer each other feedback on your subjective experiences of your relationship as you go along.

Table 2.1 provides an overview of the Stage Model, with an outline of the aims, plans and skills needed for each respective stage. The model provides an overriding theme of the work for each stage – that is, what the work is centred around. Also included is the 'relational focal point' for each stage – that is, what is going on between you and your client. Themes and the relational focus for each stage are both elaborated on in the chapters to come.

Moving between the stages

This model, of course, provides a static picture of what is usually experienced as a complex, fluid and ever-changing process. Counselling and psychotherapy skills in action are not a neat, linear operation with a defined structure and discrete stages. It is much more complicated and subtle, with both clients and therapists working in their own unique ways. The model, therefore, simply represents a guide for you. It is neither a description of how clients actually behave nor a fixed series of steps for using these skills.

However, conceptualizing use of these skills as a series of stages is an attempt to introduce some stable points into the process. These will be points at which the work begins to change by adopting a different theme and a different relational focus. In Figure 2.2, we have depicted the model in diagrammatic form. The large black arrows across the top represent the movement forward, from one stage to the next. The dotted arrows at the bottom represent the iterative nature of the process. Applicable to all stages are the foundation skills which are described in detail in Chapter 3. The entire model rests on the Ten Principles for Practice represented on the left-hand side of the figure. Client options beyond the Ending Stage are represented on the right-hand side of the figure and described in further detail in Chapter 6.

TABLE 2.1 *Aims, plans and skills within the Stage Model*

STAGE	AIMS	PLANS	CORE SKILLS +
BEGINNING **Theme:** *Focusing* **Relational focal point:** *Connection*	• To establish a therapeutic alliance • To conduct an assessment • To agree a 'working therapy contract'	Focus on the quality and strength of your developing relationship, as well as how well you collaborate together, in order to negotiate and agree how you will work, what you will need to attend to, and what can be achieved.	• Empathy • Acceptance • Genuineness • Goal setting • Holding boundaries • Working collaboratively
MIDDLE **Theme:** *Exploring* **Relational focal point:** *Deepening*	• To maintain the therapeutic alliance • To explore the client's issues at depth	Work with, open up and develop the therapeutic relationship, to enable exploration of content, process and the previously hidden or unexpressed.	• Deepening the encounter • Self-disclosure • Immediacy • Advanced empathy • Challenging to invite authenticity • Giving directives
ENDING **Theme:** *Reflection* **Relational focal point:** *Transition*	• To reflect on and review the work undertaken • To work with the client's resources to plan for the future • To close the work and say goodbye	Reflect constructively, with thought and purpose, on the issues originally brought into therapy and the work that has been conducted, to review progress and establish next steps. Mindfully and sensitively close the work, facilitate transition and say goodbye.	• Consolidation of skills • Reflection • Reflexivity • Planning • Appreciation for the significance of endings and separations as unique to the individual

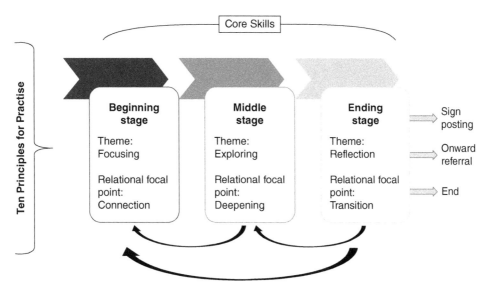

FIGURE 2.2   *Diagram of the stage model*

Summary

This chapter provided an introduction to the skills-based, Stage Model for learning counselling and psychotherapy skills on which this book is grounded. The Stage Model rests on a set of values and assumptions about people, what we believe facilitates a good learning environment, and what needs to happen for people to be able to make personal changes and heal the wounds that bring them into therapy. In this book, these values and assumptions have been summarized as the 'Ten Principles for Practice' and are described within this chapter. In the next chapter, we focus on the core skills needed in counselling and psychotherapy that underpin the subsequent stages of the work.

Further resources

For an understanding of some of the philosophical contexts from which counselling and psychotherapy theory arises, we recommend:

- Orange, D. (2010) *Thinking for Clinicians: Philosophical Resources for Contemporary Psychoanalysis and the Humanistic Psychotherapies*. New York and London: Routledge.

3

Building Your Foundations

Chapter contents

This chapter covers:

- The core skills of therapeutic work
- An integrated framework for 'active listening'
- Therapist competency
- Working with difference
- Further resources

Introduction

This chapter outlines the 'core skills' that constitute the foundations upon which your future therapeutic work progresses. They provide essential support for working successfully as a counsellor or psychotherapist and play a role at every point in the process of your work with a client. Additionally, these core skills are the bedrock from which more advanced and nuanced skills evolve and are refined as you become increasingly more competent, experienced and reflective.

Core skills

Attending to your client

What does it really mean to 'attend' to another person? Listening to them will comprise a significant and integral part of your attending (so much so, a section is devoted to this deceptively complex skill below). However, to fully attend also involves several other elements and interpersonal activities that act to enable the other person to feel they have your full attention and you value what they have to share. Attending might even be seen as the basis for listening to your client. It is a means by which you communicate, non-verbally, that you are with them. The manner in which you attend to your clients will carry powerful messages. For example, your genuineness will be enhanced when you attend well. Conversely, if your non-verbal behaviour is at odds with your words, the effect of what you say will be greatly diminished.

We rely hugely on non-verbal communication in our everyday interactions. In fact, most of our communication is conveyed through certain vocal features and nonverbal elements such as facial expressions, gestures and posture. Some researchers suggest, for example, that facial expressions are our primary mode of conveying how we feel over and above the verbal language that we use (Mandal and Ambady, 2004). Within the therapeutic relationship, the therapist's facial expressions have been identified as the most powerful non-verbal form of communication (Sharpley et al., 2006). Advances in neuroscience research demonstrate that we are sociophysiologically connected to others (Adler, 2002) and this manifests in implicit, non-verbal exchanges. Such exchanges are quick and automatic and enable us to categorize incoming information about another person to make judgements quickly (Lyons-Ruth, 1999; Schore and Schore, 2007). For example, another person's body language is picked up and processed in the brain almost immediately, leading Tipper et al. (2015) to describe our ability to identify and encode body language as an 'intuitive social awareness'. Scaer (2005) describes how subtle variations in our facial expressions, the way we carry ourselves, or the volume or tone of our voice reflect emotions such as disapproval, humour or fear, from which we make decisions about how nurturing, or conversely how unsafe, the immediate environment is. Similarly, Tipper et al. (2015) highlights how body language contains various cues regarding attitude, intention, affect and motivation.

Therefore, our facial expression, our posture, movements, the way we gesticulate and direct our gaze all provide our clients with important information about what we are thinking and feeling, and importantly how we are attending to them. As Leijssen (2006: 127) argues, 'Therapist and client are never just "talking"; they are always "bodies inter-acting"'. What does this mean in practice? There are several non-verbal, implicit ways you will demonstrate how you are attending to your clients. Each involves an internal as well as external awareness and a capacity for 'reflection-in-action':

- **Your body language** needs to be 'open'. You need to signal your receptivity, willingness to engage and warmth. This can be manifested in a posture which is relaxed, upright and centred, and movements which are natural, easy and gentle. Hunched shoulders, crossed arms and tense muscles can appear defensive, remote or unavailable. All this may seem obvious to you; however, we are not always very good at noticing how we are sitting, breathing or moving. So, what we are bringing attention to here is the need to increase your conscious awareness of your non-verbal, physical self. If you are feeling nervous or unsure, quietly focusing on slowing your breath to a steady rhythm, placing your feet flat on the ground (literally, grounding yourself) and gently rolling your shoulders can help you to find your confidence and bring your attention to where you want it to be – in the room, with your client.
- **Your eye contact** needs to convey your availability for psychological contact. This means maintaining a consistent and steady gaze. This is not the same as fixing the client

with a hard stare! Rather it involves using your eye contact to show your sustained interest in them. In other words, whenever clients return their gaze to you, they will find you looking at them and will gain a sense of you reliably being there for them. Eye contact has been shown to be one of the most salient affective, non-verbal behaviours influencing the therapist–client relationship (Sharpley and Sagris, 1995). Like your body language, your eye contact will be a natural manifestation of your attention. Therefore, it will also mean that sometimes you break eye contact. In a moment of deep thought, you may find yourself looking upwards for example. In addition, breaking eye contact temporarily may be necessary to enable some clients who feel particularly self-conscious or uncomfortable to relax a little more.

- **Your facial expression** should be congruent with what you are saying and the material you are discussing. Smiling while you talk about something difficult might seem antipathetic and undermine your authenticity. Letting clients see, by the concern on your face, that you have some sense of the pain and misery they have experienced will demonstrate to them that you are with them in their struggles, and may free them to begin to access and express those feelings. Importantly, effective therapists enhance their rapport with clients when their interest, engagement and attention is depicted in their facial expression (Sharpley et al., 2006).

- **Your voice** is a vital tool involved in implicit communication. Its pitch, tone, pace, depth and volume will convey to your client your understanding of what they are sharing and how you are attuning to them. For example, as the volume of their voice becomes quieter, dropping the volume of your own voice may act a little bit like a mirror, demonstrating that you hear not just the content of what they are saying, but the emotion and meaning behind their words.

- **Observing your client** goes hand in hand with attending to them. Observations will also shape the way you attend. Close observation of their body language, facial expression and the sound of their voice will inform how you respond verbally and non-verbally. Equally, the way they are dressed, the tone of their voice, their gestures and movements will either confirm, emphasize or conflict with their verbal messages, and so observing your client will help you understand them better. This also requires you to differentiate between 'content' and 'process' – that is, noticing not just what your client says, but the affective and physiological experience that frames what is shared. Observation needs to be non-intrusive so that your client doesn't feel scrutinized or judged. This involves a careful balance of internally noticing while maintaining a sense of connection. An effective therapist, says Schore (2003: 52), is not only carefully and consciously noticing what is being verbalized, but also 'listening and interacting at another level, an experience-near, subjective level, one that implicitly processes moment-to-moment socioemotional information at levels beneath awareness'.

- **Being mindful of the setting** that you and your client are working in contributes to their sense of the value you place on the space you share, and hence their sense that you are attending to their needs. There may be setting restrictions and limitations that you have no control over if you are working in a building or room which is not your own. However, you are likely to have control over the seating arrangements and can ensure that you are seated at an appropriate distance and that the chairs are of equal height. Positioning chairs at a slight angle, rather than directly facing one another can appear more relaxed and less confrontational. Making 'space' for clients means providing an appropriate physical environment as well as a supportive relationship and uninterrupted time.

Case example: Aleksi

Aleksi arrived for her first session late. When her therapist, Saul, answered the door to her, he noticed she looked like she had been rushing to get to their appointment – her face was flushed and her breathing rapid as though she had been running. She immediately pulled off her coat and scarf and began fanning herself with the newspaper she was carrying. She sat with her legs crossed and one arm held tightly across her chest. Underneath her flushed face her skin seemed pale and she looked exhausted. She kept smiling broadly at Saul, but her eyes darted around the room, meeting his only hesitatingly. His hunch was that she was feeling stressed and nervous. He noticed his own heart rate increasing slightly in response and took a slow deliberate breath. At top speed she launched into explaining how hectic her life was, laughing occasionally when she said, 'Life is ridiculous!'. When she paused, and looked directly at Saul, he took the opportunity to hold her gaze, smile gently and relax his shoulders before taking his time to say, 'I can hear you have very little time for yourself usually. But we have time here, today. There's no rush.' Aleksi's shoulders slumped slightly, she unwound her body and sighed deeply. A natural colour started to return to her cheeks.

In this example the therapist, Saul, noticed the incongruities between the content of what Aleksi was saying ('life is overwhelming') and her process (the non-verbal cues – laughter, smiling). Her body language, and the speed at which she spoke seemed a reflection on how busy her life was (i.e. moving around quickly, rapid breathing, exhaustion). Saul aimed to slow things down with a calming breath, by relaxing his upper body and by speaking slowly. He attempted to hold Aleksi's eye gaze to convey to her that he was with her and he was listening.

It is not our intention to imply that certain postures or gestures have certain meanings, but rather that they mean something. Your clients will be noticing – consciously or unconsciously – the degree to which you are attending to them, exhibited in your body language, facial expression, eye contact and sound of your voice. You will need to be vigilant to consistent patterns of non-verbal behaviour in your clients – for example, Aleksi's darting eye movements – and pay attention to your hunches (Aleksi is feeling nervous and stressed). By being alert to evidence from other aspects of your client's behaviour you can either confirm or disconfirm your hunch. When you sense that there is enough trust between you, you may want to share your observations. Hunches should be shared in a tentative manner that encourages exploration and is in the service of the client gaining greater understanding of themselves.

Non-verbal communication is dynamic. You and your client will be responding to one another and the implicit cues that pass between you at both a conscious and unconscious level. Any discussion of your client's non-verbal behaviour may be enhanced by a willingness to discuss your own. This involves a readiness to receive feedback from your client about how they are experiencing you in the room. Saul may, for example, have been unwittingly inviting or exacerbating Aleksi's nervousness and stress in some way – perhaps, when he answered the door to her, his internal wonderings as to why she was late showed in his facial expression and she felt judged? Perhaps she noticed Saul's heart rate quicken, and his slow deep breath and interpreted these as signs of impatience?

Listening to your client

> I have learned to ask myself, can I hear the sounds and sense the shape of this other person's inner world? (Rogers, 1980: 8)

Listening is a complex skill. It is different from simply hearing – the act of perceiving sound. Listening is a conscious action. It requires engagement, on your part, at multiple levels in which you attend to, receive and attempt to understand the messages that clients are sending, both by what they say and by what they do. Your purpose in listening will be to facilitate trust and understanding between you and your client, and to provide them with an experience of being 'met', accepted and known. However, when you are listening to them, you are not a sponge soaking up the information indiscriminately. The amount of information passing between you will be too great for you to pick up and respond to every cue and clue. Rather, you will be sorting the information coming in and deciding what to respond to; you will be forming hypotheses about what they are saying as well as what they are omitting; and you will be seeking clarification for those things that feel unclear. In other words, you will be listening actively. 'Active listening' means that you are listening with purpose and communicating that you have listened. Ways of responding to clients will be discussed in the next section. We begin by focusing on listening with purpose, using the following integrative framework.

Integrated framework for active listening

This framework outlines the multiple sources of information you will be receiving about your client as you attempt to actively listen to them. Holding this framework in mind will help you with this, as well as help you attend to your client, engage with the material they bring and respond to them in a way which helps them feel fully heard.

* **Experiences**. What is your client's experience of the world around them? What do they see as happening to them? What do they perceive others do or fail to do, say or not say? How do they encounter life?
* **Behaviour**. What behaviours does your client describe themselves engaging in? How has their behaviour changed (or not) in response to their current situation? How does your client act with you? What do they say and do?
* **Feelings**. What is your client feeling? How do they express their feelings? What is it like for them to connect to their feelings and share them with you? How do these feelings ebb and flow, both in the session and over time?

- **Thoughts**. What kind of thoughts does your client have about themselves? What sense do they make of their own and others' behaviour? What beliefs do they have about themselves, other people and events in their lives?
- **Body**. What is it like for your client to be in their body? How connected are they to their physical self? Do they describe physical sensations, or activity or health issues? How do they literally move around in the world?
- **Relationships**. What sense of connection do you have with your client? How close, or distant, do they feel to you in the room? How do they move in and out of contact with you? What relationships do they describe in their life and what is their experience of these relationships?

Working with silence

Silence is a rhythm too. (The Slits, 1980)

Silence is powerful. It can evoke a wide range of emotions and can both promote and impede the therapeutic work (Landany et al., 2004). Some degree of silence is an inevitable part of any dialogue and so it will be important for you to know how to listen to it, understand it and work within it.

- **Listening to silences**. Communication between you and your clients will continue even if one or both of you are silent. Silence can be a potent way of speaking volumes and you will need to listen to their silences as well as their words. By attending carefully to your client, and the quality of the silence, you will gain some clues about what they might be thinking and feeling when they are silent. For example, you will discern whether they are uneasy, stuck, bored, hostile or reflecting. Using the information contained within a silence will help you to decide when and how to intervene. Listening to and using silences creatively means effecting an appropriate balance between enabling clients, providing space for them to reflect and helping them to face their discomfort.
- **Sitting with silences**. Allowing space for silence can be a challenging task for both therapist and client. As a therapist, your natural inclination may be to try to fill the silence with questions or prompts as it may feel uncomfortable to sit together in what, on the surface, may seem like an empty or unproductive process. Silence can also be an uncertain space, which may be difficult to tolerate. If you find you are invariably the one who breaks silences, you may want to explore that further through reflective practice and in supervision. On the other hand, some therapists avoid interrupting silences. Landany et al. (2004) found that therapists reported using silence to convey empathy, respect or support; to facilitate reflection or client expression; to challenge the client to take responsibility or control; or to give themselves time to decide how to respond to their clients. Conversely, sustained silence may represent a form of anxiety. This anxiety may be the therapist's ('What on earth do I say next?!') or the client's ('Why isn't s/he saying anything?!'). It is important to remember that silences can arouse various feelings for the client who will have their own experience of, and attribute their own

meanings to, these verbal pauses. It is important to understand your own experience of sitting with silence as well as your client's, in order to work effectively within it.

- **Interrupting silences**. You may choose to break a silence. Interrupting a silence ought to be thoughtful and respectful. That is, your intention behind interrupting a silence should be in the service of the therapeutic work, such as helping your client to explore an issue further, to demonstrate how you are attending to them, or to help them see that they are safe and you are still with them in the room. It is helpful to start with a 'process question' – a question which makes an inquiry into the nature of the silence. Process questions can be nonintrusive ways of breaking a silence, while simultaneously aiding exploration of your client's experience and avoiding a presumptive stance. Examples include: Where have you gone to? What are you thinking/feeling right now? What's going on for you at the moment? What is happening in this moment do you think?

There is general agreement that a strong 'therapeutic alliance' is a prerequisite for using silence (Hill et al., 2003; Ladany et al., 2004). The concept of the therapeutic alliance is discussed in detail in Chapter 4. Briefly, it is the part of the client–therapist relationship that is widely agreed to act as a foundation upon which the therapeutic work can happen. Cooper (2008) asserts that therapists ought to exercise caution around using challenging interventions until the therapeutic alliance has been established. Given the fact that silences may provoke strong and possibly difficult emotions, it seems sensible to remain mindful of how your client's experience of silence may be influenced by the strength of your therapeutic alliance.

Listening to your internal responses and self-reflection

As you listen to your clients you will be thinking, feeling and intuiting. In other words, you will be responding to them internally at multiple levels. Listening to your internal responses is an important and valuable activity:

- **Your response may reflect what is happening for the client**. For example, you may experience a sense of sadness, which is what the client is feeling underneath the thoughts they are describing as having.
- **You may gain an understanding of what is happening between you and your client, and subsequently in the client's relational world**. For example, you may be aware that you are irritated with your client and the way they appear unwilling to take responsibility for their actions. This may mirror what other people are feeling towards them and why they are finding it difficult to access support from others.
- **You may be helped to disentangle material that is your own, rather than that which belongs to your client**. For example, as your client describes what it was like to grow up with an alcoholic mother, you may start to remember what it was like for you to live with an alcoholic sibling and notice that your feelings are influencing how you want to engage with the content of what your client is saying.

Reflective practice will enable you to work towards fully understanding your responses. You will utilize both your reflection-*on* and reflection-*in* action skill sets (Schon, 1983) in order to make meaning and glean insights into your responses. You may start to notice that patterns emerge from your responses and these may tell you even more about your client, or about how you react to certain situations or relational experiences. You may, at an appropriate time, decide to share your internal responses and invite your client to explore them with you. It may be that your response helps your client to understand themselves better or understand other people's reactions better. Paying close attention to the patterns of your reactions to clients and their material is the basis for behaving congruently because you will be working from a place within yourself which is known to you. Sharing your responses may require you to take a risk – there is a chance that your responses, observations or hunches do not resonate with your client. There is a certain degree of trial and error involved here. Sharing your responses therefore requires you to be open to your client's thoughts, feelings and processes to what you have shared, open to being wrong, and open, willing and curious to examine this process together.

Listening filters

None of us listens in a completely neutral, disinterested way. We use 'frameworks' to organize the vast amount of information we are receiving. These frameworks can act like 'filters' – that is, some pieces of information are attended to more than others and we inadvertently 'block' other pieces of information. Because our frameworks make up part of our individual and unique standpoint, they are inherently biased (e.g. by our personal histories, beliefs or values). In Chapter 1, we discussed how we may or may not be conscious of how our subjective standpoint may influence the experiences we have. This includes how we listen. Through reflective practice we can increase our awareness of how our subjective self can act like a 'listening filter' with our clients. This might include:

- **Culture**. Being cognizant of your own culture, and your clients' culture, as well as the differences and similarities between them will support you in understanding your clients, increase your sensitivity towards them and your developing relationship, and ultimately how you are listening to them. Examples are race, gender, sexuality, ability, age, religion and country of origin. However, cultural norms and values can be some of the most challenging to transcend. Direct eye contact, for example, is not acceptable in all cultures while in others a lack of direct eye contact may seem odd and uncomfortable. Cultural awareness also means having an appreciation for how different cultural groups are currently (or have been historically) oppressed, discriminated against and stereotyped, and importantly what this may mean for the client sitting in front of you. It may be important to discuss cultural issues with your client. For example, is it important for them to work with someone who shares something of their cultural background? What is it like for them to work with a therapist who seems culturally very different? Research suggests that some clients express a preference for therapists who are similar to them in some way (e.g. clients from marginalized social groups show some preference for therapists from a similar social group) and 'matching' therapist and client in this way may be associated with positive outcome (Cooper, 2008). However, it is also important to bear in mind that therapists' attitudes and values may be of greater importance when it comes to facilitating good therapeutic outcome than 'matching' therapist and client characteristics (Cooper, 2008).

- **Personal histories and current issues**. Our personal histories, or issues we are currently dealing with in our lives, may colour how we listen to and see the client sitting in front of us. We may find that when a client's story resonates powerfully within us, we are more or less likely to attend to certain features of the story: we may quickly jump to an assumption that we know what the client is feeling or thinking, or we may find it too challenging to focus on aspects of the client's material that we have found (or are finding) painful to confront in ourselves; we may find that we are drawn to feel close to our client, or conversely desire distance from them. Equally, current issues may preoccupy us, rendering us less open to our clients. Related feelings of anxiety, stress, fatigue, shame or mistrust can all act to negatively influence how we listen. Personal history and current issues may, perhaps unconsciously, lead us to listen well or less well, to what the client is trying to communicate about their experiences, struggles and pain.

As a result of these filters we may find we hinder our ability to listen further still by preparing what to say in advance, which thwarts any spontaneity in our interactions. Equally, we may seek confirmation of a hypothesis we have developed about a client, which leads us to ignore information that contradicts it, or become defensive or self-critical when a client disagrees with us. We may even jump to finding a solution or move towards action before we have fully understood what is going on for our client, or when problem solving is not what they want or need.

How reflective practice and supervision can help us listen more effectively

Reflective practice and regular supervision can help us become more aware of our listening filters and how they impede our ability to listen. We can also learn more about how we listen (or find we stop listening), and ultimately enhance our active listening skills, by adopting an approach known as the 'phenomenological method'. This method attempts to gradually eliminate bias, assumptions and interpretations – those things that can get in the way of listening actively – so that we can fully attend to the information we are presented with. This method can be broken down into three steps (Spinelli, 2005):

1. **Step 1: 'Bracket'**. Set aside anything and everything you think you know about whatever it is you are experiencing and suspend judgement, as far as is possible. This requires you to become open to immediate experience and work in the 'here-and-now'.
2. **Step 2: 'Describe'**. Articulate, as simply as possible and using your own words, what you are experiencing and sensing, without adding any explanation or justification. This requires you to stay with your initial, concrete impression.

(Continued)

---

3. **Step 3: 'Treat equally'**. Approach each of the different aspects of whatever you are experiencing and sensing equally, giving no weight to any particular element of that experience. This requires you to resist the temptation to give different aspects of experience a differential or hierarchical significance.

This method is demanding and challenging and indeed it might be argued that it is impossible to 'bracket' our subjective experience, to offer a description of an experience which is free of explanatory features, or to treat all elements of that experience with parity. However, Spinelli (2005) argues that this method helps us to recognize our various biases and so reduces their force. It can therefore be used as a useful starting point or guide in understanding more about how you listen. Next time you are in a conversation with someone, why not try to identify the thoughts and assumptions you are making? How easy is it to put these to one side? Is it possible to simply describe what you see, hear and feel without adding opinions or interpretations? What aspects of the conversation – the content as well as the process – do you find you are paying most attention to and/or giving more weight to?

Communicating

Attending to your client and actively listening to them, with an awareness of your personal filters, begins the process of understanding your clients. However, while these core skills constitute an essential part of this process they are not enough. Clients need more. They need you to respond in order to know that they are being heard and understood. As Truax (Truax and Carkhuff, 1967: 555) writes, 'Accurate empathy involves both the sensitivity to current feelings and the verbal facility to communicate this understanding in a language attuned to the client's current feelings'. We now turn to discuss the art of communicating your understanding of your client using the techniques of reflecting back and methods of exploration.

The techniques of reflecting back

The techniques of reflecting back are skills that enable you to communicate your understanding of the client's perspective. This is sometimes referred to as understanding the client's 'internal frame of reference', that is, how clients view themselves and their concerns. Methods of exploration, such as questioning skills on the other hand usually express the therapist's perspective or 'external frame of reference' (Nelson-Jones, 2008). For example, when you ask a question, you will be responding from your frame of reference. You will usually do this when seeking information or wanting to influence the direction of a session (see the next section for more detail).

The skill of reflecting back builds trust, encourages exploration and can help to avoid premature focusing. Reflecting back is a medium for communicating empathic understanding and acceptance because by its very nature it shows you have heard and listened carefully to what the client has said. Using these skills will enable you to track clients' thinking and feeling and to check in a non-intrusive way that you have understood. They also impose minimal direction from your frame of reference. The common element in these skills is that you are reflecting what they have said back to them in their own words or by putting it into your own words.

The three techniques of reflecting back are:

1. restating
2. paraphrasing
3. summarizing.

We will discuss each of them in turn.

Restating

Restating involves repeating back to the client either single words or short phrases which they have used. It can be an efficient way of prompting further discussion. Let's return to Aleksi's session and consider an example:

> Aleksi: My life is so busy. My schedule feels *punishing*.
> Saul: Punishing.
> Aleksi: Yes, I'm exhausted. I feel as though life is somehow out to get me … it's almost like I don't have time to breathe. And I'm on my own with all this – I have no support, no help.

Saul restated a word that was both emphasized and emotionally loaded – 'punishing'. It enabled him to stay with the client's frame of reference and encouraged further responses. It highlighted to Aleksi the kind of language she is using which helped her to connect more with her experience. Clients can sometimes be taken aback when you reflect back a particular word or phrase they have used, particularly when they are not engaging fully with the depth or intensity of the experiences they are having. Restating can act as a powerful echo that increases their awareness of self, as well as their circumstances. At other times, clients notice their words are not accurate enough (e.g. 'Actually I'm not feeling *low*, I'm really feeling *depressed*') and restating can facilitate the client to access their true feelings. In this example, Aleksi went on to share more about the kinds of thoughts she has about the world around her (a world that seems out to 'get her'), what it's like to be in her body (exhausting, barely able to breathe) and more about how she was feeling (alone, unsupported). It was a non-directional and nonintrusive intervention.

Restating is also a useful skill for maintaining the focus in a session. For example:

> Aleksi: I don't know anyone nearby who could help me with the kids. Some days I'm reduced to tears. Oh! Actually, I do know of a friend of a friend in the next street, but it would be a bit much to ask them … I don't think I have their number anyway … Where was I?
> Saul: Reduced to tears?
> Aleksi: Ah-huh; crying in the middle of the day when the kids are at school. I just seem to collapse.

Saul's intention here was to remind Aleksi of what she was sharing about how she was feeling and encourage her to continue to talk about what her life is like currently, rather than allowing her to go off on a tangent.

So, using the technique of restating stays with the client's frame of reference and can acknowledge and/or help identify the emotions underneath the content, as well as help clients to connect more with their true inner experiences in a focused way. However, we need to add a note of caution about its overuse. Imagine the following, in which Saul *only* restates Aleksi's words:

Aleksi:	I've been feeling so stressed.
Saul:	Stressed.
Aleksi:	Yes, all the time. And unhappy.
Saul:	Unhappy.
Aleksi:	Well, both really. Yes, all the time … always.
Saul:	Always.
Aleksi:	Er, yes. Always feeling stressed and unhappy.

The dialogue sounds pretty stilted and contrived. Furthermore, Aleksi starts to feel a bit stuck and there is very little increase in the depth of her understanding and self-awareness. So, as therapists we need a mix of skills. Only using one to the exclusion of others can feel tedious, sound false, and may well irritate clients and even hamper progress.

Paraphrasing

Paraphrasing is the skill of expressing the meaning of the core message or key ideas behind the client's communication, but with different words – your own words, that lets the client know that you understand their concerns, from their point of view. Paraphrasing provides a means to check your perception of what your client has said and allows both you and the client to know whether or not you share a common understanding of their problems. Paraphrasing is also an excellent information-gathering skill, because it allows you to follow clients without imposing a direction. It gives them room to say what is important for them (of course, you may certainly have occasion to ask them for information and to direct the session at some points – we will be discussing ways of doing this later in this chapter, in the section on 'Methods of exploration'). To be effective paraphrasing must, of course, be accurate. You would hardly be communicating good understanding if most of what you offered a client was incorrect or 'off the mark'. Developing the skill involves both attending well and listening accurately. It also means being open to clients and their experiences and genuinely wishing to understand them. Let's return to Aleksi's session:

Aleksi:	I suppose I've never felt like I'm getting it 'right' and now I find I'm not doing anything well. My friends are all going places – they have careers which seamlessly fit in around family life. They have husbands who support them. Perfect children. They seem to cope better … more than cope, they all seem to be so happy. They constantly post beautiful photos on social media of their family holidays and get togethers … I'm working so hard, but earning very little … I'm a single mum, I'm putting on weight … I feel like I'm failing.
Saul:	So, you're comparing yourself with your friends and telling yourself you're not good enough. And that sense of failing, of not getting it right, has been around for a while?

Aleksi: Exactly. It's like I just don't measure up. I'm 'the loser' and I always have been so I guess I always will be [*the volume of her voice drops and she closes her eyes*].

Saul: You sound sad. It's like you've been defeated.

Aleksi: … Yeah, I am. Sad. Hopeless. It feels a bit like, what's the point? What's the point in trying hard at work? What's the point in going on a diet? [*Becomes tearful*] I'm never going to be like those other mums … 'super mums'. I'm *good for nothing*.

Saul: What I'm hearing is that you imagine your efforts are futile. And you struggle to see your own worth, your own value?

Saul uses paraphrasing to follow Aleksi and to communicate his understanding of what Aleksi is sharing. He occasionally frames paraphrasing as a question, by means of checking his perceptions of what Aleksi is sharing. Paraphrasing is also used to gain more insight into what Aleksi is feeling as well as her thoughts about herself – Saul learns, through the use of paraphrasing, that in comparing herself to others Aleksi views herself unfavourably, like a failure, and her self-esteem is low. This might also be a pattern in her life.

Paraphrasing also provided Saul with a powerful way to respond in an accepting and non-judgemental way. Note that in the above example, Saul's interventions do not include opinions or value judgements (e.g. 'You are a person of worth!') or offers to 'solve the problem' (e.g. 'Would it be helpful if you stopped using social media?'). Instead, Saul stayed with Aleksi's experience in order to get as full a picture as possible of what Aleksi's struggles and pains are like for her, and to accept where and who she finds herself to be in the present moment.

Paraphrasing can also help you to become closely involved with clients, without getting hooked into an argument or collusion. It is especially useful for managing strong feelings or even attacks from clients without becoming defensive:

Aleksi: [*In a furious voice*] Well, it's alright for you isn't it? What do you know about failure? You're clearly making a success of things. You're a wealthy therapist and all you have to do is sit there and listen.

Saul: I can really hear how angry you are that I'm not able to share what you are going through.

Aleksi: Yes, I'm angry! I feel angry with everyone. *You*, my ex-husband, the so called 'friends' I have who don't see what I'm going through. *Everyone*!

Saul: And here in therapy, a space in which you so need to feel understood, it's like *I* don't see what you're going through. Like, I really don't know what life is like for you. On top of everything else …

Aleksi: [*Slowly and quietly*] I guess no one can really, and that's difficult for me.

Finally, paraphrasing is an excellent skill for helping clients to clarify for themselves what they mean. In order for you to understand clients, they also have to understand themselves. Paraphrasing allows clients to 'hear again' what they have said to you, providing them with the opportunity to understand deeply their own inner experiences. When we understand ourselves better, we are more able to sit in the driving seat of our own lives. For example:

Aleksi: I've been going back and forth over this for weeks – should I accept my ex-mother-in-law's offer to help with the kids? She's offering to take them

Saul: to school a few times a week. It would be such a *huge* help to me. But I can't
make up my mind – I don't really want her that involved. I'm afraid it will
complicate things between me and my ex … and I think it should be *him*
who is offering to help me.

Saul: So, you're in two minds. On the one hand you've got a source of practical
support which would be a great help. On the other hand, you're not sure you
want this help because of who is offering it and how it might impact your
relationship with your ex.

Aleksi: [*Pausing*] Well, hearing it back like that makes me realize – I've got to take the
help. Actually, on the whole I get on well with my ex mother-in-law and I'm
really struggling on my own. True … I am worried about how this will affect
things with my ex, but on balance the help is more important right now than
anything else.

Aleksi, hearing the therapist's paraphrase, realized that what she said was not what she meant.

So paraphrasing is an invaluable skill which can be used in multiple ways: to check
your perceptions of your clients' experiences; to gather information about them; to
demonstrate your acceptance and non-judgemental attitude towards them; to avoid collusion and manage challenging feelings; and to help your clients to clarify for themselves
what they mean. There are several things to keep in mind with paraphrasing. Firstly, it
is important to remember that paraphrasing needs to be offered tentatively (this is why
it can be helpful to occasionally phrase your perceptions as a question) because by its
very nature you are using new words to describe and reflect back to the client their own
experiences. Some words won't fit for them. As with listening, this also requires you to
be open to getting it wrong, and ready to work with that non-defensively when it happens. For example:

Saul: You're really angry with him.
Aleksi: No, I wouldn't say angry. That's not quite it … I would say annoyed.
Saul: Ok, I was a bit off the mark there – 'angry' isn't what you're feeling. So, you're
annoyed with him.
Aleksi: Yes, that's right. I'm not as mad as *angry*, but I'm feeling more than just
irritated.

Secondly, you need to avoid telling, informing or defining issues for the client. This naturally comes with being tentative. Likewise, it isn't helpful to add opinion, make assumptions or evaluate what the client shares (e.g. 'I can imagine having your mother-in-law
around a lot would be difficult – mother-in-laws are universally difficult aren't they?' or
'As a struggling single mum, I can imagine you would want to get back with your ex to
feel less alone.'). Thirdly, listening out for the depth of feeling expressed by the client is
important too. As with restating, it is important not to rely on the skill of paraphrasing
alone. If you are picking up your client's deep sadness as they speak, you will need show
you are attuned to their sadness by adjusting the way you deliver your paraphrase (i.e. in
your vocal tone, pitch, and pace) or by using a different skill entirely and not choosing
to paraphrase at all. Fourthly, it is also important to be congruent. Don't pretend that you

understand something when you don't. If you are struggling, you might say something like, 'I want to understand. Let me check with you …'.

Summarizing

Summaries are essentially longer paraphrases. Using them enables you to bring together salient aspects of a session in an organized way. Summaries focus on what the client has said. They don't involve sharing your internal hypotheses. Rather, they are used most effectively when they provide some coherence and order to what the client has been saying and provide an overview to the work so far. A possible summary that Saul might make in his session with Aleksi might look like this:

> Saul: From what you've said so far, it's as though you are pulled in several different directions at once – work, being a mum, and socially – and you're struggling with the pressures associated with that. You are rushed off your feet. You also compare yourself unfavourably to your friends and see yourself as somehow failing. Equally, it feels really difficult for you to do all this alone and sometimes you feel angry that no one seems to really know what that's like for you.

As with paraphrasing, summarizing is a useful way to clarify the content and feelings the client has shared, making sure you have grasped the salient points and you have followed the client accurately. Summarizing can also be used at the end of a session, to take stock of what has been discussed, or at the beginning of the next session to facilitate the opening of a session and provide a common starting point (e.g. 'I have been thinking about our last session and the pressures you feel you are currently under. I wonder if you would like to start there today, or if there are other issues you would like to focus on?'). When used in this way, summaries need to be offered tentatively; otherwise you might set the agenda for the session and something the client wanted to bring could get inadvertently lost.

Clients need varying amounts of help to identify what the salient issues are for them and to order their priorities. You will receive a lot of information from your clients and be forming hypotheses about what they are sharing and what they are omitting – explicitly and implicitly. You will be identifying patterns and themes as well as the 'maps' that they use to make sense of their world. Summarizing can help you *and* your client prioritize, focus and then move forward.

We now consider two specific types of summary, which are useful for focusing, prioritizing and moving the exploration forward. They are called 'forming a choice point' and 'gaining a figure-ground perspective' (Gilmore, 1973).

Forming a choice point

There will be times in sessions when you will be able to identify themes or clusters of concerns or different facets to an issue a client is exploring. Given that clients invariably have multiple concerns and will need to decide in which order they will tackle them, formulating a choice point is a way of helping clients to make that decision. It involves identifying various aspects or themes by summarizing them, and then asking the client to make a conscious choice about which issue to focus on. For example:

Aleksi: [*Exploring her concerns about being a single mum*] I feel like I'm not doing a good enough job. When I get home from work I'm so low on energy and the last thing I feel ready for is making dinner, playing with the younger ones, helping the older one with her homework … but at the same time that's the only time I have with them in the week. I feel like I'm missing out on *enjoying* my time with them. Then, there are also times I feel resentful. I don't get much of a social life anymore – in fact it's pretty non-existent because I have no-one around who can babysit. Meanwhile, my ex comes and goes as he pleases – he just doesn't take responsibility for them. That leaves me feeling angry. When he spends time with them, they do fun things together so it's like he's the fun parent and I'm the cross, tired parent.

Saul: If I'm understanding you correctly, it seems that there are several things concerning you right now: managing everything as a single mum, including the quality of time you spend with your children; your feelings about your lack of social life; and your feelings towards your ex and sharing your parenting responsibilities. Which would be useful for us to focus on do you think?

Aleksi: My feelings towards my ex. I sometimes feel so angry towards him, but I don't know what to do or what to say … so, it all just stays bottled up. I think that has a knock-on effect to everything else.

Saul's summary organized the content of the session and identified the key aspects of Aleksi's concerns. He was tentative and offered the client the choice of where to begin by using an open question. The focus for the session was then identified by Aleksi.

There may be times when you will want to disagree with clients about which issue to deal with first. You may think that they are avoiding important issues or you may believe that it would be appropriate to start elsewhere. It will be important to reflect on this difference and consider whether there is anything going on for you 'below the surface' which is taking you in a different direction to that of your client. On the one hand, it may be that your instincts are right and your client is avoiding certain issues. On the other hand, your perspective may be clouded by your own personal agenda. Reflective practice will facilitate your thinking and guide you towards focusing on what is most helpful to the client in terms of their change, growth and healing.

Gaining a figure-ground perspective   In this type of summary, the therapist offers their perception of what they think is the most prominent issue for the client. This will usually be in response to something the therapist has noticed the client talks about with heightened emotion or returns to repeatedly. The therapist may also hypothesize that one issue stands out as the crux. If that issue were managed more productively, then the client would have energy available to tackle other concerns. The notion of 'figure and ground' means that one aspect of a client's concerns is in the forefront of his or her awareness or thinking (i.e. figural), and the other aspects are a backdrop to that (i.e. in the background). What comes to the fore may vary and change. Sometimes clients are not aware of the emphases that they are placing on certain issues. Consider the following example:

Aleksi: I feel so let down by my ex … when he first told me he thought things were over between us I was shocked. I knew things weren't great, but I guess I thought it was a bad patch. Then I started to feel angry. Furious really – it was like he was just giving up on us without trying. We have three kids! The youngest is only five. How could he leave them? The oldest isn't coping – she's really struggling at school. The younger ones don't understand – they're so confused. And me … well, I'm worrying about money all the time. I don't want to move them out of their family home, but how can I manage the mortgage alone? Why isn't he helping us more? How could he do this? How *could* he?

Saul: It seems that of all the issues and changes you are dealing with as a family and as a mother, the thing that comes through as really prominent for you right now is your anger towards him. I can really hear how difficult that's been for you … you keep returning to it … I wonder, is that how it seems to you?

Aleksi: Yes, I just can't seem to stop feeling this way. There are times when I feel *consumed* by my anger and this sense of betrayal, of being let down, by him.

Saul: So, your anger has really taken you over. Would it be useful to focus on that today?

Saul used a short summary to offer his understanding of what was the most prominent concern for Aleksi. From there, he began to consider, with Aleksi, what the focus of the session should be.

Other ways you might introduce a figure-ground perspective include:

'What seems to be at the heart of your concerns is …'

'What stands out for me in what you've been saying is …'

'One aspect which is becoming clearer to me is …'

'I'm very aware of …'

Remember, it is important to offer your ideas tentatively and to invite clients to comment. They may want to disagree with you and you will need to be willing to explore their different views openly and non-defensively. This can be challenging, particularly when it seems to you as though your client is rejecting accurate reflections. We have both had experiences in which, in an attempt to attune to our clients, we have used the exact words or phrases they have used only to find our clients deny, dismiss or rebuke what we have said. To stay with the process requires patience and compassion. It involves listening out for the underlying emotions or patterns of negative thoughts that may be, perhaps painfully, clouding your exchange and leaving your client feeling vulnerable or uncomfortable.

In this section we have reviewed the reflective skills. These skills provide the therapist with some non-intrusive tools for encouraging clients to explore, clarify and focus. It is impossible not to be directive in using counselling skills. What you see as the core concern for a client and what you choose to reflect back, as well as what you leave or disregard, are all ways in which you influence both direction and content. However, in the initial stages of using counselling skills, when you are getting to know clients, you will seek to create space for them to say what they want with minimum imposition of your perspective. The reflective skills will assist you in that purpose.

We now consider methods that can be used to further explore your client's issues.

Methods of exploration

Methods of exploration include different questioning techniques, working with clients' questions, testing your hypotheses and focusing. These methods of exploration are utilized best when they are applied with an open, curious and non-judgemental mind.

It is important to hold in mind that methods of exploration convey, sometimes just implicitly, the therapist's perception of what is important to address. When using these methods, the control over content can shift away from client to therapist. Ultimately, the therapist becomes relatively more directive than when reflecting, paraphrasing or summarizing. Being able to explore what is going on for the client using these skills is an essential form of effective practice. For example, you may need to gain information from clients and encourage them to be specific; you may want to direct them to areas that you think are important to explore further; or you may want to test out new ideas with them. This needs to be approached sensitively and judiciously.

Questioning techniques

We will first look at types of questions you might use to facilitate exploration, before going on to consider some questioning 'dos' and 'don'ts', and then how to work with clients' questions.

Open versus closed questions

Open questions are the kinds of questions for which there is no predetermined answer, unlike closed questions which ask for a specific response (such as 'yes' or 'no'). Open questions demand a fuller response than yes/no type answers. Open questions are helpful in eliciting information and encouraging clients' involvement and exploration. They generally begin with 'What?', 'Where?', 'How?' and 'Who?'. For example, to a client who is talking about arguments with her partner, you might ask:

'What usually happens when you argue?'

'How do your arguments typically begin?'

'When do you usually argue?'

'Where do you argue?'

'Who is usually the first to want to make up?'

Closed questions, on the other hand, limit clients to answer in a particular way. 'Either/or' questions are examples of closed questions – they present clients with only two options and 'lead' the client if the questions are rooted in the therapist's frame of reference. Closed questions are non-exploratory and run the risk of silencing the most talkative client. Repeated use of closed questions leads to a kind of vicious cycle for both therapist and client: the client says less and less and, in order to obtain a response, the therapist asks more and more closed questions. For example, to the same client who is talking about arguments with her partner, closed questions might look like this:

Is it you or your partner who usually starts the arguments?

Do you argue late at night or first thing in the morning?

Do you argue at home or in public?

Did you argue before your session today?

A dialogue containing too many closed questions significantly restricts any exploration. However, there are times when you may want to establish certain facts, to clarify a point about which you are unclear or to check information. For example, it would be unhelpful to ask a client, 'How do you manage your depressive episodes?' if you wanted to establish something more specific, such as, 'Are you taking any medication for your depression?'

Similarly, 'open' questions must also be considered interventions – that is, they can be *too* open when they are so broad that they are difficult to answer. Examples would be, 'What have the last ten years been like for you?', 'What sort of a person would you say you are?' These kinds of questions may confuse clients or put unnecessary pressure on them to come up with an answer rather than explore their experiences. On the whole, thoughtful open questions will facilitate exploration, with closed questions being used when simple facts need to be established. Turning back to the session with Aleksi, a mix of open and closed questions might look like this:

Saul: Have you told your mother-in-law you would like to accept her offer of help? [closed question]

Aleksi: No … no, not yet.

Saul: You sound hesitant about telling her. [paraphrase] How are you feeling about her offer? [open question]

Aleksi: I thought I had come to a decision to take her help, but I still seem to be feeling reluctant … I keep thinking I can cope without her.

Saul: How have you been coping? [open question]

Aleksi: Not well really. Not well at all. I don't know why I don't just say 'Yes, please do come over and help with the kids.'

Saul: What are the feelings underneath your hesitation do you think? [open question]

Aleksi: Anxiety of some kind … I'm afraid that she'll see I'm not coping. Thing is, it's a limited time offer! She's considering taking on a new job if I don't take her up on the offer of help with the kids. I need to let her know soon.

Saul: By when do you need to let her know? [closed question]

The dialogue is exploratory and Aleksi is given the space to become aware of her feelings. However, there are also points in the dialogue where closed questions are necessary to establish some contextual information that helps the therapist and Aleksi focus on her situation.

Hypothetical questions

As the description suggests, these are questions that invite clients to hypothesize and become curious about the things they imagine and fantasize about. They are a type of open question that invite clients to speculate about future outcomes and the potential impact of their own and others' behaviours. The fantasies and fears that clients have can be debilitating and often instrumental in preventing them changing. Not unsurprisingly, clients can sometimes behave as though what they fantasize will definitely happen.

Hypothetical questions are often useful for helping clients to articulate their fears and explore them in the relative safety of the therapeutic space. Once they put some words to their fears and beliefs, they can be challenged, modified and reconsidered. If we think about Aleksi's anxiety about what she imagines her mother-in-law will think if she sees her 'not coping', using hypothetical questions could be used in the following way:

> *Aleksi:*   So, underneath my indecisiveness is this anxiety that my mother-in-law will see me not coping.
>
> *Saul:*   What do you imagine she would think if she could see you weren't coping? [hypothetical question]
>
> *Aleksi:*   I guess ... she'll think I'm a terrible mother.
>
> *Saul:*   And then what would happen? [hypothetical question]
>
> *Aleksi:*   She would get angry. She would disapprove of me.
>
> *Saul:*   And in this scenario, what would you be feeling? [hypothetical question]
>
> *Aleksi:*   Like an even bigger failure ... although I have to say the reality is, she's actually always been quite supportive of me. I've never felt judged by her ... I don't know where these thoughts are coming from, but I do know her opinion seems to matter to me.

Through the use the hypothetical questions, Saul helps Aleksi identify what she fears and she begins to explore how likely it is that her mother-in-law will judge her, and what any judgement would mean to her.

Hypothetical questions are also valuable for helping clients to visualize positive outcomes and to imagine acting differently. For example:

> *Saul:*   If you felt certain that your mother-in-law wasn't judging you, that her offer to help was rooted in her genuine understanding of the pressures you are under, how would you be feeling about the decision?
>
> *Aleksi:*   Completely differently! I wouldn't hesitate to have her help me. It might even be nice for the kids to see their grandmother more ...

Hypothetical questions essentially ask the client to construct an imaginary picture. Exploring that picture may give them some insight into aspects of their concerns that they are overlooking, anxious about or avoiding. Examples of hypothetical questions include:

What do you imagine would happen if ...?

What is the worst thing that you imagine might happen ...?

If you were feeling confident about that, what would you be doing differently?

If you were in control of this situation, what would you be saying?

If you imagined yourself doing things just as you would like, how would that look?

'Why' questions

'Why' questions are tricky. They can be unhelpful to the extent that they can put pressure on clients to justify or to find causes or reasons for the way they are feeling or thinking. Eliciting justifications may entrench the client in an existing position rather than helping them to see new possibilities. 'Why' questions can also convey a hint of criticism. What may be heard is, 'How come you got yourself into these difficulties? In addition, you may notice that if you ask a 'Why?' question, your clients often respond as if you had asked either 'What?' or 'How?', so they don't always land the way you intend.

However, clients often do want to understand why they behave as they do, think the thoughts that they have, become depressed or have unsuccessful relationships. It is also one of the aims of using counselling and psychotherapy skills to help clients gain greater self-understanding and insight into themselves and the possible ways in which they invite others to behave in certain ways towards them.

So, 'Why?' questions need to be asked with a great deal of care. Prefixing or incorporating a statement or view that demonstrates your openness, compassion and curiosity, into a 'Why?' question can help turn an unhelpful 'Why?' question' into one that is more facilitative of gaining insight, understanding and achieving growth. For example, an unhelpful 'Why?' question might look like this:

> *Aleksi:* I just exploded. I shouted at him, I threw my wine glass across the kitchen …
> I am so upset by the way I behaved, but I was just so furious!
>
> *Saul:* Why did you behave like that?
>
> *Aleksi:* I don't know! Like I said, I felt furious!

Whereas a more helpful 'Why?' question might look like this:

> *Aleksi:* I just exploded. I shouted at him, I threw my wine glass across the kitchen …
> I am so upset by the way I behaved, but I was just so furious!
>
> *Saul:* I can hear how furious you were and also how unhappy you were with the way you responded … I'm wondering, do you have any thoughts as to why you acted that way?
>
> *Aleksi:* Everything just got on top of me. It's no excuse, but I felt like I couldn't take any more of his excuses … I was reminded of how my dad was never around for me and would never apologize – it would just be excuse after excuse.

In the first example, Saul's question sounded accusatory and unempathic. Aleksi then became defensive and was unable to explore the meaning behind her behaviour. She became stuck. In the second example, Saul shared an understanding of what Aleksi had been feeling. He also invited her to explore (rather than justify) what was behind her reaction. This facilitated Aleksi to find some insight into why she behaved as she did.

Reflection point

Effects of questions

Questions will have both positive and negative effects. Generally, well-timed, relevant and clear and questions will have several positive effects. They can help clients to focus and be specific, assist you both in information gathering and open up previously unexplored areas. However, overuse of questions can also produce negative effects. For example, they can increase the therapist's control and hence the therapist's personal agenda can be the driving force behind the session. For example, there is always a risk that the questions the therapist asks are not the questions the client wants or needs to answer. At times questions may even skew exploration when the session becomes more like an interview with a question-and-answer feel. In these instances, very little mutual understanding is developed.

Questioning 'Dos' and 'Don'ts'

Do

- **Be clear and concise**. Specific, brief questions are usually easier to respond to.
- **Understand your purpose**. The intention behind your question should be in the service of facilitating exploration and understanding.
- **Share your purpose**. For example, 'I'd like to be clear. What exactly happened when … ?' or 'I'm asking this because I think it might be useful to take an alternative perspective for a moment. What do you imagine might happen if … ?'
- **Consider paraphrasing the client's response** to check that you understand before asking another question.
- **Consider linking your question to what the client has said** with a bridging statement – for example, 'You mentioned feeling very angry. What happened next?'

Don't

- **Ask multiple questions all at once**. It will be difficult for the client to know where to start and they may lose the thread of what they are sharing.
- **Prevaricate**. The draw to excessive qualification is usually an indication that your questioning is becoming unhelpful in some ways.
- **Lead or insinuate**. Leading and insinuating, explicitly or implicating, imposes a view. For example, questions that begin, 'Don't you think …?' or, 'Doesn't everyone feel …?' restricts exploration and may even leave the client feeling criticized or in the 'wrong'.

Working with clients' questions

Clients may pose their own questions to you, the therapist. Clients' questions arise for a variety of different reasons – not just because they want information from you (though of course this is sometimes true). Sometimes, clients will ask a question as a way of introducing an issue, or sometimes because they are feeling a growing sense of desperation about their situation. Sometimes clients ask questions as a defence against exploration, or as a means to avoid an issue they are struggling to confront (that is, by asking you a question they hand the issue over to you). Of course, clients may also pose questions to you because they have no previous experience of therapy and imagine they will simply be on the receiving end of your advice and opinions. You will need to 'tune in' to what the covert or underlying message in the question might be. When you are attuned in this way, clients' questions can be source of rich information about them, their experiences and what they most need. Their questions often provide access to their real concerns. Your responses, in turn, need to work with what you are sensing and encourage further exploration. Always remember that it can take courage to ask questions of a therapist and you need to work respectfully and sensitively with any possible anxiety which your client may be experiencing. This may mean that you start by being transparent about the fact that you are not going to answer their question, or are not going to immediately answer their question – for example, 'Before we look at the answer to that, I'd really like to understand more about what is behind your question.' Or, 'I can hear that you really want an answer from me, but first of all let's just pause and think about what this means to you.' Equally, it might be important to be really explicit about why you're not going to answer their question – for example, 'There are so many possible responses to your question, the problem with me providing you with an "answer" is that it might suggest there is a "right one".' Or, 'I truly believe that the most meaningful way to answer your question is to explore your thoughts around it, rather than mine. Perhaps we can look at that together?'

We have included below a sample of common questions that we have been asked many times by our clients, along with some possible underlying meanings and options for responding.

Question 1: 'Do you think I'm crazy?'
Possible underlying meanings:

> 'You think I'm crazy. You are judging me.'
>
> 'There is something wrong with me.'
>
> 'Therapy is only for crazy people.'

Possible options for responding:

> 'You sound worried about yourself. Will you say some more about that?'
>
> 'I think you are unhappy and confused. I don't think you're crazy.'
>
> 'It sounds like it might be important for you to know how I see you?'

Question 2 'What do you think I ought to do now?'
Possible underlying meanings:

> 'You know better than me.'
>
> 'I'm feeling lost.'
>
> 'I should be going about this in a certain way.'

Options for responding include:

> 'What would you like to do?'
>
> 'I think that's our purpose here, discovering what you might do.'
>
> 'What do you imagine yourself doing?'

Questions 3: Do you think I'm being unreasonable [or too demanding, unfair, weak, irresponsible, arrogant, etc.]?
Possible underlying meanings:

> 'I really don't know how I'm coming across.'
>
> 'I'm worried about my relationships with others.'
>
> 'I need reassurance.'

Options for responding include:

> 'It sounds as if some aspect of your behaviour is concerning you. Is that right?'
>
> 'What is it about what's going on that leads you to think that of yourself?'
>
> 'What would you really like me to know about how you are feeling in this situation?'

Reflection point

Considering clients' questions

Questions 1 to 3 represent a small sample of possible questions clients pose, their possible meanings and some possible responses. Working with clients' questions will require you to attend to your client and actively listen to them at multiple levels, in order to ascertain if there is more to their questions than the literal question itself.

- What kinds of things might you need to know about your client in order to get a sense of any underlying messages they might be communicating?
- What other possible meanings can you identify in the questions posed above?
- What other response options can you think of to the above questions?
- How do you imagine yourself responding to a client who posed such questions to you?

Questions do not have to be answered directly or immediately. We are not implying that you should avoid either giving information or telling clients what you think. However, in the early stages of the therapeutic work, when clients are often at their most vulnerable, they may invest you with 'expert power' and want advice or even to be told what to do. You will need to acknowledge their questions and be aware of how your responses may be interpreted as either implying a course of action or a 'right' way of thinking, feeling or doing. At the heart of what you do and say needs to be the therapeutic relationship and developing and maintaining a sense of trust and of safety.

Testing hypotheses

As your therapeutic work progresses with a client, you will develop hunches about them – what they are feeling, thinking, imagining and so on. You will begin to draw a picture in your mind of who they are, how they find themselves in the situation that they do, how they view the world, what their struggles and pain are, how they can be resourceful and creative, how and why they can self-sabotage, etc. You will start to generate hypotheses, which may contain what you believe to be useful insights about their problems and concerns. Reflective practice is a vital tool in helping you to notice how your subjective lens influences what you sense about your client and will challenge you to remain open to multiple possibilities and perspectives about them. Armed with the insights you gain through reflection and a deepening level of self-awareness, you will make decisions about what, when and how to share your hypotheses. An important rule of thumb in sharing your hypotheses is to tentatively test them out in the first instance, always remaining open to other possibilities and multiple layers of truth. Rigid adherence to any one theory is the antithesis of exploration, curiosity and respect.

Statements which begin, 'I'm wondering if …' or, 'I'm getting curious about …' or, 'I'm imagining …' demonstrate your curiosity in a respectful way. Such statements are also useful alternatives for the occasions when you think questions might be seen as intrusive or inquisitorial, but you are looking to deepen the exploration in some way. These statements also open the door to tentatively sharing a hypothesis or idea. If we return to Aleksi's session, for example, Saul, who has now developed some hypotheses about Aleksi, might test them out in some of the following ways:

Saul's hypothesis 1:	Some of Aleksi's anger towards her ex may also contain previously unexpressed anger towards her dad.
Saul's intervention:	You have talked about how your ex's behaviour reminds you of your dad's behaviour when you were growing up. I'm wondering if there are any ways you link the two of them?
Saul's hypothesis 2:	Aleksi becomes preoccupied with thoughts of what her friends are doing to such an extent that she disconnects from her own experience.
Saul's intervention:	You have talked a lot about what your friends' lives are like. I'm curious as to what it's like for you to talk about yourself?

Saul's hypothesis 3:	Aleksi puts a lot of pressure on herself to be a 'super mum' and doesn't often get a chance to talk about the realities of motherhood.
Saul's intervention:	I can hear that you have a number of thoughts about what being a 'good mother' entails. I'm imagining that there are a lot of feelings – potentially difficult feelings – around what it's like for you to be a mother.

Focusing

It may, at times, be necessary to focus the client in a particular way and ultimately shift the direction of dialogue. It is more directive than any of the techniques of reflecting back. So, once again, it is important to be mindful of what this may mean for the client as you will, at some level, be communicating to them what you believe is important to address. Focusing brings the client's attention to the central themes of the work that need to be explored and avoids tangential patterns of expression. For example, it may be necessary to move the client's focus from others to self; to help them move from making vague statements to more concrete ones; or to shift the session from content-driven, to process-orientated. In response to Aleksi, Saul might use the skill of focusing in any of the following ways:

Saul: I have a clear picture of what your ex says and does. I wonder how you respond to him? [Moving Aleksi's focus from others to self.]

Saul: You have talked about your worries about running a family home without your ex around. I wonder, specifically, what those issues are. [Moving Aleksi from vague to concrete statements.]

Saul: I can hear how unsupported you feel on a daily basis and that other people just don't seem to understand what life is like for you. I wonder how you feel when you are here, in therapy? [Moving the session from content-driven to process-orientated.]

So far in this chapter we have considered the core skills of attending, listening and communication. We now turn to consider therapist's competency and working with difference.

Competency

Your therapeutic competency – that is, your ability to work with clients skilfully, creatively, ethically and knowledgeably – will develop over time as you build on the core skills we have discussed in the chapter. Currently, within the UK the SCoPEd project (SCoPEd, 2019) is being conducted jointly by the BACP, the BPC and the UKCP to agree a shared, evidence-based competence framework for counsellors and psychotherapists. Established competency frameworks will typically outline the knowledge, skills (including personal qualities and capacities for reflection), abilities and ethical understanding needed to work as a counsellor or psychotherapist. Competency frameworks that are tailored to specific groups (e.g. working with children and young people), ways of working (e.g. telephone and online counselling) or particular therapeutic modalities (e.g. integrative or person-centred) are also available. It is worth visiting the websites of the aforementioned organizations to view these frameworks and to keep abreast of developments in the field.

Working with difference

In the UK, the Equality Act 2010 introduced a legal framework intended to protect the rights of individuals and promote equality of opportunity for everyone. Nine 'protected characteristics' are listed in the Act – these are characteristics that are legally protected against discrimination. They comprise age, disability, gender reassignment, marriage and civil partnership, pregnancy and maternity, race, religion or belief, sex and sexual orientation. However, as the BACP (2016) highlights, while these protected characteristics encompass fundamental individual attributes, it is essential to remember that their importance to each individual client will vary. To work ethically with difference in practice requires that we are mindful of how concepts of equality, diversity and inclusion manifest in unique ways for all of us, client and therapist alike, and within the therapeutic relationship.

Working ethically and sensitively with difference demands a rigorous evaluation of our own personal values and assumptions. We must first understand how these influence and shape how we view our clients, ourselves and the world we inhabit. We must therefore approach our reflective practice with integrity. Understanding and working with difference is also about having an appreciation for the numerous ways culture and personal experiences affect our clients' expressions of distress and the way they make meaning. Similarly, as therapists, we need to be cognizant of the way political and cultural landscapes contribute to the clinical and ethical thinking we do about our clients. What makes each human being different goes beyond the protected characteristics referred to above and includes individual experiences of belonging, 'normality/ abnormality', judgement and freedom. However, there are of course groups who are (or have been) privileged or disadvantaged, empowered or subjugated. Developing and exercising robust moral fibre is not a choice point for the therapist, it is a prerequisite for the work. Working within an ethical framework, such as that developed by the BACP and the UKCP (see Chapter 1) is not a tick-box exercise. It involves conscious, active engagement with social, cultural and political layers of experience.

Summary

In this chapter we have described the core skills for working successfully as a counsellor or psychotherapist. They are considered to be the foundations upon which your future therapeutic work progresses and have a central role at every point in the process of your work with a client. We broadly grouped these core skills as those relating to attending, listening and communicating. We also considered your ability to work with clients skilfully, creatively, ethically and knowledgeably — capacities which are collectively known as 'therapist competency'. We briefly introduced 'competency frameworks' which you can use to guide your thinking, reflecting and professional development. Finally, we looked at the importance of being ethical and sensitive to issues of difference in the therapy room and drew your attention to the necessity of working mindfully around concepts of equality, diversity and inclusion. These may manifest in unique ways for all of us, client and therapist alike. In the next chapter we start to explore the very first stage of the therapeutic process, and look in detail at the aims, plans and skills you will be considering as you enter into your work with a client.

Further resources

- Cozolino, L. (2016) *Why Therapy Works.* New York: W.W. Norton & Company.
- Reeves, A. (2018) *An Introduction to Counselling and Psychotherapy: From Theory to Practice* (2nd edition). London: SAGE.
- Spinelli, E. (2005) *The Interpreted World: An Introduction to Phenomenological Psychology* (2nd edition). London: SAGE.
- SAGE Counselling in Action series.

Online resources

Visit https://study.sagepub.com/staffordandbond4e to watch:

Video 3.1   Expressing Warmth and Care

Video 3.2   Active Listening

Video 3.3   Reflecting, Paraphrasing, Summarizing

Video 3.4   Asking Open-Ended Questions

4

The Beginning Stage

Focusing and Connection

Chapter contents

This chapter covers:

- Aims, plans and skills for the Beginning Stage
- Establishing a therapeutic alliance
- Conducting an assessment
- Agreeing a working therapy contract
- Preparing for and managing your first session
- Checklist and worksheet for preparation and management of the first session
- Further resources

Introduction

In this chapter we discuss the aims appropriate to the Beginning Stage of the therapeutic process. We consider the plans you will implement in order to realize these aims, and the skills you will employ to help you do this. We also include a section on preparing for, planning and managing your first session with a new client.

The key theme for the Beginning Stage of the work is 'focusing'. This reflects the key activities of the work at this stage – defining, pinpointing and prioritizing the client's presenting issues and how you will collaboratively address them, as well as drawing your attention towards beginning to develop your relationship with the client. Your main intention behind this focus, at this stage, will be to create a sense of trust, positive regard and warmth. Hence the relational focal point at this stage is defined as 'connection'.

Aims, plans and skills for the Beginning Stage

Aims

The following three aims characterize the work of the Beginning Stage:

1.   To establish a therapeutic alliance
2.   To conduct an assessment
3.   To agree a 'working therapy contract'

Plans

Let's look at the plans you will need to develop and implement in order to achieve your aims for the Beginning Stage, considering each aim in turn.

To establish a therapeutic alliance

As we discussed in Chapter 1, therapy is fundamentally a human activity. While this relationship has much in common with other relationships – for example, close friendships – it is a unique relationship with specific characteristics that distinguishes it from other forms of support. In the Beginning Stage of your work with a client you will be starting to form this special kind of relationship. For many therapists, the therapeutic relationship is the central agent of change, growth and healing. As Yalom (1989) writes, 'It's the relationship that heals, the relationship that heals, the relationship that heals' (ibid.: 91). Research demonstrates that psychotherapy outcomes are influenced, to a considerable extent, by the therapeutic relationship (Norcross and Lambert, 2019) and hence the establishment of a good, collaborative relationship with your client is an essential feature of the work you enter into together.

In the Beginning Stage, you will plan to establish a 'therapeutic alliance' (or 'working alliance'), a key component of the therapist–client relationship. This is a concept that describes the quality and strength of the relationship between therapist and client, and degree of collaboration that exists between them. Bordin (1979) proposed the therapeutic alliance (what he called the working alliance) as a pan-theoretical construct, which is now widely adopted within the field of counselling and psychotherapy, wherein the alliance is measured in terms of an agreement about the therapeutic goals of the work, unanimity on the therapeutic tasks, and the development of a relationship bond.

The therapeutic alliance

This can be defined as:

- **Goals**. The purpose of the therapeutic work, what can be achieved and what the outcome(s) might look like
- **Tasks**. What will happen in therapy including in-therapy behaviours and processes
- **Bond**. The experience of a positive emotional bond between therapist and client, including attributes such as the degree of trust, respect and sense of affinity between them.

For Flückiger et al. (2018: 318), 'the alliance represents an emergent quality of mutual collaboration and partnership between therapist and client [and] infuses every interaction throughout psychotherapy'. It is therefore not an endpoint, goal or outcome of therapy. Rather, it unfurls over time, being forged, shaped and sculpted according to each unique dyadic encounter and interaction. Planning to develop a therapeutic alliance is imperative for the success of counselling and psychotherapy (Flückiger et al., 2019) as it is 'the part of the client–therapist relationship that enables [them] to work together even when [they] experience some desires to the contrary' (Clarkson, 1995: 31) Numerous research studies show that a robust and positive relationship exists between the therapeutic alliance and therapy outcomes (e.g. the degree to which people feel better, symptom alleviation, wellbeing and drop-out rates) (Flückiger et al., 2018).

To conduct an assessment

Planning an assessment is an integral part of any counselling and psychotherapy process. There are competing perspectives on assessment (and diagnosis) in the psychotherapeutic world. In our view, the most recent and significant contribution from the field comes from the work of Lucy Johnstone and Mary Boyle (2018), *The Power Threat Meaning Framework*. It is not within the scope of this book to discuss in depth the wide variety of approaches and techniques available to therapists undertaking an assessment. However, we present a basic introduction and overview to the assessment process in order to help you plan this part of your work.

Assessment is an important aim for the Beginning Stage, although it is an ongoing, continuous process featuring at every stage of the work. It is not a linear activity – clients' views of themselves, others and their problems often change as the work progresses and they gain new insights. During the preliminary assessment, it is therefore important to hold this in mind and keep decisions and hypotheses under review. Supervision will help you to maintain an open perspective and iteratively evaluate your judgements. The methods you will employ to help you conduct an assessment can vary and most therapists will draw on a mixture, including semi-structured interviews, questionnaires, current research, intuition, listening to the narrative process and observation. Here we outline the key elements you will need to consider in your assessments and encourage you to access the resources provided at the end of this chapter for further support.

To agree a working therapy contract

A 'working therapy contract' can be defined as a specific commitment from both therapist and client to a clearly defined course of action. Using counselling and psychotherapy skills requires the assent of the client to be effective. This means that the client actively engages with the opportunity to reflect on an issue or problem in greater depth, and more systematically than is usually the case when receiving informal support from friends and relatives.

It is important to plan to negotiate and agree with your client the working therapy contract that your subsequent work with them will rest upon. This contract will formalize some of the key differences between relationships that provide informal support and their relationship with you, their counsellor or psychotherapist. As discussed in Chapter 1, some of these differences include a purpose and agenda for the work which is predetermined, setting clear boundaries and clear role specification. A 'working therapy contract' is important to the client psychologically, therapeutically, ethically and possibly legally because it manages client expectations and provides criteria by which you can both assess what is happening as the work progresses and to decide when the work is completed. Contracting is empowering for clients when negotiated collaboratively.

The process of discussing the working therapy contract with your client will also involve determining the tasks and goals of the work, both of which contribute to the therapeutic alliance (see above).

Skills

We now turn to the skills that you will need to learn in the Beginning Stage to support your work, meet your aims and put your plans into action. We consider each aim in turn.

Skills needed to establish a therapeutic alliance

We will first consider what is needed to develop a relational bond. An agreement about tasks and goals is discussed in the section below on 'defining the focus, process and direction of your work'. You will be building on your core skills in order to develop a relational bond, in particular listening and communicating skills. These will be expanded on in the ways discussed below.

Much has been written about how to develop the kind of intense personal connection necessary for therapeutic work to proceed. Carl Rogers (1902–1987) described an effective therapeutic relationship as characterized by certain core qualities. While these qualities have been variously described, the common thread is the significance and worth ascribed to clients themselves, their experiences and our contact with them. In the Beginning Stage you will plan to demonstrate certain attitudes and ways of experiencing and being with your client that encapsulate these qualities. In particular, we consider here three qualities, which are, 'values and attitudes, but also skills which can be taught, learnt, practised and supervised' (Clarkson, 1995: 40):

- Empathy
- Acceptance
- Genuineness

The skills you employ to demonstrate these qualities will build on the core skills outlined in Chapter 3. The purpose of communicating these qualities is to facilitate a transformative relationship that engages the client in the therapeutic process. It is not enough to expect clients to know that you accept and understand them. You will need to demonstrate and communicate these values both verbally – in what you say – and nonverbally – in how you say what you say, and how you orientate yourself towards them.

It is important to note that empathy, acceptance and genuineness are not stage-specific – they are fundamental throughout the work. However, we introduce them here as they are enormously influential in developing a good rapport and sense of connection with your client.

Empathy

Empathy is 'the capacity to think and feel oneself into the inner life of another person' (Kohut, 1984: 82). It is about deeply understanding another person and attempting to grasp as fully and accurately as possible the messages they are trying to convey verbally and non-verbally. For Rogers (1980: 142), who wrote extensively on the subject and considered empathy to be one of six 'necessary and sufficient conditions' for change, empathy was a process rather than a state. It was 'a way of being' with another person:

> It means entering the private perceptual world of the other and becoming thoroughly at home in it. It involves being sensitive, moment by moment, to the changing felt meanings which flow in this other person, to the fear or rage or tenderness or confusion of whatever that he or she is experiencing. It means temporarily living in the other's life, moving about in it delicately without making judgements.

Empathy involves striving to sense your client's world from their perspective, and to be open, sensitive and aware of their experiences. It is a cognitive, emotional and embodied vicarious imagining. Empathy is therefore different from sympathy. Sympathy can be seen as an experience of similarity or agreement with another, to feel compassion, commiseration or support for them. Sympathy often also involves an assumptive understanding of what is happening for the other person. It is about 'looking on' (experience-distant) rather than 'looking from within' (experience-near), which is what you are attempting to do when you empathize. Let's consider an example:

> Jermaine has sought therapy, with a therapist called Liz, to help him understand his feelings about his girlfriend's pregnancy. While he and his girlfriend had recently talked about wanting children in their future, they hadn't made any decisions or plans, and the news is unexpected.

> *Jermaine:*   I'm still in a state of shock. On the one hand I'm really excited, on the other I'm *so, so* scared … sometimes I feel nothing at all, like it's not quite real, like is it true? Is she really having a baby?

Example 1: Expressing sympathy

> *Liz:*   I understand completely. I would be shocked too. Everyone feels some degree of shock when they realise they're going to have a baby.

Example 2: Communicating empathy

> *Liz:*   I can really hear what an impact this news is having on you … you're feeling all sorts of different emotions, which sound overwhelming at times. And sometimes you feel none at all. You're asking yourself, 'Is this really happening?'

In the first example, the therapist, Liz, has some sense of accord with Jermaine. Her response is sympathetic in the sense that it identifies some commonalities that often (but not definitely) exist for expectant parents and uses them to try to offer something supportive. However, in expressing her sympathy Liz makes presumptions about Jermaine by drawing on what she thinks she knows happens generally, rather than focusing specifically on Jermaine's individual, unique experience. In the second example, Liz draws out the features of what Jermaine shares specifically, in an attempt to enter his private perceptual world and look from within his experience.

Empathy is almost universally understood to be central to therapeutic understanding. This is supported by research investigating effective elements of the therapeutic relationship, which has demonstrated that empathy is a robust predictor of client outcome (Elliot et al., 2018).

Because we are all separate, unique beings, it is impossible for us to understand our clients completely. We cannot experience another person's life just as they do, because of the uniqueness of each individual's experiences; however, empathic understanding is an essential component for building rapport. It demonstrates 'communicative attunement' – an intentional, active engagement with the client's experience moment to moment (Elliot et al., 2018). Empathy opens up a reflective space for your client – being understood and affirmed provides the support and safety needed for self-expression and exploration (DeYoung, 2015). Clients no longer feel alone or alien because they have someone moving alongside them in their experience. From this perspective empathy can also be seen as a way of normalizing your client's experiences. Through empathic understanding you are able to show them that there is nothing shameful or unnatural in human distress.

Acceptance

Acceptance is akin to what Rogers (2004) termed 'unconditional positive regard' (UPR), what Egan (2006) referred to as 'respect' and what Mearns and Cooper (2018) described as 'affirmation'. Essentially, acceptance means valuing and affirming others because they are human. Mearns and Thorne (1988: 59) write, 'The counsellor who holds this attitude deeply values the humanity of her client and is not deflected in that valuing by any particular client behaviours. The attitude manifests itself in the counsellor's consistent acceptance of and enduring warmth towards her client' – that is, an attitude of acceptance is not conditional, rather it is inherently non-judgemental. Accepting another human being as they are stems from an underlying belief that we all have reasons for behaving, thinking and feeling as we do. It is also an acknowledgement that the way our clients behave, think and feel may be reflective of the means they have found to survive, cope and adapt to life's challenges, disappointments and pain. Even if these behaviours, thoughts and feelings do not seem to serve them well, they are manifestations of 'creative adaptations' to the world around them. Acceptance is not about colluding or agreeing with everything your client says, does and feels – colluding and agreeing are intrinsically judgemental acts after all. Rather, it is about respecting and being open to the whole person sitting in front of you, not just those parts of the person that you understand, like or feel resonance with. Let's return to the work with Jermaine to tease out how Liz might demonstrate her acceptance for who he is and where he finds himself with the unexpected pregnancy:

Jermaine shares with Liz that, on receiving the news that his girlfriend was preg-
nant, he felt angry and started an argument with her. He blamed her for not taking
precautions. The disagreement escalated and he stormed out.

Jermaine:	In that moment all I could feel was anger and I just started shouting all this horrible stuff ...
Liz:	Your first feeling was anger and you reacted to it – you lashed out.
Jermaine:	Yes exactly [*sighs deeply*].
Liz:	That's a big sigh, I wonder what's happening for you right now? Now you're reflecting on that moment?
Jermaine:	I'm feeling frustrated with myself that I behaved like that. I don't really blame her, it's not her fault – it's no-one's 'fault'. I should never have said the things I did!
Liz:	You felt angry in the moment and now you're regretful of how you behaved as a result. I wonder whether there were other feelings involved too that might help us make sense of what happened? Earlier you described yourself feeling scared ...
Jermaine:	I am scared. I just don't know how I'm going to support us. It's such bad timing – I'm in between jobs, what if I don't get another one? It's a frightening prospect.

Liz recognized that his behaviour towards his girlfriend didn't serve him well. His
behaviour may even have been evocative or challenging to hear. However, Liz attempts
to resist judging Jermaine's behaviour, without suggesting she approved of it either. She
does this by acknowledging the feelings Jermaine reported to experience. She tries to
demonstrate her acceptance by working with her belief that there were reasons underlying his behaviour, as yet unacknowledged and out of awareness to either of them, that
reflected his distress in the moment of hearing the news. She does this by being open
to the whole person sitting in front of her, including the Jermaine that is sitting across
from her sighing deeply and able to reflect on what happened with hindsight. This
includes accepting that Jermaine has multiple feelings that may appear in conflict with
one another and yet are all valid.

Clients may experience a variety of emotions at the prospect of discussing what
concerns them. For example, they may feel ashamed, fearful, sad or antagonistic. Often,
they judge themselves harshly and anticipate criticism from others. We believe that
clients who feel judged or blamed are unlikely to feel secure enough to begin exploring concerns and disclosing painful issues. It is therefore vital that you aim for, and
work to maintain, a relationship that is accepting of who they are. However, it would
be absurd to suggest that you are, or can become, judgement-free. Firstly, in order to
work effectively with your clients, you will need to be continually hypothesizing and
making assessments. This will involve making judgements about the content your clients bring, their process, and the process between you. Secondly, as therapists we bring
our subjective self into the room which influences how we listen, experience and
respond to our clients (see Chapter 3). What we can do, however, is approach our work
with clients from a place of empathic understanding and with an appreciation that

clients – just like us – are doing the best they can and therefore deserve neither blame nor condemnation.

Acceptance is a key aspect of an effective therapeutic relationship. Research in this area suggests a significant correlation between therapists' unconditional acceptance for their clients and positive outcomes (Norcross and Hill, 2004), with studies indicating that the experience of a 'warm' and 'positively regarding relationship' are among some of the most valued aspects of therapy (Cooper, 2008).

To accept clients means appreciating and celebrating their differences and acknowledging the validity of their perceptions. Acceptance is neither a bland nor a resigned attitude. It is a strong, potent quality that recognizes the worth of your clients, receives and gives credence to what they disclose to you and believes in their ability to change.

Genuineness

Analogous to congruence and sincerity, genuineness is about how real we are as people in response to, and in relationship with, our clients. This quality demands authenticity, openness and 'visibility' without hiding behind a professional role. As Tolan (2017) writes, 'Congruence is that aspect of ourselves that is open and flexible – not given to distortion and denial' (ibid.: 44). The genuine therapist is, 'freely and deeply himself' (Rogers, 1957: 97).

Genuineness does not carry an imperative to voice all our feelings and thoughts about our clients. It is not an act of promiscuous self-disclosure. Rather, to be genuine in a therapeutic relationship means being aware and connected to your internal responses. Clients do sometimes act in ways that we don't like or get on with very well leaving us feeling, for example, irritated, frightened or bored. Having an awareness and connection with your inner feelings means that if you feel impatient with a client, you can identify and locate your impatience; if you feel angry with a client, you can own your anger. Genuineness is about being able to reflectively and reflexively consider the impact your client is having on you, paying close attention to the patterns and themes that emerge. Crucially – and this is one of the reasons why supervision is so helpful – it means separating what belongs to you and what belongs to clients. From this place of internal integrity and integration you are able to make choices about what you communicate about your internal responses to your clients, and what you do not. These choices involve sharing relevant aspects of your experience of clients with them in ways that they can both accept and use (Mearns and Thorne, 2007). This should be at the heart of your disclosures. This is discussed in greater depth in Chapter 5.

In the example of Jermaine's work with Liz, communicating her genuineness Liz might share something like this:

Liz: You know Jermaine, on hearing about how you reacted to your girlfriend with anger and blame, I found I was responding with some anger myself. I also felt a little frightened. I wonder if these feeling tell us anything about what was happening between you both?

Jermaine: I think she felt angry too … she shouted right back at me. I think I really hurt her … and the argument was frightening for us both. We've never argued like that before.

Research in this area has found that there is a significant relationship between the 'real relationship' (i.e. the extent to which therapist and client are genuine with one another and perceive each other in ways that are realistic) and therapy outcomes, suggesting that therapists need to attend to and strengthen this aspect of the therapeutic relationships with their clients (Gelso et al., 2018).

Being genuine and transparent promotes trust and safety. Some research studies have found that therapists' 'trustworthiness' is considered by clients to be one of their most important qualities (Cooper, 2008). In a genuine encounter, clients learn that their experience with you is trustworthy. This in turn cultivates a sense of trust in their own perceptions (Tolan, 2017). When clients trust in themselves, they can begin to learn more about the real 'inner me'. Genuineness also provides important modelling for clients. As you demonstrate authenticity, you implicitly provide your clients with opportunities for connecting to and expressing their own authenticity. Futhermore, as Evans (1994) argues, clients will pick up inauthenticity early and may withdraw. There is no 'fake it till you make it' in therapy – we cannot give our clients the impression of one thing (e.g. strong and authoritative) if we are actually feeling something quite different (e.g. frightened), imagining this to go unnoticed and as without impact. Clients are more likely to sustain their work with you if they have confidence in you and experience you as genuine.

The interrelatedness of the three qualities

Empathy, acceptance and genuineness are inextricably bound together, and we have abstracted them here for the purposes of discussion. They are the fundamental values that you will need to express explicitly and implicitly in order to build a strong therapeutic alliance. Clients may arrive in therapy feeling inept, powerless and unworthy. However, a relationship in which they are empathically understood, respected and acknowledged, and experience another human being as genuinely interested in them can be powerful. This frees clients to become engaged authors of their own wellbeing and help them to move from a position of alienation from both themselves and others to one of intimacy.

Empathy, acceptance and genuineness are not without challenges. Empathy requires us to not be afraid to feel – we must actuate our courage and resilience (De Young, 2015). To be accepting of our clients requires us to start with acceptance of ourselves (Tolan, 2017) and this is not always an easy task for many of us. Additionally, acceptance means meeting another exactly where they are and holding the creative tension between being a facilitator of change and having no expectations or conditions around that change. Genuineness demands a high level of self-awareness and honesty. This is why personal therapy, considered critical to the training process by all accredited training courses, can be so useful. Self-awareness and honesty may involve confronting aspects of ourselves that are uncomfortable or painful: 'For therapists as well as clients, therapy is a place where shadows can be confronted' (Bager-Charlson, 2010: xiii). These qualities are not about being perfect either – this would be an impossible and even unhelpful aspiration. In fact, 'misattunements' in therapy, which are followed by a process of repair and 're-attunement', teach us that we can not only survive moments of difficulty and pain, but also return to a psychological and physiological state of calm with a renewed sense of resilience and courage (Schore, 2011). Clients do not need the perfect therapist; they need a relationship in which the other is available, open, understanding and reliable.

Finally, while your aim at the outset will be to create a therapeutic alliance, attending to the relationship will be a continuing and important task extending throughout your work together. This relationship will change as your work progresses. You may experience unsteady beginnings or go through periods of confusion and turmoil before free and open dialogue can begin. Your relationship will be one of the most valuable sources of information that you both have. Clients will show you much by the manner in which they relate to you about the shape and patterns of other relationships in their lives. In the Beginning Stage of working together you will be laying down secure foundations from which to stand, grow and thrive.

Skills needed to conduct an assessment

Assessment starts from the moment you and your client are in contact and begin forming ideas about one another. As well as making an assessment of what your client needs and whether you can help them, your client will of course be making an assessment of you. Your ability to build a good rapport and the quality of your developing relational bond will be important aspects of assessment, as these things will indicate to you both something about how you will work together. Therefore, you will be building on the skills outlined in the previous section, as well as the core skills outlined in Chapter 3 – in particular, attending, using the integrative framework for listening, listening to your internal responses and considering your listening filters. As the development of a relational bond has been discussed in the previous section, we focus here on other important aims of assessment. These are pictorially represented in Figure 4.1.

- What is the presenting issue?
- What are the contextual issues?
- How motivated is the client?
- Are there any risk issues to consider?
- Do you have the right level of competency to work with this client?

What is the presenting issue?
You will first need to understand and establish the issue(s) your client is bringing. By 'presenting issues' we mean issues which are uppermost in the client's mind. They may or may not be clear about their issue(s), or they may feel confused or overwhelmed by them. You will need to be able to tolerate these feelings and help the client towards greater clarity. This means neither seeking to neatly package clients' concerns nor assuming responsibility for defining the issues for them when frustration or anxiety builds. Rather, it requires embracing uncertainty, staying with complexity and ambiguity, being open to new information, and avoiding premature actions and conclusions based on minimal exploration. Equally, when clients present their problems in a precise manner it should not deter you from seeking further clarification. You will need to provide the

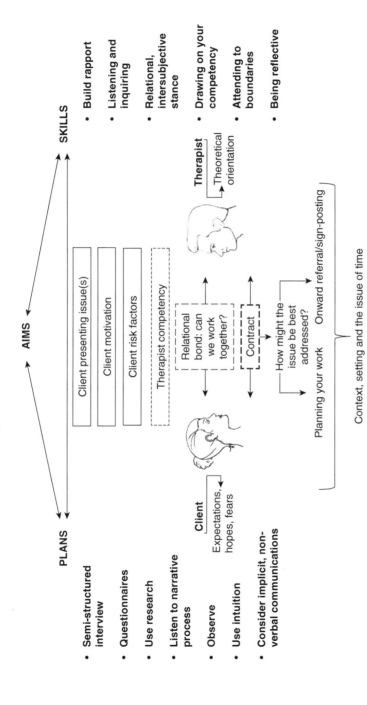

PLANS

- Semi-structured interview
- Questionnaires
- Use research
- Listen to narrative process
- Observe
- Use intuition
- Consider implicit, non-verbal communications

AIMS

Client presenting issue(s)

Client motivation

Client risk factors

Therapist competency

Client

Expectations, hopes, fears

Relational bond: can we work together?

Contract

How might the issue be best addressed?

Planning your work   Onward referral/sign-posting

Therapist

Theoretical orientation

Context, setting and the issue of time

SKILLS

- Build rapport
- Listening and inquiring
- Relational, intersubjective stance
- Drawing on your competency
- Attending to boundaries
- Being reflective

FIGURE 4.1   *Assessment and contracting*

time to explore their opening statements. Clarifying and reaching a common, working understanding with clients is an important activity, begun at the outset and forming the basis for subsequent deeper exploration, goal-setting and action.

Understanding your clients' presenting issue(s) will include understanding the particular meanings and beliefs they have about them, how they view themselves and how they feel they are impacted by them. This can be enhanced by obtaining contextual information (see below) and a history of the issue(s).

You will also need to be alert to signs of significant emotional and physical distress that may point to needing either the involvement of, or a referral on to, another professional such as a psychiatrist or medical professional (Palmer and McMahon, 1997; Daines et al., 2007). For example, if someone refers to physical pain, dizziness or headaches that do not have an obvious explanation in their account, it is worth asking if they have had a medical assessment and encouraging them to obtain one. Persistent feelings of anxiety or depression – especially if accompanied by changes in patterns of sleep or eating, repeated acts of self-harm, suicidal ideas or possible delusions – may indicate the need to involve another mental health professional. This is not to assume a pathology. Rather, it is to recognize that some coping mechanisms are more or less functional and may require the involvement of different kinds of support. Clients may be understandably anxious about seeking medical or psychiatric assessments. They may have chosen to discuss their concerns with you because you are 'outside' the medical world and they wish to explore alternative ways of addressing their problems. Care needs to be taken about raising the issue of further assessments in order that your client feels supported and respected.

Questions to help you understand your client's issue(s) include:

- How does the client define and describe the issue, and what do they share about its duration, persistence and possible trigger(s)?
- How does the issue affect the client?
- Are there any issues the client may be avoiding, dismissing or overlooking?
- What does the client believe about themselves, others and life?

What is the context?

Understanding the context within which your client lives means learning about their cultural context; current circumstances, including such things as whether they are in work and what their current living circumstances are; whether they have close and supportive relationships; and what is important to them. This is a good point at which to assess what resources they have, and lack, and what their current coping mechanisms are. As Joyce and Sills (2014: 191) write, 'The fact that our clients have survived so far means that they have already found enough resources to manage their situation and symptoms to some extent, even if these resources carry a heavy "downside"'. Their resources and ways of coping can help shed light on their issues, and also help you identify 'gaps' and strengths to build upon. It also means gaining some information about their past including their childhoods, previous relationships, history of health issues, and any events they ascribe particular significance to.

Questions to help you understand contextual factors during assessment include:

- How does the client invest their time and energy?
- What is important to know about their cultural context?
- What support systems does the client have (or lack)?
- What events, past and present, are important to them in terms of how they understand their current issues?

How motivated is the client?

Client motivation is a crucial element of the change process in counselling and psychotherapy and has been shown to be strongly associated with positive therapeutic outcomes (Cooper, 2008). You will need to develop an understanding of how driven your client is towards making changes in their lives. This is often a hugely complex area for evaluation as clients may desperately long for things to be different while simultaneously feel fearful about what change will involve and how it will affect their lives and relationships. This is understandable – therapy shakes things up! As well as being potentially healing, positive and transformative, it can have far-reaching consequences that can be challenging to manage. It will be useful to find out what has brought the client into therapy at this time and how realistic the changes they would like to see happen actually are. It will be equally important to evaluate the client's sense of personal responsibility around making changes, the support they have around them, and what they are expecting to happen in therapy and from you.

Questions to help you understand your client's motivation to change include:

- Why now? What has prompted the client to seek therapy?
- What are they expecting therapy to be like and how will they make use of it?
- How might they stop themselves from getting what they want?
- What have they previously tried to do to resolve their issues?

Are there any risk issues to consider?

'Risk' in counselling and psychotherapy refers to the risk of harm a client poses to themselves and/or others. This includes risk of self-harm or suicide. It is an extremely important element in any assessment as it helps you to make decisions about how to work safely with clients within a psychotherapeutic relationship (van Rijn, 2015). As with the assessment literature in general, it is beyond the scope of this book to discuss risk assessment at depth; however, we provide an overview here of some of the salient features of a risk assessment.

The *Cross-Government Suicide Prevention Workplan* (HM Government, 2019), led by the Department of Health, identifies groups of people who are at high risk of suicide. These include men, people in care of mental health services, those in contact with the criminal justice system and people with a history of self-harm. In addition, specific occupational groups have been found to be at greater risk of suicide than the national average for those within the age range 20–64 years. They include males working in the lowest-skilled occupations; individuals in culture, media and sport occupations (particularly females); females in health professions, particularly nursing; and male and female carers (Office for National Statistics, 2017). Non-fatal deliberate self-harm is more prevalent than suicide, but is also associated with increased risk of suicide (Christiansen and Jensen, 2007; Hawton et al., 2003). Larkin et al. (2014) identified several factors that consistently showed associations with repetitious self-harm, which included previous self-harm, a diagnosis of personality disorder or schizophrenia, a sense of hopelessness, a history of psychiatric treatment, alcohol or drug abuse/dependence and living alone. Van Rijn (2015) suggests that an assessment of risk always needs to consider whether your client belongs to any of these at risk groups; whether your client is experiencing high levels of stress and how they are coping with that stress; and what protective factors play an active role in your client's life. These are factors which change, in some way, a person's response to the aforementioned areas of risk and act to guard against harm, such as personal resilience or having a reason to live.

Questions to help you assess your client's level of risk include:

- Does your client belong to any groups of individuals considered to be the most vulnerable to risk?
- Has your client experienced any stressful life events in their recent past?
- In terms of severity, how would your client describe their problems?
- What are your client's usual coping strategies, and what are their planned strategies for coping with the issues they have reported?

Do you have the right level of competency to work with this client?

As discussed in Chapter 3, therapist competency refers to the knowledge, skills, abilities and ethical understanding needed to work therapeutically. Questions and thoughts you may have around your level of competency to work with any particular client should be considered in supervision. As part of an assessment, you will need to be considering what you are able to bring to the work with the individual client sitting in front of you, and what your limits of competence are. These may include such things as needing specific training and experience with a particular issue (e.g. addiction), your capacity to work within a multidisciplinary team of professionals (e.g. working in particular settings such as the NHS) or an understanding of particular cultural values important to your client (e.g. understanding certain religious beliefs your client holds). Assessing your own competency with ethical awareness also requires you to consider what clients you feel you couldn't work with at the current time for personal reasons. These may be temporary (e.g. you may decide that while you are dealing with your own bereavement, you would struggle to work with another person's) or fundamental (e.g. you feel that the values you hold around animal welfare mean you are unable to work with someone who is cruel to animals). Paying close and candid attention to the impact the client has on you will invariably provide you with valuable insight into your level of competency.

It will also be important to consider your client's preferences for the kind of therapy they are looking for and assessing whether you are able to offer it, and if not what that may (or may not) mean for your work together. The client's preferences may include therapy method, format, therapist's relational style and characteristics, and therapy length (Norcross and Wampold, 2010). In light of the research suggesting that client preferences are linked to the success of therapy, Norcross and Wampold (2002) suggest explicitly discussing a client's strong preferences whenever it is practically possible to do so.

Questions to help you assess your competency to work with a client include:

- What kind of knowledge and/or experience will you need to work with the issues the client is presenting?
- Do you feel the client needs any form of specialist input for the issues they have brought?
- Does the client express any strong preferences for a particular style or type of therapy or therapist?
- What do you feel about this client and the issues they have brought?

Assessment is not and should not be viewed as a procedure that is 'done to' clients as passive recipients. It typically involves intensive and extensive exploration, during which clients will hear themselves describe themselves, their concerns and their lives, perhaps for the first time. It is important to foster an environment in which they feel able to be participants in this process, engaged to a greater or lesser extent, and remain mindful that, as a result, they may be affected and challenged by what you are discussing. Involving clients may be accomplished not only by using your skills and clinical experiences but also more concretely by encouraging them to develop self-assessment and self-monitoring techniques (Nelson-Jones, 2008). While assessment is intended to lead to working hypotheses and a plan for the way you work together, it is important that you preserve an open and flexible view of their issues. The most effective assessments are the result of collaboration between client and practitioner. It is important to remember that clients will also be making assessments of you, and this is an opportunity for them to see if you feel like the right therapist for them.

Assessment at the Beginning Stage means that both you and your client are working towards a shared 'good enough' understanding of what the issues and concerns are for them. It is an opportunity for the client to become clearer about their concerns as they put them into words to an attentive listener. It also means that you have started to acquire enough relevant information about how the client sees themselves and their concerns in order to make a preliminary assessment and to facilitate contracting.

Reflection point

'Ian'

Consider the following client referral:

Ian is a 40-year-old father of two, currently working as a scaffolder. Recently, he consulted his GP because of persistent low mood over the previous four months. He was prescribed anti-depressants and his GP referred him to the community counselling and psychotherapy service within which you work. A brief assessment was conducted over the telephone by one of your colleagues. Ian provided them with the following information.

(Continued)

Along with 'low mood', Ian also says he has been struggling to get to sleep at night despite feeling 'exhausted' by the end of the day. He also reported feeling 'really stressed out' about his working life as he may be facing redundancy.

Ian and his wife separated a year ago. Ian says he has often 'felt lonely' now that he lives alone. The only accommodation Ian could afford when he moved out of the family home was on the other side of town, further from both his children (aged six and nine) and many of his friends. He sees his children every other weekend and misses them a great deal. At the weekends he is pleased to have a break from work, but simultaneously he doesn't know how to spend his time when he isn't visiting his children. He used to enjoy playing football on a Sunday with his local team, but he doesn't feel motivated to join in anymore. He has two close friends who he meets with once a month. They frequently invite him to meet more often, but Ian says he doesn't want to 'intrude' on their lives and imagines them to be 'far too busy' to make time for him in reality.

Ian would like to 'feel normal again instead of constantly down and depressed, or stressed out'. He has never been in therapy before and doesn't know what to expect, but he is 'willing to give anything a go if there's a chance it will help'.

The colleague who is managing Ian's referral has asked you if you are available to meet with Ian for a formal, in-person assessment with a view to working with him should therapy seem appropriate.

- What do you understand to be Ian's presenting issues and what else do you need to ask him to clarify them?
- What features of Ian's story so far are you noting in terms of important contextual factors?
- What kinds of questions might you ask in order to establish Ian's motivation to be in therapy and to engage in change? Is there anything in your colleague's report that already speaks to that?
- Does Ian fall into an at risk group? If so, how might you use that information to inform the questions you ask him?
- Based on the information your colleague has provided so far, how do you feel about the prospect of working with Ian in therapy?
- What other questions do you find you are asking yourself about this prospective client?

Skills needed to agree a 'working therapy contract'

A discussion about the working therapy contract should involve at least three elements:

1. The type of help you are offering
2. The focus, process and direction of the work
3. The practicalities of your work

In order to do this, you will be building on the core skills already outlined, with a particular focus on working collaboratively with clear boundaries. Let's look at each element of your contract in turn.

Agreement for the type of help you are offering

What will probably matter most to your client is that you are trustworthy. You will begin to speak to this by being explicit and clear about interpersonal boundaries and exactly what kind of support and help you provide as a counsellor or psychotherapist. This may require you to clarify what you are offering and avoiding confusion with other types of relationship – for example, friendship, a sexual relationship, or one that offers support or assistance in the form of advice or practical action. Potential clients may have little direct experience of therapy and this aspect of a contract should entail clarifying what is likely to be involved for them should they decide to work with you. This will also involve being clear about the confidential nature of the work, including the limits of confidentiality. Confidentiality is one of the basic conditions of counselling and psychotherapy. It is essential for enabling someone to talk openly and freely about personally sensitive issues. The boundaries of confidentiality need to be stated clearly and, where appropriate, negotiated with clients. You will need to be alert to the non-verbal clues (body language, hesitancy, facial expression) that may communicate the client's desire for further discussion or information about this aspect of the contract.

A clear general statement on confidentiality might sound something like this:

Therapist: What you say and do here is confidential. However, I want to say something to you that I say at the outset to every client. If I think you are in danger of harming yourself or anyone else, I may take steps to involve others. I will, if possible, discuss this with you first. Are there are any questions you want to ask me about that?

After responding to any questions or comments about how you will respond to risk issues, you may wish to open up discussion to anyone who may be routinely informed about your work together. For example a receptionist, or anyone involved in providing you with professional support on a confidential basis, such as your supervisor or experienced colleagues. These are all people who might be thought of as falling within a 'circle of confidentiality' that support your practice and for whom it would be impractical to seek a client's consent every time the client might be discussed.

Therapist: There are a small number of people with whom I may discuss our work together on a strictly confidential basis in order to provide you with the best possible work. They are … Are there any questions you would like to ask? Are you willing for me to do this?

It is so much better for trust building to be clear at the earliest possible opportunity about how confidentiality will be managed and to have given the client an opportunity to raise any issues that concern them.

If you are working in an agency setting, the limits to confidentiality may be clearly outlined in policy and practice guidelines that will inform how you approach discussing confidentiality with your clients. It is important to familiarize yourself with important ethical issues on confidentiality and we have included suggestions for further resources below.

Clients will arrive with their own hopes, fears and expectations. Typically, clients will be asking themselves: Can I be confident that this therapist will be putting my best interests first? Will this therapist work to good standards of care and competence? Can I trust this therapist to respect the sensitivity of any personal information I share? Equally, clients may not be able to articulate their hopes, fears and expectations this neatly, but have more vague fears and hopes as to what it will be like to be in therapy and to work with you. These are all matters which can be considered and discussed explicitly and sensitively when negotiating the working therapy contract.

Defining the focus, process and direction of your work

The second aspect of the contract, defining focus, process and direction, is twofold. Firstly, you will need to determine what clients want to achieve (the goals of the work). Secondly, you will need to discuss the process of the work (the tasks). These are two key elements of the therapeutic alliance. We discuss each below.

Goals Agenda-setting and ordering of priorities are typical features of goal setting because clients often have multiple issues to deal with or problems with many facets. Client goals may be interpersonal (e.g. to develop greater intimacy in relationships, to find support from a therapist during a crisis), symptom related (e.g. to manage anxiety, to sleep better) or related to personal growth (e.g. to increase self-awareness, to identify and express feelings). Goals should be orientated to the client – that is, they are goals the client wants to achieve as opposed to goals you think they should have or other people in their life want for them. This may mean helping clients to discover what they want and value most. Making changes takes time and energy, and we are all more likely to work harder for goals that are our own, and less likely to sustain our investment in pursuing ends we do not value or which we see as imposed upon us. For example, a client's engagement and motivation towards achieving the goal 'My partner wants me to start working part time' will be fundamentally very different from their engagement and motivation towards the goal 'I really want to start working part time.'

At the start, clients may be vague about what concerns them. For example, they may know they are feeling uncomfortable but be unable to discriminate further, or they may have hunches that some of their behaviour is unhelpful or self-defeating but be unclear why. They may also use vague statements to protect themselves from the discomfort they anticipate they will experience when they describe in specific terms what their problems are. For example, a client might begin by stating, 'My partner and I don't see eye to eye any more and that's the problem' when what they want to say is, 'Our sex life is grim. We don't have sex as often as I would like and when we do it's boring. I'm thinking of leaving him.'

Two important things to keep in mind when considering a client's goal are: How realistic is the goal? and How will you know when the goal has been achieved? One way to help you and your client start to think about these questions is the SMART goal setting system, an acronym to help you assess how **S**pecific, **M**easurable, **A**chievable, **R**elevant and **T**imely the goal is.

Clients will need to distinguish what they can control from what they cannot and take responsibility for themselves and their actions. This is not to deny that clients have legitimate grievances and very real constraints, such as lack of money, poor housing or lack of qualifications, or that the social/cultural/familial context to which a client belongs should be ignored. Clients do not live in a vacuum and helping them to focus on themselves does not mean discounting the contexts in which they live and work.

It is not possible for clients to deal with every concern at once, and they will often need to prioritize. The following questions may be helpful in assessing priorities:

- What concern is causing the most distress?
- What concern would, if tackled, lead to the greatest positive outcome?
- Are there any concerns that could be relatively easily addressed immediately, and subsequently might give the client a greater sense of control and success?
- Which concerns can be dealt with through individual counselling or psychotherapy, and which may need to be addressed elsewhere (e.g. with a social worker, a GP, a psychiatrist, a physiotherapist, a lawyer)?

Ideally, priorities should be agreed in collaboration with the client and kept under review. As clients explore what is important to them, their priorities may change. They may also experience positive or unwelcome changes in their lives that necessitate some re-ordering.

Reflection point

Thinking about goals in therapy

Can you think of a goal you would like to set yourself, perhaps related to your interest and/or training in counselling and psychotherapy, or related to another aspect of your life? Try applying the SMART goal setting system to help you articulate your goal and assess your progress.

Specific: What exactly do you want to achieve?

Measurable: How will you measure goal achievement? (What will you see, think, feel, know or hear once the goal has been reached?)

Achievable: Is your goal genuinely and realistically attainable?

Relevant: Is this goal orientated to what you need and want, and is the focus of the goal you and your actions, thoughts and behaviours?

Timely: What timeline are you setting yourself for reaching your goal (and is this realistic?)?

Tasks   The second element of defining this part of the contract involves a discussion and an agreed, mutual understanding of the process and 'in-therapy behaviours' of the work – that is, the *tasks*. These might include who takes the lead and sets the agenda for the session, the therapist's degree of directiveness, how much challenge the client wants or needs, or whether there will be any exercises for the client to do outside of the sessions such as completing a questionnaire. Because the tasks of the work also include an agreement on a commitment to meet, how frequently and over what period of time, there is some overlap between agreeing tasks and negotiating some of the practical elements of your working therapy contract.

Let's look at how a client Amal and her therapist Gayle considered the goals and tasks of their future work together.

Amal begins by telling Gayle that her relationship with Julia has been going through a 'rough patch'. They have been together for nine years, but for the last two years things between them have felt 'increasingly platonic'. She tells Gayle, 'I love Julia very much, but we feel more like friends than girlfriends these days.' Amal says they no longer have sex, they rarely socialize together and she can't remember the last 'date night' they enjoyed with one another. Amal has felt anxious about trying to talk to Julia about these issues as she has the strong impression that Julia is unconcerned, holding the belief that all long-term relationships end up this exact same way. Amal is aware that Julia's job is causing her a lot of stress and her low wage leaves her financially dependent on Amal to pay many of their bills. This all leaves Amal feeling guilty whenever she contemplates ending the relationship as she worries about how Julia will cope without her. Gayle begins by asking Amal what she would like for herself.

Amal: [*Sighs deeply*] I would like our entire relationship to change. I'd like to go back to how things were when we first met – we were all over each other back then. We had so much fun – travelling, festivals, dinners out with friends …

Gayle: Amal, I can really understand how much you must yearn for how things were … and yet I'm thinking about the place you find yourself in now and what you might realistically be able to do in the present.

Amal: I know, I know … can't turn back time, can we?

Galye: [*Smiles appreciatively*] Alas, no – therapy can't turn miracles.

Amal: Ok. Well, I guess I *do* want our relationship to change. Not to go back in time, but to become 'unstuck' and move forward. Whatever forward looks like – either together, or … ugh! This is really hard, but maybe even apart.

Gayle: Right, so I can hear you want your relationship with Julia to change. As Julia isn't here with us – this is individual therapy for you – I'm wondering what we need to focus on in *you* that might help you to feel less 'stuck'. You have talked about feeling guilty, for example, whenever you think about leaving the relationship …

Amal: Yes, I think my guilt would be an important thing to understand more. At the moment it's like I'm responsible for everything which feels unfair. I end up feeling a weird mixture of resentment and … like, sort of afraid – I find it so hard to talk to Julia about how I'm feeling.

Gayle: I wonder if we can be even more specific? You would like to examine your sense of responsibility in your relationship which at the moment feels one sided. You would also like to feel able to have an honest conversation with Julia about your feelings. How does that sound to you – about right, or do we need to tweak those goals?

Amal: Yes, that's it. Exactly.

Gayle: So, the next question is, how will we know when you have reached these goals? When I ask that I'm wondering, how will Amal feel? What thoughts will she have? How will her life be different?

Amal: I guess I'll feel like a weight has been lifted – freer! And I won't be having these awful thoughts about how I'm ruining Julia's life … I'm not sure what life will look like, but at a minimum I guess I will have had a conversation with Julia about how I'm feeling.

Gayle: I'm aware we have 12 sessions planned Amal. To your mind, do these sound like realistic aims within that timeframe?

Amal: I think so. I mean, I'd like to start by talking about how guilty I've been feeling and my sense of responsibility towards her.

Gayle: How about we start there and in a few sessions time, we check in to see how you're doing?

Amal: That sounds good.

Gayle: Ok. So Amal, in terms of how I work, I usually take my cue from clients – that means, I allow you to set the agenda for each session and we go from there. Therapy isn't about giving advice, it's more about exploring and thinking together. How does that sound?

Amal: That sounds OK … although I'm aware I have a tendency to go off on tangents. I managed to avoid a lot of difficult stuff with my previous therapist! I would appreciate it if you could 'rein me in'.

Gayle: I'm happy to try and identify, and tell you, when I think you or I have lost focus. How does that sound?

Amal: Good. And – will I have to do anything in between our sessions?

Gayle: I don't give you any concrete exercises to do … but it can be really helpful if you could find time to reflect on our sessions and share any thoughts you've had in between them. As we'll be meeting on a weekly basis, on the same day and at the same time, that'll mean committing some of your time to reflection every week. Does that sound feasible?

In this example, the therapist, Gayle, used the SMART goal-setting system to guide Amal in setting out her aims for therapy. Amal began with an unrealistic goal to go back to how things were when she met Julia, and Gayle makes an important point – 'therapy can't turn miracles'. This may seem obvious, but clients frequently arrive in therapy imagining that therapy, or the therapist, will be able to wave a magic wand. Arguably we can all be susceptible to longing for a magic fix to our problems, and this can often be seen in the therapy room. Gayle then prompts Amal to consider how relevant her aims are ('this is individual therapy for you – I'm wondering what we need to focus on in *you* …'), and when Amal talks about her feelings in response to her situation (guilt, responsibility, fear) she helps Amal specify exactly what she wants to achieve ('I wonder if we can be even more specific?'). Gayle then turns to considering how Amal can measure her progress towards her goals ('how will we know when you have reached these goals?') and whether Amal feels it's reasonable to expect these goals to be achieved in the time they have available. Once Gayle has a 'good enough' sense of their mutually agreed upon goals for the work, she prompts a discussion about the tasks of their work. She does this by sharing with Amal a bit about how she normally works and aims to make this collaborative by checking out what Amal's thoughts are ('How does that sound?') and by taking into account Amal's request to help her stay focused.

Agreeing the practicalities of your work

This is sometimes referred to as the 'business contract' because it specifies the terms on which you will work together. However, in a working therapy contract it represents far more than that. The practicalities of working together, on which you agree, speak to the boundaries of your work and your relationship, albeit in a different way to the inter-personal boundaries. The way you both commit and adhere to them will contribute to the sense of mutual trust, safety and respect you have for the work you are undertaking together. These practicalities include: when and where you will meet; the frequency of your sessions; the fee; any administration that may need to be completed; the length of time you will work together (if this can be predetermined) and whether you will sched-ule review points in advance; your cancellation and holiday policy; and how you manage communication between sessions, including electronic communication.

Some or all of this aspect of your contract may be predetermined by the setting you are working in. Community counselling services and the NHS, for example, will have their own policies and procedures which you will need to adhere to and communicate to the client. The essential elements of a basic contract can be found in any relevant professional codes and ethical guidance. Remember that contracts are neither engraved in stone nor something to keep clients in line. You will need to be mindful about the power dynamics in your relationship with your client. Whether we like it or not, clients often see us as ideal, powerful and expert. Some clients may need to invest you with power, while others might want to compete with you. You will need to be sensitive to that when making an agreement with them; do so in the spirit of negotiation rather than imposition.

Preparing for and managing the first session

In this section, we propose a framework to guide you in preparing for and conducting your first session with a new client. The framework contains three broad components:

1. Consideration of client and therapist expectations
2. Making contact
3. Managing the first session

Consideration of client and therapist expectations

Prior to your first meeting, in the mind of your prospective client, you may have been given a form and a personality; they may have imagined themselves in a relationship with you and have fantasies about you as an individual. Clients are likely to have a plethora of expectations, including hopes and anxieties, about the therapy process (Oldfield, 1983; Mearns and Dryden, 1990). They may, for example, hope for a quick solution, advice or the 'right' answer. They may believe that you are the only person who can help them, or that no one can help them. Clients also experience feelings of relief and a renewal of hope and energy at the prospect of resolving their problems. Deciding to contact a specific therapist or accept a referral is often the start of a client taking control of their life.

It is important to acknowledge these expectations and provide opportunities for your client to explore them. They often provide valuable clues to understanding a client's internal world and how they might use the opportunity to work with you. For example, a client who expects you to have all the answers may be hampering their own progress by regularly looking externally, to others, to solve their problems.

Equally, as therapists, we are not immune to pre-meeting expectations, including hopes, fantasies and anxieties. We will probably imagine what clients will be like and how it will be to work with them. Our fantasies might begin with a voice on the telephone ('sounds angry') or might be fuelled by remarks made on referral – for example, 'This is a really difficult case. I thought of you immediately because you'll be able to help him through!' You will need to be aware of your own fantasies, the pressures you place on yourself, and the expectations of others such as referral agencies. Separating all this out as far as is possible will free you to connect honestly with clients and work with them to meet their needs for development and change. (For a discussion of transference see McLeod, 2009.)

Making contact

While you may establish the first session as the 'assessment session', it is worth observing the process of the client making contact with you and noting anything that may contribute to your overall sense of them. For example, if you have the opportunity to talk over the telephone in advance of your first meeting, you will be listening not only to what they say but also to the ways in which they are speaking – for example, are they hesitant or tearful? Pre-session contact is also an opportunity to consider with clients what they want, and to communicate to them that you are an empathic, accepting listener.

You may also want to encourage clients to use the time between your initial telephone conversation and the first face-to-face meeting by inviting them to do some pre-session work (Elton-Wilson, 1996; Dryden and Feltham, 2006) – for example:

- 'Will you give some thought to what you want to get from therapy. If it helps to write it down and bring the notes along with you, that's fine.'
- 'Between now and when we meet, will you notice the times when you feel more or less stressed out and what was happening at those times. It could be useful to our work if you noted down your observations.'

These kinds of interventions encourage clients to become more aware of themselves and their behaviours, thoughts and feelings. It is also possible that these kinds of interventions foster and promote their participation in, and responsibilities within, the process of therapy.

Managing the first session

You will have numerous responsibilities to attend to in the first session. Below we provide a 'Checklist and worksheet for preparation and management of the first session' which is intended to guide you through this process (Table 4.1). We begin by detailing the process. Firstly, you will need to *help your client feel welcome* and as settled as they can. This may include acknowledging any anxiety they are feeling in meeting you, or the importance of their decision to enter therapy. This demonstrates a level of respect which we feel is essential in building the foundations of a good therapeutic alliance. Settling in questions, such as asking them about their journey to your place of practice, or how they are feeling about arriving, can help to alleviate any anxieties. Starting in this way can also help set the pace for the session and avoids launching into discussing difficult and painful experiences too quickly.

Secondly, it is helpful to *provide the client with an overall sense of what your session will look like*, including the plan and aims for the first meeting. This removes any sense of mystery, decreases uncertainty (which may in turn decrease anxiety) and sets boundaries around your time together. You might say something like this:

> *Therapist:*   We have 50 minutes together today. The purpose of this first meeting is to get to know each other a little. I would like to hear about what has brought you here today, and in turn you may have questions for me. I suggest we use the last ten minutes or so to discuss some of the practicalities of working together, but feel free to ask me any questions you might have as we go along. By the end of the session today I would like you to have a good idea of what having therapy will involve so some of your questions for me might be related to that.

In this introduction, the therapist sets out the time boundaries, plan and aims for the session. They attempt to ensure the client is very much part of the process of assessment by inviting them to ask questions. The therapist also leaves the discussion of practicalities to the end of the session and in this way the first session starts with what is most important – the client and the issues they bring.

A third task of this first meeting is to *acknowledge any pre-meeting contact you have had*, or information you have been given about the client from a referrer. This communicates a level of transparency in the process, which invites trust and offers a sense of safety. It will be important to keep the client at the heart of the process and remain mindful of the influence of any pre-session expectations you may have. It is therefore useful to start in the here-and-now and begin the process of exploration from there. You might do this in the following way:

> *Therapist:*   I know that you have already met with … and I was given some notes
> about your meeting. However, I would really like to hear about what
> brings you here today in your own words.

Alternatively, if you have absolutely no information about your client, you will need to acknowledge this too. In this way you are immediately responding to any expectations they might have about what you know about them:

> *Therapist:*   This is not only the first time we are meeting face to face, but also the first
> opportunity I have had to learn anything about you. It would be useful to
> start with what brought you here today.

It is important to bear in mind that clients may not know how or where to start. Reading and hearing about others' experiences is very different from actually being a client. There are problems with saying things like say 'start where you like' or 'start where you feel comfortable' because clients may neither like what they are doing nor feel very comfortable. These sorts of questions may also be *too* open and so broad they are difficult to answer. A client may begin with, 'I don't know where to start', or 'What do you need to know about me?' Responses that help them to begin the process of sharing something about themselves and exploring their issues include:

- 'What would be useful for me to know about you?'
- 'It's difficult for you to begin now that you're here. It might be helpful to start with something specific – perhaps you could tell me how you found out about this service?'
- 'You said you wanted help with … so perhaps you could begin with that?'

A fourth task for the first meeting is to *provide your client with some information about you and the therapy you offer.* Clients may want to know what theories you espouse or what techniques and strategies you use. They may have clear ideas about what they want from a therapist. For example, they may favour an active approach that focuses on what they can do now to resolve their problems and do not want to focus on their early past. They may have concerns about particular approaches or have previous experience of similar kinds of therapy and found it unhelpful. You will need to be able to describe how you work clearly, concisely and without recourse to jargon. You will need to be prepared to answer clients' questions meaningfully and non-defensively. It is worth considering how you might describe your work in advance of your first session. You might say something like:

> *Therapist:*   I'm interested in helping you to find ways of handling what is troubling
> you. I can best describe the way I work as listening carefully to what con-
> cerns you as well as what you are already doing to cope. I think that by
> talking your concerns through in some depth and having the opportunity
> to stand back from them, together we'll be able to find options for doing
> something positive about them and making changes.

Rather than:

> *Therapist:*   Well, basically I have humanistic/existential/psychodynamic/CBT orien-
> tations (have you heard of any of these?), although not totally, so I borrow
> from other approaches if needed. In the early stages, I'll be empathizing
> with you and later on I'll confront any distortions I pick up. I'm really
> interested in the work of Freud/Klein/Rogers/Pearls. Lately I've become
> more interested in facilitating goal-directed behaviour. The research
> around this is really interesting …

The latter is confusing rather than clarifying. It is about the therapist's interests rather
than what is going to be useful for the client. Jargon and technical language may be
meaningless to potential clients and make you sound like a textbook. It also distances
you from clients, and language that obscures can make already vulnerable clients feel
even more intimidated. A good rule of thumb is – keep it simple.

A fifth task of the first session is to *formulate a provisional agenda or plan moving forward*. This will require discussing priorities with clients and negotiating the focus for the
immediate work. The balance to be struck here is between developing a workable broad
aim and subsequently formulating some interim or sub-goals that help clients to move
towards that aim. The decision to work together along with aspects of the provisional
agenda and the broad aim for the work will form an important element of your working
therapy contract (see above).

The sixth and final task of the first session is to *manage the end of the session*. This needs
to be done in such a way that you communicate your commitment to them moving forward. Acknowledge the effort, and for many courage, they have shown in attending. Set
clear boundaries from the outset. Provide clarity on what happens next. And begin to
give clients a positive experience of ending. This can be achieved in the following ways:

- Remind clients of the time available and give some notice of the ending. Covert
  glances at a clock do not signal open communication. Instead, you might say, 'We're
  doing fine, we have 15 minutes left. Let's recap on where we've got to so far.'
- Confirm the days and times for subsequent sessions.
- Make a commitment to begin with a particular issue in the next session – for
  example, 'That feels important to discuss. Let's pick that up next week.'
- Discuss and agree any interim tasks – for example, completing any administration.

The ending of the first session is a strategic moment in working together in which
the therapist's respect for the client and the possibility of purposeful progress can be
affirmed. This is a temporary ending until the next session.

There is a balance to be struck in the first session to ensure you are attending to the various tasks in hand. You will need to provide information and ask relevant questions, but also
avoid talking too much yourself and ensure that the focus remains on your client. You will also
need to respond to their questions in such a way that they remain involved and encouraged.
You may also want to state explicitly that any decisions made, goals set or action taken will
be theirs, that you will be helping them and not deciding for them or acting on their behalf.

TABLE 4.1 *Checklist and worksheet for preparation and management of the first session*

Pre-session	☐
Consideration of any information I have prior to the first in-person meeting (e.g. a conversation I have had over the phone with the client, or referral information I have received from a colleague or other professional):	
• What features of this client's story have I been struck by?	
....	
....	
....	
• Is there specific information I need to clarify with them?	
....	
....	
....	
• How have I been reflecting on this client? What expectations do I have of them? How have I been feeling about meeting them?	
....	
....	
....	
In-session tasks	☐
The things I need to do during the session are:	
☐ Be clear about the structure of the session, including the amount of time available	
☐ Provide information about confidentiality	
☐ Ensure the client has enough time to talk through their most pressing issues	
☐ Establish the notion of shared responsibility for working together	
☐ Provide information on how I work	
☐ Discuss and/or clarify the fee, scheduling of future sessions, administrative tasks and any relevant policies	
Post-session	☐
Consider all the information I have obtained during the meeting, and reflect on the following ready for my next supervision session:	
• How have I understood the client's key issues and did we have a shared understanding of those?	
....	
....	
....	
• Are there any risk issues I need to think about with my supervisor?	
....	
....	
....	

(Continued)

TABLE 4.1 *(Continued)*

• Did I feel we made a reasonable connection? Do I feel we have the potential for a good therapeutic alliance? .... • Is there any information I think I need about this client that I didn't manage to obtain? .... • How do I feel about working with this client? ....

Summary

This chapter has been concerned with the Beginning Stage of the therapeutic work, which is principally about establishing a therapeutic working alliance, conducting an assessment and agreeing a working therapy contract. In this chapter we have introduced some key concepts for working therapeutically in this early stage with a client. These have included the relational (or therapeutic) bond, and the qualities of empathy, acceptance and genuineness. We have discussed how the skills you employ to demonstrate these qualities will build on the core skills outlined in the previous chapter. We have also outlined important areas to consider when undertaking assessment, including presenting issues, context, client motivation, risk factors and your own competency. In addition, we considered how to agree a working therapy contract, which we divided into three areas for discussion with your client: the type of help you are offering; the focus, process and direction of the work; and the practicalities of your work. This included a discussion on therapeutic tasks and goals. Finally, we looked at how you might prepare and manage your first session with a client and we have offered a 'Checklist and worksheet for preparation and management of the first session' to help guide you in this process. In the next chapter we consider the Middle Stage of the work and helping clients to explore their concerns in a purposeful way.

Further resources

- Johnstone, L. and Boyle, M. with Cromby, J., Dillon, J., Harper, D., Kinderman, P., Longden, E., Pilgrim, D. and Read, J. (2018) *The Power Threat Meaning Framework: Towards the Identification of Patterns in Emotional Distress, Unusual Experiences and Troubled or Troubling Behaviour, as an Alternative to Functional Psychiatric Diagnosis*. Leicester: British Psychological Society.
- Rogers, C. (1980) *A Way of Being*. New York: Houghton Mifflin Company.
- Safran, J.D. and Muran, J.C. (2000) *Negotiating the Therapeutic Alliance: A Relational Treatment Guide*. New York: The Guilford Press.
- Van Rijn, B. (2015) *Assessment and Care Formulation in Counselling and Psychotherapy*. London: SAGE.

Online resources

Visit https://study.sagepub.com/staffordandbond4e to watch:

Video 4.1	Can You Help Me? – Scenario
Video 4.2	Can You Help Me? – Discussion
Video 4.3	Contracting – Scenario
Video 4.4	Contracting – Discussion
Video 4.5	Being Non-Judgemental
Video 4.6	Client Autonomy – Scenario
Video 4.7	Client Autonomy – Discussion

5

The Middle Stage

Exploring and Deepening

Chapter contents

This chapter covers:

- Aims, plans and skills for the Middle Stage
- Maintaining the therapeutic alliance
- Exploring the client's issues at depth
- Principles for self-disclosure and immediacy
- Principles for challenge and giving directives
- Further resources

Introduction

This chapter discusses the aims, plans and skills for moving the work beyond the initial stage of making a connection and focusing on the central issues your client brings. The Middle Stage is concerned primarily with helping clients to explore their concerns in a new and meaningful way. As discussed in Chapter 2, counselling and psychotherapy are complex and fluid processes. The transition from one stage to the next is not a neat, sequential operation. There is likely to be overlap between stages or a cyclical feel to the process. However, to move from the Beginning Stage to the Middle Stage, you and your client will have a sense that the essential aims of the former stage will have been met to a 'good enough' degree such that you can turn your attention to deepening your exploration of 'the what' and 'the who' of the client in the room, evolving the work of the Beginning Stage.

The key theme for the Middle Stage of the work is 'exploring'. This reflects the key activities of the work at this stage – examining what is going on for your client at depth. Your intention behind this focus, at this stage, will be to help your client gain insight and meaning into themselves and what is troubling them, and finding new perspectives and experiencing new ways of being with themselves, others and the world. You will be doing this by aiming to maintain and strengthen the therapeutic alliance, expanding and strengthening the sense of mutual trust and connection between you. Hence the relational focal point at this stage is defined as 'deepening'.

Aims, plans and skills for the Middle Stage

Aims

The following two aims characterize the work of the middle stage:

1. To maintain the therapeutic alliance
2. To explore the client's issues at depth

Plans

Let's consider the plans you will need to develop and implement in order to achieve each aim for the Middle Stage.

To maintain the therapeutic alliance

Your plan to maintain the therapeutic alliance will be twofold. Firstly, you will look to strengthen the relational bond. The relationship that you will have developed with your client will be the 'interpersonal power base' from which you facilitate in-depth exploration of their issues. By this, we mean that clients have experienced you as an accepting, competent, trustworthy therapist and as someone who is demonstrably 'with' them – that is, someone who is providing the safety of a containing relationship that allows for and accepts often painful or shameful disclosure without censure. You will be planning to strengthen this sense by deepening the encounter and using self-disclosure and immediacy (see 'Skills needed to maintain the therapeutic alliance' below). In the second part of your plan, you will look to work to the contract. This will involve planning regular reviews of your work and monitoring progress with your clients.

To explore the client's issues at depth

At this stage in the counselling and psychotherapy process, you will plan to explore the client's issues at depth. Deeper exploration at this stage has a quality and intensity that exploration in the Beginning Stage does not have. For clients, it carries the potential both for renewed energy as they gain clearer self-understanding, and for discomfort as they begin to relinquish old perspectives. At its core, deeper exploration implies a change in focus from the evident to the cloaked. The focus turns to what clients are either unaware or dimly aware of, as well as what they may be avoiding, ignoring or overlooking. It has been usefully described as helping clients overcome 'blind spots' (Egan, 2006). Deeper exploration will involve process orientated planning, specifically with regards to 'advanced empathy', challenge and giving directives (see 'Skills needed to explore the client's issues at depth' below).

Skills

We now turn to the skills that you will need to learn in the Middle Stage to support your work, meet your aims and put your plans into action. We consider each aim in turn.

Skills needed to maintain the therapeutic alliance: Strengthening the relational bond

Maintaining the therapeutic alliance will require skills in strengthening the relational bond, and working to the contract – that is, reviewing the agreed tasks of your work, and assessing progress towards the client's goals. We begin by discussing three elements involved in strengthening the relational bond, before turning our attention to the contract. These three elements are:

1. Deepening the encounter between you and your client
2. Self-disclosure
3. Immediacy

Let's look at each in turn.

Deepening the encounter

> As they move, they pass through an emotional narrative landscape with its hills and valleys of vitality affects, along its river of intentionality … and over its peak of dramatic crisis. (Stern, 2004:172)

Let's return to the first premise of this book as outlined in Chapter 1 – that is, the idea that human beings are innately relationship-seeking creatures who depend on others for their psychological, physiological and spiritual survival. In Chapter 4, we looked at how this idea is used to understand one of the key ingredients for healing and change in therapy – relational connection to another human being. It is a very particular kind of connection containing specific qualities. One of the pivotal tasks of the Middle Stage is to maintain this special and important connection and to be open to, and strive towards, developing, deepening and living within it.

This depth of experiencing with another, within a therapeutic space, has been variously described (e.g. Buber's concept of the 'I–Thou' world of relating (1958), Hycner and Jacobs's concept of the 'dialogical-interpersonal' (1995), Stern's 'moments of meeting' (2004) and Mearns and Cooper's 'relational depth' (2018)). It can be defined as 'a state of profound contact and engagement between therapist and client' (Mearns and

Cooper, 2018: 44) within which certain relational qualities (empathy, acceptance, genuineness and attunement) are offered, experienced and received.

In the Middle Stage, you will be working with the potential for your relationship to deepen in this way. This level of engagement is one of resonance and accord. It can be impactful for both client and therapist. For Buber (1958) this kind of encounter was one in which the therapist emerges personally affected and changed. It can therefore feel risky for us, as therapists, to open ourselves up to this kind of experience. Like our clients, we enter into the therapeutic relationship, not knowing where the journey will take us, with no guarantees as to what we may find or who we will become. Allowing ourselves to be impacted, influenced or even transformed by our clients is essentially what is needed to truly experience empathy and acceptance – these things intrinsically shape and alter us as we experience them. This requires a willing and open spirit.

By definition a meeting is a coming together of more than one person. For Buber (1958: 11), 'all real living is meeting'. An encounter with a sense of deep connection is therefore not one-sided. As Rogers (1957) asserts, for therapeutic change to occur, the therapist and client need to be in 'psychological contact'. Therefore, clients too, are required to enter into the therapy relationship with you, with a similar spirit of openness and willing to meeting you. That is, not just being open and willing to examine themselves, but also to receiving what you offer. Clients need to allow themselves to experience their therapist's response (Rogers, 1957) – your response alone is not enough to achieve this state of deep encounter. Siegal (2007) considers an essential feature of human relatedness to be the experience of 'feeling felt', and as such clients are not only connecting with their experiences powerfully in these moments, they are also (and crucially) receiving the response of the therapist – a response that is empathic, attuned, affirming and real.

With this in mind, we begin to see how a client is impacted by their therapist who is in turn impacted by their client. This leads us to the idea that the therapeutic relationship is co-created – both parties contribute, influence and are affected by what happens in the room and what passes between them; together they create and engage in a synergetic, receptive experience. This has been described as a 'reciprocal, mutual influence' by Stolorow et al. (2002) and a 'bidirectional' process by Murphy and Cramer (2014).

Research investigating the experience of 'relational depth' has found it to be concurrent with gaining insight, self-knowledge, understanding and acceptance (Mearns and Cooper, 2018). Mearns and Cooper (2018) suggest that the more relational depth clients experience, the more improvement in therapy they show overall. To facilitate this kind of experience, Mearns and Cooper (2018) suggest 'letting go' of your agenda and trying to make it happen, or of trying to *do* something *to* your client; and instead attempt to meet your client wherever they are in their own journey towards an intimate connection with another human being.

Self-disclosure

Self-disclosure promotes interpersonal intimacy. When we are facilitating our clients' self-expression and encouraging them into narrative dialogue, we are supporting them to self-disclose. In Chapter 1, we discussed what has become known as the 'relational turn' in counselling and psychotherapy – a movement towards viewing human beings as fundamentally connected, experiencing each other in a co-created field of relating. From this perspective, how do we understand what the therapist shares of themselves? When therapists are called on by their clients to explicitly communicate something of themselves, how can this be used therapeutically and what might be the impact of therapist self-disclosure? We consider some of these questions below.

In one sense, of course, you cannot avoid disclosing yourself to clients, both by your self-presentation and what you say and do. However, 'therapist self-disclosure' usually refers to the therapist actively and explicitly disclosing something personal from his or her own experience. While a therapist's self-disclosure is inherently transparent, it differs qualitatively from a therapist's congruence in that, 'self-disclosures are an event rather than a quality' (Cooper, 2008: 114). A therapist may make an autonomous decision to disclosure something about themselves to their client, or they may be asked a direct question by their client which may necessitate some form of disclosure (e.g. 'Do you have experience with this issue?', 'Have you been through a divorce?', 'Do your religious beliefs inform how you work?').

Hill and Knox (2001) found that, in terms of immediate outcomes (e.g. gaining insight), therapists' self-disclosures were perceived by clients as helpful rather than unhelpful, but in terms of the ultimate outcomes of therapy (e.g. symptom reduction), the effects of self-disclosure were unclear. Cooper (2008) concludes that carefully considered self-disclosures, in moderate amounts, may be more helpful to clients than a complete absence of self-disclosure. It is important to keep in mind that whatever the reason for your self-disclosures, they should always be in the service of the client, 'to validate reality, normalize, model, strengthen the alliance, or offer alternative ways to think or act' (Hill and Knox, 2001: 416).

Therapist self-disclosures can therefore be used effectively at times. They may be used to strengthen your therapeutic alliance for example. They may also be a useful way to help your client explore their issues at greater depth. We include discussion of therapist self-disclosure here to highlight some of the ways in which it can enhance your relational bond and the sense of a safe space for your client to explore themselves in.

- **Creating hope that improvement is possible**. Appropriate self-disclosures can be very helpful when your client feels stuck with something and has lost hope that any improvement will be possible – for example, 'I remember how challenging personal therapy can feel at times.'
- **Breaking down a sense of isolation and shame that may be associated with a particular problem**. When someone feels alone and this sense is reinforced by shame or self-blame, one way to cope is to turn inwards, inadvertently corroborating an existing sense of alienation from the world. A sensitive self-disclosure can provide both comfort and encouragement – for example, 'When I was treated for cancer, I noticed that everyone seemed to be in their own little bubble. We were all going through the same treatment but couldn't talk about what it meant to us. I know how lonely it can feel.'
- **To make contact**. Personal communications can be more powerful than theory. That is, self-disclosure may be much more helpful to clients than referring to

research or theory. It is the experience of being understood as a person that matters most to us in the height of emotional turmoil – for example, 'I remember just how helpful it was to me to be able to talk to someone who was detached and uninvolved during my divorce.'

- **Modelling**. Some clients may be completely unused to sharing anything about themselves with another person. This may be for numerous reasons, but the lack of 'know how' can result in anxiety, getting stuck or feeling ashamed. Demonstrating how to appropriately disclose something about yourself may provide a useful model for sharing, connecting and creating intimacy – for example, 'There have been times in my life when I've not known where to begin describing what I feel or what I'm going through.'

It is always important to remember that self-disclosure changes the focus from the client to the therapist, even temporarily. It is therefore not without risk. It is very easy to drift from self-disclosure to a general social conversation or for the therapist to become the focus of attention. Sometimes clients will collude in the shift of attention away from themselves in order to avoid talking about difficult issues. Depending on the type of disclosure, some clients may also feel drawn to taking responsibility or feeling anxious about the therapist.

An example of how this may look in practice is in Arjun's therapy with his therapist Gary. Gary senses that Arjun is putting on a brave face, as he was taught to do with his emotional pain by his father in particular. Arjun is being stalwart in describing a particularly painful episode in his childhood.

Gary: I imagine you felt sad.

Arjun: These things happen, don't they? That's life ... and you just have to get on with it. Moaning on about my feelings won't help. That's what my dad always said.

Gary: It seems like you believe feelings will hamper you in some way? Instead of feeling, you just get on with it ... stop 'moaning'.

Arjun: Dwelling on the past won't change anything.

Gary: Arjun, I think that if I'd experienced the rejection that you experienced, I would feel sad and hurt.

Arjun: Do you? I suppose feeling sad seems weak – I don't want to seem weak.

Gary: There have been times in my past when I've also wanted to avoid looking 'weak', and I've ignored painful feelings as a result. I wonder if that's how it is for you?

Arjun: Well, my dad always saw being 'weak', being emotional, as such a failing in a man. I've never wanted him to see me as failing ... so I guess I just shove feelings 'under the carpet'.

Here, Gary uses self-disclosure to model talking about feelings. Sometimes clients lack the skill of making feeling statements. They have had little practice at identifying, labelling, allowing and expressing their feelings. Gary's self-disclosures ('I would feel sad and hurt', 'There have been times in my past when I've also wanted to avoid looking "weak"') enabled Arjun to feel safe enough to begin to explore his responses and his relationship with his emotional self.

Reflection point

Clients' requests for therapists' self-disclosure

Take a look at the following list of client questions and consider how you feel about answering them:

- How long have you been working as a therapist?
- In your professional opinion, what is the best way to address my problem?
- Have you got any children?
- Where did you train to become a therapist?
- What is your sexual orientation?
- Where else do you work?
- Have you had any personal experience of depression?
- Do you believe in God?

In reviewing this list, were there any questions you would find particularly easy to answer, or conversely you would be uncomfortable answering? Is there any pattern to the questions you found 'easy' and those you found 'uncomfortable'? How did the thought of answering each question leave you feeling?

Let us turn now to the concept of immediacy – a strategy that focuses on what is happening in the relationship between you and a client. It often feels risky and yet is surprisingly powerful.

Immediacy

Immediacy means focusing on the 'here and now' of the therapy, specifically how the therapist is feeling about the client, about the therapy relationship or about themselves in relation to the client (Hill, 2004). Therapeutic schools of thought which place a particular emphasis on the interpersonal dynamics within the therapeutic dyad postulate that clients often 're-enact' with their therapist interpersonal conflicts that have brought them into therapy (e.g Safran and Muran, 2000; Yalom, 2002). This means that, at an unconscious level, the client and the therapist create echoes of the client's relational concerns or conflicts that are going on for them (or they have previously experienced) in their everyday lives outside of the therapy room. It is almost as if they are 'acting out' the parts of the story or the roles of the main characters that make up the concern or conflict, and the therapy relationship parallels the client's external relationships in some respect. If therapists are able to bring what is happening into conscious awareness, immediacy can enhance open dialogue about these interpersonal conflicts, which in turn may help the client to make changes to their unhelpful relational patterns.

Karpman (1968) developed a model to explain unhelpful relational patterns that keep us stuck and/or in conflict: the 'Drama Triangle'. The Drama Triangle is one way of helping us to think about the interpersonal conflicts that clients experience and help us increase our awareness of what may then play out in the therapy room. The Drama

Triangle consists of three positions or 'roles' – these are styles of relating and represent different perspectives on the conflict or issue at hand. The roles are 'persecutor', 'rescuer' and 'victim'. Each role signals some form of inauthenticity – they do not reflect the real positions people are in, in life. The Drama Triangle is depicted in Figure 5.1.

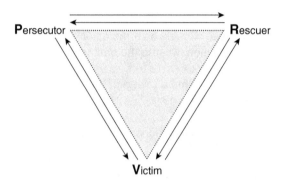

FIGURE 5.1   *Karpman's Drama Triangle (1968)*

The 'persecutor' puts others down through criticism, judgement, dismissiveness or overt oppression. They seek, and may be seen as, being 'all powerful'. The 'rescuer' offers help, tries to 'fix', problem-solve and protect. They seek to be, and are often seen as, caring and sensitive. However, in their own way they are disempowering of others because the implicit message in the way they are relating is, 'I am helping you because *you are not capable of helping yourself.*' The 'victim' puts themselves down, they feel helpless and blameless. They are dismissive of their self-agency and seek out answers to their problems outside of themselves. The roles within the Drama Triangle are co-dependent and require the other two roles in order to maintain their own position. We are all susceptible to 'stepping into' any one of these roles in times of interpersonal crisis. However, there may be a role that our clients (or indeed we) are particularly familiar with when we find ourselves caught in a relational conflict.

Reflection point

Stepping into 're-enactments'

Consider a disagreement or conflict you have had in a relationship or relationships with others in which you found yourself stuck and struggled to find resolution. Consider the Drama Triangle:

- What position did you start in? Did this change as the process went on?
- How were you feeling and what were you thinking about the other person(s) involved in the conflict?

- Was the 'role' you had familiar to you in any way?
- If you found resolution, what happened or what did you do to address the 'stuckness'?

If we are able to recognize such patterns when they are happening in our relationships with our clients, through the use of immediacy we have an opportunity to use live material to help our clients reflect on their feelings and thoughts, consider ways in which they may get themselves stuck and experiment with new ways of being. Kasper et al. (2008: 282) write that 'Immediacy seeks to promote the here-and-now awareness of problematic interpersonal patterns and to create a corrective emotional experience by establishing new interpersonal patterns.'

There are some research studies that point to the effectiveness of immediacy in therapy and have found that it is often used to resolve such things as misunderstandings between therapist and client; it may even be useful in encouraging clients to talk about immediate, often negative, feelings towards their therapist or the work, which in turn may facilitate change (Kasper et al., 2008). Additionally, clients may gain new awareness by staying with and exploring their thoughts and feelings as they occur now in relation to you and to what they are revealing. Immediacy requires the therapist to be transparent, profoundly in touch with what they are experiencing, and effectively communicative in the moment. It can therefore significantly deepen the relational bond between therapist and client because 'such relating requires the therapist as well as the client, to speak from "deep within their very soul"' (Mearns and Cooper, 2018: 153).

However, immediacy can be a difficult skill to master, taking time and experience to develop. It often requires the ability to 'reflect-in-action', a reflective skill that many trainees and qualified therapists alike can find tricky. In addition, clients may not always understand why you are choosing to focus on the here-and-now and/or are not always aware of how they are feeling right now. They may feel that focusing on what is happening out there is more relevant and more likely to help them address their issues. You need to be clear with yourself, as well as prepared to articulate to your client, why you are sharing your subjective responses in this way.

The power of immediacy is that it enables you to capture the moment. You and your client are required to face the dynamics of your relationship, providing clients with a potentially different experience of dealing with their issues in a non-defensive way.

Some important principles regarding self-disclosure and immediacy include:

- **Be clear about your intention with yourself and your client**. This requires you to be self-reflective and honest with yourself. Your aim is to assist your client, not to serve your own needs. For example, if you are seeking to unburden yourself, gain sympathy or to relieve your own feelings, then it is more appropriately discussed in supervision and/or in your personal therapy. Being clear with your client ensures the process remains transparent and helps to return the focus to them. This can be achieved by making a link back to the client's experience or inquiring about their perspective.

- **Understand your client** so that you feel reasonably confident that your self-disclosure, or use of immediacy, is likely to be helpful and is not going to be perceived as intrusive, confusing or burdensome. This can only be evaluated on a case-by-case basis.
- **Own what you share and accept that your experience is subjective.** Your client may have different experiences to bring to bear on what you are discussing. Take responsibility for what you say and use 'I' to describe your experience clearly and directly.
- **Observe the impact of your intervention on your client and your relationship.** You will need to work responsively. This may include directly inquiring into the impact of what you have shared or considering how the space between you feels. Your observations and inquiry will help you to judge how effective your intervention has been and whether it will be useful or appropriate to use self-disclosure or immediacy in the future.
- **Self-disclose infrequently and be brief to avoid shifting the central focus from your client to yourself.** Additionally, it is worth remembering that if you cannot be brief, the disclosure is likely to be too complicated or you may be too emotionally involved in what you are sharing for it to be useful.
- **Restrict self-disclosure to experiences over which you have a reasonable level of self-awareness.** Only disclose things about yourself that you have been able to work through to the point that you feel reasonably resolved about them. It is best to avoid self-disclosures that raise strong feelings that will distract you from hearing your client's experience and feelings.
- **Work with immediacy non-defensively.** Be open. Immediacy is not about pointing out the unproductive aspects of a client's behaviour or criticizing what is happening in the room. If a pattern is developing between you and your client – for example, a pattern of avoidance, collusion, cosiness or hostility – then you will need to consider the part you are playing in that.
- **Remember that clients are not bound to confidentiality.** Only share what you are willing to have communicated to others.

Let us look at an example of immediacy in practice. Harry is talking about supporting others, especially his mother, who has a disability, and his girlfriend, who is struggling with a bereavement. He says that one of his strengths is being able to listen to others and help them solve their problems. His therapist, Nina, thinks that he supports others at a cost to himself. She notices that he is looking exhausted and has been irritable, and she notes that he has complained about lack of sleep and that he is overeating.

Nina: I'm thinking, I wonder who supports Harry?

Harry: [*Sharply*] I've got friends – you know that, but they have got enough on their plates without listening to me all day for goodness sake. It's not as if I'm very depressed or homeless or living in a war zone, is it?

Nina: I don't think receiving support is conditional on severe problems.

Harry: [*Angrily*] Well, you would say that – you make money out of other people's 'petty' problems!

Nina: [*Pauses*] What do you make of what's going on between us right now Harry?

Harry: [*Accusingly*] What's that supposed to mean?

Nina:	You seem angry. Perhaps angry with me.
Harry:	[*There is a pause and then, in a more moderate, but tired tone*] I just don't want to have to think about all this stuff and I feel like you're pushing me to … [*rubs his eyes*] I feel overwhelmed by all your questions and I don't know what to say or where to turn.
Nina:	Ok, that's important for me to hear. Perhaps I've moved in too close and too quickly and not respected your pace enough?
Harry:	Yes, in a way … [*Long pause*] but at the same time I'm here in therapy to learn something about myself. I know I need to deal with things 'out there' better, but I don't know how to … [*Looks up at Nina*]
Nina:	Would it be helpful for you if I shared what I think happens between us sometimes? It might help us think about how you deal with stuff 'out there' …
Harry:	Alright.
Nina:	I've noticed that you seem to find it hard to receive support from me … if I really try to understand you, it feels as though you push me away – with a laugh or throwaway line. Does that fit with what you see happening at all?
Harry:	Yeah, that sounds familiar. My girlfriend says that I push her away when she's trying to help me too …
Nina:	And what usually happens then?
Harry:	Well I guess usually she keeps trying to help … but then I get annoyed because I feel she's 'too much', like she won't leave me alone. Then she gets upset …

Nina uses immediacy, the here-and-now relational dynamics between herself and Harry, to help explore Harry's experience and also focus on an interpersonal pattern in his life. A possible parallel is in process in which Harry is offered help and rejects it – with his girlfriend and with Nina. Nina is transparent about why she thinks it might be helpful to focus on the therapeutic relationship ('Would it be helpful for you if I shared what I think happens between us …') and attempts to work non-defensively and responsively to create a space in which Harry can start to identify and examine some of the themes of his relationships which cause him difficulty ('Ok, that's important for me to hear. Perhaps I've moved in too close …').

We now turn to the second part of maintaining the therapeutic alliance – working to the contract.

Skills needed to maintain the therapeutic alliance: Working to the contract

The Middle Stage, with its emphasis on the shift to deeper levels, may also be a time when contracts are reviewed and re-negotiated. You and your client need to be asking yourselves the questions: 'Is what we're doing helping fulfil our contract? and 'At this stage of our work together, are we understanding the issues and revealing possibilities for change?'

During the Middle Stage it is therefore advisable to agree to have a 'review session' (or sessions if you are working with a long-term or open-ended contract) so that you are both able to check your progress and responsiveness to the goals and tasks you agreed on at the outset. This is not intended as a test of your adherence to your working therapy contract in which you pass or fail; rather, it is an opportunity to assess progress and what is working well between you. A review session can also help keep the client's needs at the heart of the process and provide space, if needed, to generate new goals, tasks and time frames (Reeves, 2018). Reeves (2018) argues that it is important to agree review points at the start of therapy, and in the process of reviewing consider all aspects of the therapy relationship. For this reason, he suggests, it can be useful to prepare for your review in supervision and explore some of the following questions yourself that could then be usefully posed to your client during your review session:

- Compared to when we started, how are you feeling now?
- Do the goals we set at the beginning of the process still feel relevant?
- What do you feel has changed for you, for better or worse, and what has stayed the same?
- Do you feel able to share all that is on your mind when you are here?

Reviewing your work may involve a reassessment of the client's issues. Often this process is called 'reframing'. Reassessment or reframing is important because it enables the client to consider a new perspective in relation to the problems or issues that are causing them concern. This often releases a new sense of hope and energy that can contribute to overcoming any obstacles to change. Clients who are unable to reframe their problem or develop new insights are more likely to remain stuck with the disabling perspectives that may have prompted them to seek help. The intention is to stimulate a shift in clients' assessment of both the meaning and significance of their concerns so that the possibilities for change begin to emerge. Reassessment moves clients towards the brink of action and can represent the point at which clients withdraw energy from problems and start to invest in resolutions. Reframing does not involve either disputing or contesting concrete information. It is concerned with interpretation and illumination.

Case example: David

A client, David, has recently retired. He tells his therapist, Charlotte, that he feels miserable and depressed. His voice is full of regret as he recounts how retirement is a landmark for him. He had spent over 40 years in the same industry where he had built a good reputation and was well respected. At work he found friendships and fulfilment. He believes that by not having a job any more, his life is 'basically over'.

In facilitating David to reframe what he believes to be the central problem (retirement), Charlotte will not be disputing either David's age, the fact of his retirement or his feelings about it. Nor will it mean placating or sympathizing. Instead, Charlotte will be attempting to involve David in reassessing his situation and help him to consider multiple possibilities. Retirement from his job of 40 years does not mean David can no longer work if he wants to; friendships may be continued outside of previous employment and new relationships may be formed outside of working life; David can still find respect from others, aside from the respect he experienced in his previous position. Reframing works best when it is born of collaboration between client and therapist. In David's case, it might well involve helping him to acknowledge and mourn the loss of his working life before beginning to help him shape a different and more revitalizing view of what retirement means. In other words, it is his view of what being retired means that is imprisoning him, not the fact of his retirement.

A metaphor that illustrates this complex and important process is the simple one of framing a print. Different borders and types of frames will enhance different aspects of the picture. Certain colours and hues will either become more prominent or appear more subdued. Some frames will do nothing to enhance the picture and render it drabber and less interesting to our eyes. In all of this, the picture itself will not have changed; rather, different aspects of its colour and form will have been intensified and, consequently, we will perceive it differently.

What makes reframing so powerful is that once we have been faced with alternatives, it is less easy to return steadfastly to our former view of reality. If we return to the picture metaphor, once we have seen a border and a frame that really suits the print, it is hard to envisage or accept it framed in a different way.

It can be painful for clients to acknowledge the extent to which they have been the architects of their own unhappiness. It can take courage for them to face squarely what they may have been dimly aware of and yet overlooking. They need the security of a trustworthy relationship in which to take the risk of looking afresh.

In their research, Etherington and Bridges (2011) found that reviews which are designed and implemented well can be a useful method for both clients and therapists to focus on their aims, encouraging the client to implement changes, collaborate in deciding when to end (where there is choice) and ask for what they want, and reflect on their relationship with their therapist as well as their progress.

Strengthening the relational bond and working to the contract – two key activities involved in maintaining the therapeutic alliance – may involve exploration and reflection at a deeper level than in the Beginning Stage. As a consequence, both of you may feel more vulnerable as well as more invigorated. Clients will be 'opening themselves up to you' in qualitatively different ways – approaching the edges of their awareness, sharing profoundly personal material and collaboratively developing a more intimate space with you. You will be 'holding' their disclosures and your relationship will become expressively closer. This has rewards and responsibilities. Your clients' ways of managing closeness will become palpable. Maintaining the boundaries of the therapeutic relationship is not only ethical but also vital to helping clients to express, tolerate and manage any discomfort, to feel free enough to question themselves and to look at what feels risky.

Skills needed to explore issues at depth

There's a room where the light won't find you

Holding hands while the walls come tumbling down

When they do, I'll be right behind you. (Tears for Fears, 1985)

Deeper exploration at this stage evolves from the work of the Beginning Stage. This means that it is rooted firmly both in a clear mutual understanding of how clients view their concerns together and in your appreciation of their concerns based on your perspective. In this section we look at three ways in which deeper exploration can be achieved:

1. Through 'advanced empathy'
2. By challenging your client to invite authenticity
3. By giving directives

We look at each one in turn.

Advanced empathy

In practice, you will need to learn to listen and attend to what and how clients are communicating, as well as to what they are implying, hinting at or omitting. It is listening for the hidden, the unexpressed or the ulterior message, and understanding the possible significance of that. Egan (2006) refers to this as 'advanced empathy', meaning the ability to discern and understand 'covert' or deeper meaning. Essentially, as you communicate your deeper understanding of clients, you will influence them towards more profound exploration and greater self-understanding.

It is hard to illustrate in writing how a practitioner develops an understanding of the ulterior and hidden aspects, because much of the significant interaction is both subtle and non-verbal – for example, facial expression, voice tone, pace of speech, body posture or a fleeting glance. Accurately reflecting what your client is communicating relies on your ability both to sense and to distil the important kernel from the packaging that may surround it.

Let's consider an example from practice to consider how this might look and sound in therapy with Naomi. Nine months ago, Naomi started a prestigious graduate programme for a city finance firm. She had felt under huge pressure to work long hours and meet strict targets. Six months into the programme she started experiencing panic attacks and her doctor signed her off work with anxiety and referred her to therapy with Carlita. Naomi told Carlita that she had always been 'a perfectionist' and driven to excel. She felt her parents, both successful in their respective careers in the law and medicine, expected her, like them, to have a lucrative career just as her older brother had. She had previously described to Carlita her feeling of 'shame' at being signed off work and considered herself 'a failure and a disappointment' to her family. Carlita sensed there were also other emotions and thoughts Naomi had about her situation that were as yet unexplored.

> Naomi: [*Softly spoken, eyes downcast*] My mum asked me yesterday how I was going to cope without a career. Not, how I was going to cope without a *job* – she used the word 'career'. [*Sighs deeply*]
>
> Carlita: [*Matches the volume and soft quality of Naomi's voice*] What did that word – 'career' – mean to you?
>
> Naomi: Well, it's different from 'job' isn't it? A job pays the bills. A career – it's like an identity ... it tells the world how successful you are ... [*Long pause, then*

slightly louder in volume and sharper in pitch] It was like she was saying, 'You had your one and only chance at making a success of life and *you blew it!*'. [*Looks up and makes eye contact*]

Carlita: There's a lot behind that word for you. As well as connotations, I'm sensing a lot of emotion … can you tell me more?

Naomi: [*Even louder now and with a flush in her face*] It was so … it was so … ugh! I don't know! How *could she* say that? She knows how stressed out I am – I'm embarrassed to be signed off work, I'm worried about money, I'm worried about my future and then *BAM!* She hits me with 'You're nothing but a failure!'

Carlita: I'm hearing a lot of anger in your voice … would that be right word for you right now?

Naomi: Yes! I feel angry! Maybe even something even bigger than anger!

Carlita: Anger … really big … like rage, like fury?

Naomi: *Fury* – yes, that's a good word. *Fury*. I felt … I *feel* furious with her right now.

In this segment, Carlita helped Naomi express her previously unspoken anger which she had sensed running alongside Naomi's shame. Carlita tried to facilitate deeper exploration by paying attention to the sound and volume of Naomi's voice as well as her words and noticed a change in volume and pitch as Naomi recalled her mother's words. She listened out for the covert meaning behind Naomi's words (i.e. 'career'), as well as the implicit emotion. Carlita also communicated what she was sensing affectively – Naomi's anger – and tentatively checked this out with Naomi. In this way Carlita was sensitive to the fact that often unexpressed emotion has been unhelpfully bottled up for some reason, such as shame, stigma, confusion or fear, and therefore needs to be worked with carefully. She then tried to convey her acceptance of Naomi, by staying with the anger and helping her find more authentic words to describe her experience.

When you are attending carefully to clients, you may discern patterns or themes that permeate their lives and which provide an explanation for what is going on for them in the present. Themes and patterns can be likened to our 'default' positions or 'blueprints'. They are the habitual responses, feelings and thoughts that we fall back on irrespective of what the situation demands. Carefully listening for the hidden, the unexpressed or the ulterior message behind what the client is sharing may help to uncover some of their unhelpful patterns. Let's return to Carlita's work with Naomi.

Carlita believes she may have identified a theme, or pattern, in Naomi's life in which she never quite 'measures up' to other people. Despite Naomi's academic success, for example, Naomi focuses on the things she thinks she didn't do well in at school, compared to her parents and brother. Naomi tells Carlita about a memory she has of arriving home from school, excited and proud to tell her parents that she had achieved 97 per cent in a Maths exam, and her father responding by saying that her brother had gotten 100 per cent in the same exam the year before.

Carlita: Do you remember how you felt back then?

Naomi: [*Sounding flat and unemotional*] Nothing. How silly that I had felt proud of myself. [*Shrugs and looks away*]

> Carlita: You almost sound indifferent … and yet I'm thinking, it's obviously a memory that has stayed with you – you're recalling it all these years later and so it sounds pretty important …
>
> Naomi: I guess I wasn't surprised by my dad's response to be honest. I was never as clever as my brother – I was always being reminded of that – and I never will be.
>
> Carlita: It's like you're saying more than that. It's as if you're saying, 'Compared to others, I'm no good'.
>
> Naomi: Uh-huh … I guess I've never felt equal to others.

Carlita thought about the package around the kernel of what Naomi was saying. Even though Naomi said she felt 'nothing' and shrugged, Carlita recognized the meaning behind Naomi sharing her memory and looked to explore that with Naomi to help her gain greater clarity around its significance. Clients may give clues about their particular patterns – for example, recalling certain events or experiences, or saying something like 'Here I go again' or 'It feels like this happens all the time.' While patterns give us familiarity and a sense of control, some also stunt creativity and spontaneity. Clients may have patterns that are destructive to themselves and to others (Lister Ford, 2002; Stewart, 2007) and the work may involve revealing them, the function they have served and how they are unhelpful in the present.

Challenging to invite authenticity

> True change can be very painful because you have to let go of part of yourself. We knew from experience that by changing, we gained more than we lost. We got more awareness. We got more compassion. We used to call it 'raising our consciousness'. (Woodfox, 2019: 264)

Your exploration in the Middle Stage will seek to increase your client's self-awareness and self-reflection on who they truly are and where they find themselves to be. Helping clients to become more in touch with themselves, and to develop authentic self-expression can be supported through genuine contact and your own authentic self-expression. As we discussed in Chapter 4, being authentic with your clients implicitly offers them space to connect to their true selves.

Being authentic and genuine is usually easy enough when you are feeling naturally warm, accepting and interested in your client, but presents various difficulties when your experience of them, or what you are hearing about the way they act, think or feel jars with you in some way. For example, how able would you feel to share with a client that they leave you feeling bored or angry? How would you go about sharing your sense of them as someone who is overly critical of others? It is not uncommon for trainees and qualified therapists to worry about the impact of their congruent, more challenging responses on their clients ('What if I hurt their feelings?', 'What if they aren't ready to hear it?', 'What if I've got this wrong?'). There are good reasons why we try to avoid upsetting people in our everyday interactions – we are usually driven to act in socially acceptable ways or to avoid harm. However, in order to galvanize the change process, our clients – with our support –

need to learn to work with and process difficult feelings and confront aspects of themselves or their lives that may be initially very uncomfortable to face, and 'if we tread on eggshells around our clients' feelings, we might block rather than facilitate change' (Tolan, 2017: 55). Here we look at a particular kind of intervention that calls on the therapist to access their authentic, subjective self and work from a place of integrity: challenge.

To challenge means to question, to stimulate and to arouse. Challenging in counselling and psychotherapy is intended to invite clients to reflect on and become curious about their current views with the intention of adopting different, more empowering perspectives. Clients' appraisals of their situations are often potentially restricting; in other words, they may be using out of date or faulty maps which they may not be consciously aware of. However, we are in a position to spot erroneous or self-defeating ways of being and share our thoughts in an authentic and caring way that enables them to construct different and less obstructed views of themselves or their world. It is from these different views that they will be able to increase their self-awareness, capacity for authenticity, and identify possibilities for constructive change.

Sharing your views and challenging clients by inviting them to examine things differently does not imply that there is a right way of looking at situations or that there is a reality which the therapist operates within and which the client must be helped to espouse. Rather, the intention is to facilitate the kind of deeper exploration that stimulates clients to reassess themselves and their concerns. Essentially, you will be focusing on the ways in which your client understands their world – that is, make sense of both their own and others' behaviour and the situations they are in. Deeper exploration that increases authenticity can be facilitated through challenge in the following ways:

- **Making connections and noting discrepancies**. For numerous reasons, clients may not make connections that would enable them to gain a deeper understanding of themselves and their concerns. Making connections is like completing a jigsaw. The individual pieces have meaning and significance when they are put together, which they do not have when they are viewed separately. Equally, as you listen and attend to clients you will become aware when things do not add up. Holding up a mirror to the games, distortions and discrepancies which clients employ to keep them from effective change calls attention to perceived incongruities, inconsistencies or camouflage they are using to hide from themselves.

- **Identifying personal resources and limitations**. Often clients do not have clear and up-to-date pictures of themselves. As you listen to clients, you may hear how they overlook the skills they have or how they dismiss what you hypothesize might be genuine constraints. If clients are to begin to take control of their concerns, then being clear about their resources and limitations will be important. Challenging clients in this way encourages them to become more *reflective* and *reflexive* about themselves, in the same way that that reflective practice can facilitate your own journey of self-awareness as a therapist (see Chapter 1).

- **Increasing clients' awareness of themselves**. Clients may be unaware of how their behaviour impacts on others. Equally, clients may not understand the influence of their beliefs. They may have irrational (and unreasonable) beliefs that both inhibit and disturb them. Beliefs are often expressed as a 'should' or 'must', as if signifying an immutable rule rather than a choice. Often, clients put themselves under a lot of pressure with 'shoulds' and 'musts', which can then become self-defeating: 'I must be liked by everyone' or 'I should get everything right and never make a mistake.' These beliefs may come with a set of inferences which increase the harmful power behind the belief: 'I should get everything right and not make a mistake; *anything else makes me unlovable and I will end up alone.*'

- **Accessing unexpressed feelings**. Clients may find feelings difficult; they may be difficult to experience, to make sense of, to own, to label and to express. They may act as though certain feelings are wrong or they may deny expressions of certain feelings such as joy. Sometimes too they will mask one feeling with another – for example, laughing to cover pain or expressing sadness instead of anger. Feelings have resonance and meaning for clients if they can allow their feelings to surface, understand what their feelings are communicating to them and let them guide the way. Challenging clients to explore their feelings gives them useful insight into themselves and their current situations.

- **Diminishing blame and promoting responsibility**. You may want to encourage clients to confront themselves in a responsible way, as an alternative to self-blame or blame of others. Blame can feel ostensibly palatable as its binary logic makes things seem easier to understand. However, some clients may punish themselves, or others, in ways that hamper insight, and lose touch with the richness, complexity and ultimately real tapestry of life. You might ask them to talk to themselves as a person who is interested in understanding, rather than condemning, what they do or perceive others as doing.

Often, clients have developed beliefs and ways of behaving, feeling and thinking because these are the things that have provided protection from censure, abandonment, shame and deprivation. Some of their unconscious strategies for coping have been and remain helpful. Others may once have been helpful but have outlived their usefulness or have even become self-defeating and harmful. Clients are often unaware, or only dimly aware, of how they disempower themselves. As Tolan writes:

> A line between material which is in awareness and out of awareness suggests that it is either one or the other. It is perhaps more useful to imagine a band, or 'grey area' of experience which is rather dimly sensed and which can be brought into sharper focus by paying attention to it. (Tolan, 2017: 53)

Helping clients to appreciate the purposes these strategies have served, as well as the way they may now be self-sabotaging, is the start of helping them to become more self-compassionate, open and empowered.

Change can feel threatening. We are all susceptible to employing methods, consciously or unconsciously, to resist change and keep ourselves safe from the unknown. We might consider these strategies and methods to be like 'psychological protective devices'. Often, in our work with clients, we will notice some of the following ways in which clients explain their positions in order to avoid their pain or how threatened they feel:

- **Rationalizing**. Clients may justify their position by intellectualizing or applying logic to what is happening (e.g. 'It makes perfect sense I was the one who was fired – last one in, first one out. There is no point in feeling angry about it').
- **Dismissing**. Clients may diminish the importance of their experience (e.g. 'It is what it is. That's life – I could be so much worse off').
- **Delaying**. Clients may avoid accepting the urgency of a situation (e.g. 'I'm snowed under at work, there'll be plenty of time next week to see my doctor about these symptoms').
- **Externalizing**. Clients may blame others, focus on changes others need to make or attribute their problems to contextual factors (e.g. 'If she sees me as aggressive, that's really her problem').

Case example: Jade

Imagine the following scenario. Jade has been referred to you for therapy by her GP whom she consulted for depression following the breakdown of her marriage of 15 years. Jade has described feeling 'low' most or all of every day, with occasional 'bouts of severe irritability' in which she shouts at her kids, snaps at her neighbours and in one instance when her ex-husband visited, threw a glass of water across the room at him. Jade says she feels 'exhausted and ashamed' after she has gotten angry with people. So far you have had six sessions together. Jade's usual mood has been depressed and she has been very tearful. However, on a few occasions you have experienced her as impatient, sometimes blunt and sometimes cutting in her remarks to you. On arrival at her next session, she storms past you in the hallway leading to your therapy room looking worked up. She drops the fee for her session on your coffee table dismissively and remarks in an accusing way, 'I suppose you'll want paying!'

Reflection point

How might you respond to Jade?

- How does Jade's behaviour leave you feeling?
- Would you consider challenging Jade on the way she has arrived and how she has paid you?
- What kinds of things are you thinking about as you consider whether or not to challenge Jade?
- Can you articulate a response to Jade that she could find helpful in exploring her issues?

In Chapter 1, we discussed the art of giving and receiving feedback as an important tool in learning counselling and psychotherapy skills. In many ways, the skill of working with feedback is at the heart of learning how to challenge. We build on this here, with some principles for challenging clients authentically:

- **Go gently**. Clients will be more likely to listen to challenge if it is expressed tentatively. Telling or informing may seem dominating and suggests that you are the expert when, in fact, you are sharing a subjective view. Being gentle does not mean diluting your message or prevaricating with 'ifs' and 'buts'. Rather it means conveying that what you are saying is open to exploration and modification. You might communicate this by saying, for example, 'I'm wondering if …' or 'How does this seem to you …?' or or 'My hunch is …'. As with self-disclosure and immediacy, it is helpful to use 'I' statements when sharing something about your own experience.

- **Remember your purpose**. Your aim is to help clients to reassess themselves, gain greater awareness and explore, with honesty, the concerns they bring in order to effect some change. You will need to monitor whether your challenging interventions are helping them to do that. The decision about what to share, challenge a client about or invite them to consider should be based on the agreed contract and not on the therapist's inquisitiveness.

- **Consider whether the client is able to receive what you're saying**. Sometimes clients are raw and vulnerable. They need time to let themselves heal a little and regain their emotional balance before being able to face aspects of themselves or the issues they are struggling with, even though they are well aware that they will have to do this sooner or later. As a colleague once remarked, 'If your skin is raw, even a small puff of breeze stings.' In these circumstances, the most skilled and insightful challenges are not going to further the work if clients are able neither to hear nor use them.

- **Avoid blaming**. Effective challenging involves neither blaming nor finding fault. Clients are more likely to use challenges that are free of criticism. Recognizing and acknowledging unhelpful beliefs and behaviour, owning and taking responsibility for what is legitimately theirs to take is not the same as condemning. If you sense that clients experience your challenges as criticism, then you will need to address that openly. This can be done by using immediacy (see above).

- **Be open to challenge yourself**. In other words, be open to receiving feedback as well as giving it. You may not always agree with other people's feedback and challenges; you may initially find it difficult to hear or perhaps find it confusing. However, you cannot expect clients to receive your challenge with openness unless you are prepared to do the same. It is important to remember that challenges are not about uncovering some objective truth; they are about furthering exploration, promoting freedom of expression and increasing authenticity. This will require you to listen as non-defensively as you are able to when a client points out ways in which they have experienced you as unhelpful, openly sharing with your clients when you think the process has been inhibited (e.g. by collusion or competition) and owning your part in that (you may need to own your defensive response at times too), and learning to challenge yourself and explore your own behaviour in supervision.

It is also important to remember that simply stringing basic skills together does not develop effective challenges. Your perspectives will be based on careful listening and attention to your clients and will be explainable in terms of whichever counselling and psychotherapy theory you espouse. Several other books in the Counselling in Action series provide different theoretical perspectives which you might use to assist your understanding of what clients bring. Of course, supervision also provides an opportunity for exploring how and in what areas to challenge clients.

Let us look at an example of challenge in practice. Hannah is under review at work because of problems she has been having managing her team. Her own manager is concerned that junior colleagues are scared of her and have stopped approaching her for help and guidance. Hannah conveyed 'surprise' at receiving this feedback as she sees herself as honest and straightforward with other people, which she feels is what's needed to get the job done. Her therapist, David, experiences her quite differently. David feels Hannah comes across as critical, negative and anxious about getting things right. David's aim is to encourage Hannah to explore her behaviour and impact on others and to challenge her to view herself from a different perspective.

Hannah: [*Sighs and looks annoyed*] I'm pretty irritated to be honest … I just want to get on with the job and this 'review' is just getting in the way. All I've done is be honest with people – I'm a straight talker, that's just who I am.

David: It sounds like being direct and honest is important to you … and when people don't understand that you feel irritated. As you talk about it, you sound impatient.

Hannah: [*With a sharp tone in her voice*] Yep. Seriously, I've got no patience for this … Constructive criticism is important if you want to progress! Don't any of them see that?!

David: So, from your perspective you are trying to help them, to support them to do well …

Hannah: [*In a more moderate tone*] Well, yes. So, yesterday, I gave a colleague feedback on their report. I told her straight that it was disappointing and full of errors. If the report had been sent to the Head of Department without corrections she would have been in trouble. So, what else was I supposed to say?

David: Hannah, from the way you described the feedback you gave your colleague, it sounded to me like you focused solely on what was wrong with her report … so you didn't find anything good about it?

Hannah: [*Slowly, contemplatively*] Well, no … that's not entirely true … Some parts of it were good, excellent even.

David: I'm curious about that Hannah … it seems like you only shared 'half' of your honest thoughts on her report – your thoughts on what was wrong with it, rather than your thoughts on what was excellent. Does that make sense to you?

Hannah: Yes, I get you – I guess I hadn't really noticed that I was doing that! To be honest, I'm so anxious that, as a team, we get it right I become completely preoccupied with what we might be getting wrong.

David: I wonder what that's like for your team?

Hannah: I guess my anxiety gets passed around like a hot potato! It can't be easy for them … there may even be times when my feedback appears unkind.

In this session, David used challenge to explore the impact of Hannah's behaviour on other people. He starts by trying to understand things from her point of view ('It sounds like being direct and honest is important to you …') which is a non-judgemental, gentle way in to looking at the issue. By naming Hannah's implicit affect (impatience) David facilitates Hannah to access another emotion underlying what is happening for her at work – her anxiety around the performance of her team. David avoids condemning Hannah's behaviour and instead gently challenges her to become curious rather than blaming herself and others ('So, from your perspective you are trying to help them …', 'I'm curious about that …') and ultimately to consider the issue from another perspective ('I wonder what that's like for your team?').

What happens if you do not challenge clients? Challenges usually result in a process of gradual 'cognitive shifts' within the client rather than a single 'light bulb' moment. A complete absence of any challenge may mean that the client becomes aimless and does not gain the new insights essential for change. In one sense, the therapeutic process is challenging from the outset, because clients are brought face to face with their concerns from the start. However, unless you encourage clients to try on different perspectives, they are unlikely to move beyond their present limiting views, those views that are keeping them stuck or immobilized. Challenging is demanding of clients, requiring them to look differently at themselves and their concerns as a necessary precursor to change.

Sometimes failure to challenge is to collude with clients' self-defeating behaviours and beliefs. Additionally, silence on a subject can be ambiguous. Your client may take silence as affirmation that you are supporting that aspect of their behaviour or belief. You will need to have established a therapeutic alliance and developed a reasonable understanding of your client and their issues before using challenge, and therefore in the Beginning Stage it is usually right to avoid direct challenges. In the Middle Stage it is appropriate to offer challenges and unusual not to be challenging, but it should be used sensitively and gently.

Giving directives

As the description suggests, giving directives involves the therapist openly directing the client to do something, or directing the therapeutic process in some way. This is in contrast to a non-directive stance, in which the therapist attempts to refrain from instructing the client or process in any way. Cooper (2008) highlights the research evidence that supports both directive and non-directive practices. For example, there is clear evidence that directive interventions are associated with positive therapeutic outcome and may even be necessary to help clients reach deep levels of processing (Cooper, 2008). On the other hand, high levels of directivity can be experienced as 'being told what to do' – also viewed as unhelpful to clients (Cooper, 2008). Cooper concludes that:

> The key question … may not be so much whether directivity or non-directivity is better, but about finding a way of working that avoids either extreme, and which has the potential to incorporate both directive and non-directive elements in a way that is responsive to individual clients. (Cooper, 2008: 140)

The kind of directives we want to focus on here are those that are intended to guide clients to areas that the therapist believes would be a fruitful source for deeper exploration and understanding, and aim to aid clients' self-expression and increase their self-awareness. Such directives arise organically out of the work, as the therapist learns more and more about the client sitting in front of them. Examples of directives include:

- suggesting that your client focus in on a particular aspect of their narrative
- inviting a client to try and stay with a particular emotion that has arisen
- encouraging the client to describe what is going on in their body as they talk through an issue
- offering to do an exercise or role-play
- recommending a particular between-session activity.

In a similar way to self-disclosure, which changes the focus from the client to the therapist, directives are rooted in what the therapist thinks the client should focus on, not necessarily what the client thinks they should focus on (though of course there may be an agreement). Directives can be very powerful and influence the work in significant ways. There are therefore important principles guiding the use of directives:

- **Do not overuse them**. Clients may feel bossed around, criticized, intruded upon or even persecuted if they are constantly on the receiving end of directives. Too liberal a use might rob clients of any sense of control and may encourage over-dependence.
- **Be clear about your intention and what you are suggesting**. As with self-disclosure and immediacy, you need to be able to clearly link the interventions you are using with the overall aims of the work. Sharing why you are being directive with your client also offers you both an opportunity to work collaboratively. Providing clear guidelines, for example, describing exactly what an exercise might entail, will avoid confusion and again ensures that your client is part of the process rather than having something 'done to' them.
- **Check in with your client**. Ask them their thoughts on what you have suggested or recommended. Inquire about the helpfulness of your interventions, or how willing they feel to try an exercise, role-play or between-session activity, and be prepared for clients to say no! Your directive may not suit them, they may feel resistant, uneasy or not ready. Exploring their 'no' may be a useful route of exploration, but you may also need to accept and respect where they are at.

The following example demonstrates giving directives in practice: Amy has been working on being more assertive in her therapy with Rahul. She has described an overbearing father who she found frightening growing up. She remembers 'keeping her head down' and not bringing attention to herself as a teenager in attempts to avoid interactions with him. She thinks this is linked to her problems asserting herself at work and in her friendships. Amy is telling Rahul about a situation at work in which a male colleague, Ben, has put pressure on her to swap her annual leave with him at the last minute, which would be really inconvenient for her.

Amy: So, Ben just stared at me – y'know, looking really annoyed. And I could feel my face go red, but I just froze up. I couldn't speak!

Rahul:	And now? Are you able to speak to what was going on for you?
Amy:	Oh, I don't know! I was just wanting to get away from him … just didn't want to be in that situation. I don't know how to say no to him!
Rahul:	[*gently*] Amy, put some feelings to your words.
Amy:	Um, don't know … maybe anxious?
Rahul:	Stay with that feeling for a moment … experience what you feel … what comes up?
Amy:	OK … [*sits quietly for a moment*] I feel anxious, yes … a bit wobbly. I feel kind of annoyed actually – oh! I don't know where that's come from!
Rahul:	I think it might be useful to try and stay with these feelings some more – are you OK to do that?
Amy:	Yes, I think so …
Rahul:	OK, where can you feel that annoyance in your body?
Amy:	[*Long, reflective pause*] The wobbly feeling is right here [*places a hand on her stomach*] … and here, sort of in my throat … do you know what? I think it's more like anger, not annoyance.
Rahul:	And again Amy, I'm going to ask you to speak to that – what words go with that anger?
Amy:	I want to tell Ben – go away! What you've asked of me isn't OK!

In this example Rahul uses directives to help facilitate deeper exploration, and to help Amy articulate what she feels. By inviting Amy to stay with her feelings ('Stay with that feeling for a moment …') and encouraging her to try and describe what was happening in her body ('where can you feel that annoyance in your body?'), Amy shifts from describing herself as frozen up to accessing her anxiety and anger. Rahul made several checks to see how his interventions were 'landing' with Amy ('are you OK to do that?'), as well as trying to make sure he was transparent about why he was directing the session the way that he was ('I think it might be useful to try and stay with these feelings …') which ensured the process remained collaborative and didn't push Amy beyond a point she was ready to go to.

Summary

In this chapter we have looked at moving from establishing the essential aims of the Beginning Stage to deepening your exploration of what the client brings into the therapy room in the Middle Stage. We outlined two key aims for this stage – to maintain the therapeutic alliance and to explore the client's issues at depth. We considered the important skills involved in evolving the work in these respects to include deepening the encounter between you both, self-disclosure, immediacy, advanced empathy, challenging to invite greater authenticity, and giving directives. Within this chapter we have provided important principles for working with and developing these skills. Finally, we have also looked at the importance of regular reviews to support your ability to work to the contract, which may include a reassessment of the client's issues. In the next chapter we consider the final stage in the process of therapeutic work – the Ending Stage – concerned with reflection and transition.

Further resources

- De Young, P.A. (2015) *Relational Psychotherapy. A Primer*. New York: Routledge.
- Mearns, D. and Cooper, M. (2018) *Working at Relational Depth in Counselling and Psychotherapy* (2nd edition). London: SAGE.
- Yalom, I. (2002) *The Gift of Therapy*. New York: Harper Collins.

Online resources

Visit https://study.sagepub.com/staffordandbond4e to watch:

Video 5.1   An Empathic Stance

Video 5.2   Self-Disclosure in Psychotherapy

Video 5.3   Bringing Things into the Here-and-Now

Video 5.4   Trustworthiness and Resilience – Scenario

Video 5.5   Trustworthiness and Resilience – Discussion

6

The Ending Stage

Reflection and Transition

Chapter contents

This chapter covers:

- Aims, plans and skills for the Ending Stage
- Reflecting and reviewing the work
- A model to guide reflection
- Working with the client's resources and planning for the future
- Closing the work and saying goodbye
- Tips for ending
- Further resources

Introduction

In this chapter, we begin by discussing the aims of the Ending Stage and continue by reviewing the plans and skills by which these aims will be achieved. By this stage in the therapeutic process, you will have made a strong and meaningful connection with your client which will have facilitated a focused and explorative approach to the issues they have brought to therapy. Through this relationship, they will have had an opportunity to shed light on those issues, examine and gain insight into them, as well as experience catharsis, understanding and healing. In the Ending Stage you will be turning your attention towards reflecting on that process and making decisions about ending the work and looking to the future.

The key theme for the Ending Stage of the work is 'reflection'. This describes the key activities of the work at this stage – thoughtful and constructive consideration of the therapeutic work, the client's progress and learning for the future. Your intention behind this focus, at this stage, will be to help your client consolidate their learning and plan how to apply it going forward. You will also be supporting and guiding your client to find closure in the work they have undertaken with you – this may mean ending therapy, finding support elsewhere or beginning a new piece of work with you. Whatever the final outcome chosen, there will be a deliberate and conscious movement from one stage in their journey to another. Hence, the relational focal point at this stage is defined as 'transition'.

Aims, plans and skills for the Ending Stage

Aims

The following three aims characterize the work of the Ending Stage:

1. To reflect on and review the work undertaken
2. To work with the client's resources to plan for the future
3. To close the work and say goodbye

Plans

Let's consider the plans you will need to develop and implement in order to achieve each of your aims for the Ending Stage, considering each aim in turn.

To reflect on and review the work undertaken

In Chapter 1 we discussed reflective practice as a personal resource for learning counselling and psychotherapy skills. During the Beginning and Middle Stages of your work, one of the key capabilities you will have been facilitating your clients to strengthen within themselves is their own ability to think reflectively and reflexively about themselves, their relationships, their issues and the context within which they are living. Your plan at the Ending Stage will be to build on their reflective capacities and guide them through a process of review for the work you have done together. This is closely linked to the two further aims for this stage – working with the client's resources and closing the work – because being able to reflect and review on their journey, progress and who they find themselves to be as they say goodbye to you will support them in identifying their resources and finding closure.

To work with the client's resources to plan for the future

You will plan to establish with them what their strengths and healthy coping strategies are, as well as staying aware of those things that have previously stopped them from doing what they need to do. This will involve looking towards the future and considering referral options, other sources of help or continuing onwards without professional support.

To close the work and say goodbye

Finally, a key and obvious aspect of planning at this stage, is to plan for the ending of therapy with you. This includes planning when to end, being mindful of different types of endings and appreciating the individual significance each client, as well as you, the therapist, place on the ending.

Skills

Let's consider the skills that you will need to utilize in the Ending Stage to support your work, meet your aims and put your plans into action. At this stage you will bring together all the skills you have been learning throughout the book. For example, in facilitating reflection and review, you will be using the integrative framework for active listening to hold multiple sources of information your client is giving you about how they view the work they have done and how they will use it in the future. This will require you to honour the courage they have had in coming into therapy and the changes they have made, as well as acknowledging any disappointments or frustrations they have about what hasn't changed. To work with client resources and plan for the future, you will employ methods of exploration to test hypotheses and identify what they are doing really well as well as how they may self-sabotage, or alternatively how they need help to manage their own expectations of what may be possible post therapy. Throughout, you will be attempting to convey your empathy, acceptance and genuineness. This is particularly important in helping clients to close the work and say goodbye.

Therefore, in terms of skills, this is a stage of consolidation for you as a therapist. Below, we look at each aim for this stage and present some key concepts and ideas to guide you in achieving these aims.

Skills needed to reflect on and review the work undertaken

> Reflection is our human way of making meaning in life. [It] is the bridge between information and wisdom. (Carroll and Gilbert, 2011: 95)

Through the development and strengthening of your therapeutic alliance, in which your clients will have experienced your empathy, acceptance and genuineness, they will have had various opportunities to explore their issues at depth, identifying and naming what was 'wrong' and starting to make sense of, and make changes to, their lives. They will have been invited to increase their self-awareness and self-reflection and become more in touch with an authentic sense of themselves. We might conceptualize the Ending Stage as the pinnacle of those reflections – that is, the point at which the client's learning becomes 'transformative' (Bager-Charleson, 2010). This represents the stage of reflection and learning where 'the initial problem has become an asset, something to be incorporated as a valuable experience; almost like "recycling" something that was previously useless' (Bager-Charleson, 2010: 149).

Carroll and Gilbert (2011: 86) suggest that confronting a problem (as our clients will hopefully be doing by entering therapy) leaves people 'ripe for reflection'. They argue that 'uncertainty, confusion and surprise are often emotional pathways to helping us reconsider

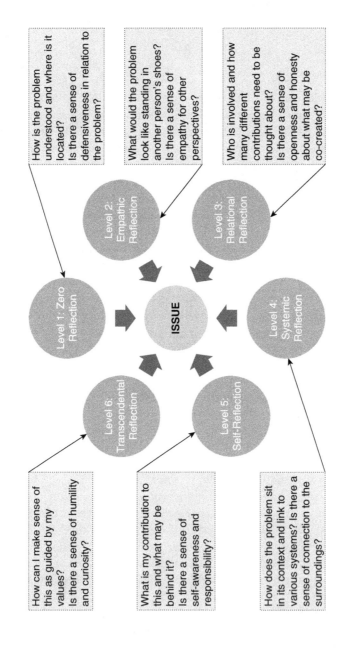

FIGURE 6.1 *Levels of reflection*

and think through what we have never thought through before. Wake up calls, high-wire moments, shocks and traumas – all are potential triggers for processes of reflection.' Clients will have been developing their reflective capacities throughout their work with you, and so this kind of open inquiry into themselves and their issues is not unique to the Ending Stage. However, we draw on a model for guiding reflection here as part of the Ending Stage involves clients reviewing and looking back with a purposeful focus on the therapeutic work, their progress, any changes that have taken place and their relationship with you. The model proposed by Carroll and Gilbert (2011) considers six levels of reflection (see Figure 6.1). These levels can be used to guide your own reflective practice, as well as guide your clients in considering their issues and how they have engaged with them over the course of their work with you from several different angles. Importantly, as Carroll and Gilbert (2011: 104) write, 'each level of reflection brings valuable learning pertinent to its own stage'.

- **Level 1: Zero Reflection**. This is a position of non-reflection and a place which we are all susceptible to start from. It is difficult to examine ourselves honestly or look at the bigger picture. Typically, from this position we are defensive, resistant or rigid in our thinking, which can result in seeing the problem as being out there or as someone's else's fault. At this level of reflection there is very little movement and instead a sense of stuckness prevails.

  o   When my client Ali suddenly and angrily tells me he finds my time boundaries 'too rigid' we find ourselves in disagreement about why time boundaries are in place. Internally, I initially respond by feeling defensive of my way of working, feeling annoyed and blaming him with thoughts such as 'He lacks awareness' and 'He doesn't respect the space'. In other words, 'This disagreement is all his fault!'.

- **Level 2: Empathic Reflection**. This is a position of observation of the issue at hand, where we are able to acknowledge the perspective of another. By and large, the problem is still out there. However, we can experience some empathy for alternative perspectives. Carroll and Gilbert (2011) describe this is as 'blame plus understanding'. At this level of reflection there is some movement and loosening of black and white thinking.

  o   In considering Ali's perspective that I am 'too strict' when it comes to beginning and finishing our sessions on time, I remember his military school upbringing and how his time was dictated by stringent timetables and strict disciplinarians. I remember Ali telling me how he lived with a mixture of anger and fear at school and longed for his time to be his own. I feel less defensive and more compassionate. I think to myself, 'I understand his need to retaliate against the time boundaries given his school experiences.'

- **Level 3: Relational Reflection**. This is a position of sharing responsibility. Reflecting with this lens is about recognizing and appreciating the co-created nature of relationships, narratives and issues. As we face a problem, we begin to see our part in that problem – 'our part' may reflect a way of contributing to the problem occurring or be more about the influence of our subjective view of the problem itself. We are freed from the blame game, and more open in our thinking.

○ As Ali and I talk about the time boundaries I begin to recognize that my initial reaction, from a place of zero reflection, contributed to his feeling he had little say in how we worked together. Without meaning to, I shut down any discussion or exploration about how he experienced the time boundaries of our sessions. Ali recognizes that he can lash out when he feels he hasn't any control over things. He knows this can leave other people feeling attacked. He recognizes that he didn't share with me that his sense of having no agency left him feeling frightened. Together we can see how we both contributed to the disagreement and hostile feelings.

- **Level 4: Systemic Reflection**. This is a systems position, which allows us to see how the problems at hand are created, viewed and influenced by context. Carroll and Gilbert (2011) describe this as the 'helicopter view' of the small and large systems that affect our lives. These systems might include the organizations we are a part of, our family backgrounds, our community, culture and heritage, the current political field or religious group we belong to, for example. This level of reflection moves us into an appreciation of the bigger picture.

  ○ I consider the context within which Ali and I work – private practice – and think about the potential power imbalance which might be at play: I'm on home turf, I set the contract and the fee, I may be seen as an authority figure with expertise. Equally, Ali, who works as a policeman, represents a different kind of authority figure to me. How has this affected the way I have engaged with him and understand the balance of power in the room? Ali comes from a large family in which he needed to assert himself (usually loudly) in order to be heard above his siblings. In contrast, I am unused to arguing and overt displays of anger in my background – was there a clash of familial cultures when we disagreed about the time boundaries?

- **Level 5: Self-Reflection**. This is a position of internal reflection and personal responsibility. It is about using self-insight and increasing self-awareness. Looking through this lens helps us to see our particular contribution to the issues and problems we are facing, and perhaps the patterns and re-occurring themes we find ourselves dealing with. This level of reflection helps us to examine our assumptions and the way we make meaning and gets us in touch with our self-agency.

  ○ As I start to reflect from this perspective, I consider why time boundaries have been so important to me in my work. While I recognize that my professional belief is that time boundaries help establish a therapeutic frame and create a sense of safety, I can also see that there is a personal piece of the puzzle at play – as a child in a therapy that I hated having to go to, I watched the clock anxiously waiting for the time to be up. Unlike Ali perhaps, scrupulous attention to the time reminded me of my freedom to leave rather than feeling forced to stay. I begin to see how my initial defensiveness to Ali's challenge was – just like Ali – rooted in fear.

- **Level 6: Transcendental Reflection**. This is a position of meaning making, transcending the individual, dyad or system. For some this is a spiritual or religious stance, for others a philosophical perspective. It might be thought of as an expanded perspective – it is not taking the helicopter overview of the level of systemic reflection in that it is not looking down on the systems we are a part of. Rather, it is looking down, up, through, inside and outside in a multidimensional way. It looks for the overarching meaning in the issues being faced and requires us to be willing to enter a space of uncertainty.

o   As Ali and I continue our discussion around the time boundary, we begin to talk about Ali's belief in human beings as fundamentally free, an idea he became engaged with at an early age. He found his school days punitive and restrictive, and thought of his teachers as trying to oppress his self-agency. Equally, in working with me, Ali found the boundaries of the work threatening to his inner sense of freedom. We begin to examine how his inner sense and long-held beliefs could be respected while holding a space for boundaries and an acknowledgement of the limitations of our contract.

This model of reflection can be used throughout the work and in review of the work in the Ending Stage. It provides different angles for thinking about the issues the client brings. Questions to help guide reflections at each stage might be asked directly or used to guide your thinking.

Case example: Helena

Let's consider Helena's journey through therapy and how her reflections developed to a point of 'transformative learning' during the Ending Stage, by using the model put forth by Carroll and Gilbert (2011):

Beginning Stage. When she began therapy, Helena described herself as 'unusually unmotivated at work', suffering headaches and frequent colds that stopped her going to work and left her feeling 'unhappy and depressed'. Helena worked as a food writer for a popular national magazine. Ordinarily she loved her job, which felt like a 'perfect fit' for her and her interests. She was creative and bright and received encouraging and supportive feedback from her boss who had recently assigned her a coveted writing project which would have involved travelling to Asia. Despite her love of travel and the prestige associated with the project, Helena had made excuses not to go. She reported to her therapist that in the last six months she had increasingly felt ignored and rejected by some of her colleagues at work social events and over coffee breaks. Recently she had overheard someone remarking that she was unfairly singled out and favoured by their boss. She blamed her colleagues for her lack of motivation, ill health and decision not to take the writing project on (Level 1: Zero Reflection).

Middle Stage. Helena identified feelings of shame and hurt in relation to her experiences with her colleagues. However, alongside this she also started to recognize that her colleagues may have envied her when her boss awarded her the writing project (Level 2: Empathic Reflection). She shared with her therapist that at work she had come to feel very isolated. She began to recognize that her response was to withdraw

(Continued)

from others, even her work friends, which compounded her loneliness. Helena started to become aware that the hostility that existed between herself and some of her colleagues was co-created – in part, their envy and in part, her withdrawal from them (Level 3: Relational Reflection). Helena considered the culture of the organization. Ambition and individualism were prized and teamwork tended to be undervalued. Helena could see that both she and her colleagues were working within a very competitive environment and could often see each other as rivals (Level 4: Systemic Reflection). She also reflected in one session that, even though she didn't intend to get ill, she had to admit that headaches and colds provided her with a legitimate excuse to avoid the office and the peers she had come to fear. Helena began to consider that her lack of motivation was like a form of self-sabotage and that it was possible that she had excused herself from the project her boss had offered her to avoid any more feelings of social rejection and isolation. She initially felt sad and then started to feel angry that she had allowed herself to miss out on this opportunity (Level 5: Self Reflection).

Ending Stage. At this point in the work Helena and her therapist built on Helena's increased self-awareness, and insights into her place of work, to transform her presenting issues into a valuable experience Helena could learn from. Helena could see that her fear of being envied by her colleagues meant that she had distanced herself from everyone at work and, without realizing it, deliberately undermined herself and her contribution. She could also see that she had blamed her colleagues without thinking through her issues from other angles and had cast all her colleagues in the same light. She knew that, actually, there were some who had seemed genuinely pleased for her when her boss had offered her the writing project. Helena wanted to apply this learning in practice. She began to consider the deeper meaning in her experience. She felt that part of her angst was related to a clash of the organization's ethos of individualism versus her own values around community and connection (Level 6: Transcendental Reflection). Helena began by setting herself a goal to try to reconnect with work friends. Despite her fear of envy and social rejection, Helena wanted to progress in her career and moving forward she aimed to try to recognize when fear and envy were holding her back.

Reflection point

Using the Six Levels of Reflection model

Consider a recent experience with another person that has caused difficulty for you – it could be at work, with your therapist or a peer. Write a description of the experience in terms of its basic content or describe it to a friend or peer. Then consider the following questions:

- How did you behave?
- What thoughts did you have?
- How were you feeling at the time, and how do you feel now as you reflect-on-action?

- Were there other, contextual factors that influenced the situation in your view?
- How would you describe the relationships involved?
- What level(s) of reflections have you been working at as you consider the answers to these questions?
- What have you learned from the experience about yourself, and about the other(s) involved?

Skills needed to work with the client's resources to plan for the future

> The way to minimize suffering is to approach pain and create a way of understanding it and sharing it with others. (Cozolino, 2016: 256)

In the Ending Stage with your client, you will be identifying and drawing on your client's inner resources as well as possible external resources that will support their journey moving forward, outside of therapy. Inner resources may include such things as resilience, courage, tenacity and optimism. External resources may include things like activities, daily routines and supportive relationships. Research studies in the field of child psychology and development suggest that resilience in particular is linked to problem-solving skills, social competence and having a sense of purpose, as well as enabling individuals to recover and even flourish following setbacks and adversity, and avoid future risk-taking behaviour (WHO, 2017). In the contemporary health field, the concept of resilience is not only a central feature of children and young people's health but is considered important in understanding the health of adults and elderly people too. In fact, the World Health Organization (WHO) considers resilience so vital to good mental and physical health, it is at the core of their European policy framework for health and wellbeing for 2020 (WHO, 2017).

During the Beginning Stage and at the assessment point, you will have identified your client's resources and coping strategies and had a sense of what might be missing or unhelpful (e.g. excessive use of alcohol to deal with stress, socially isolating themselves when they feel depressed) as well as what they do well (e.g. reaching out when they need help). During the Middle Stage, you will have been helping your client to build up healthy resources and personal resilience in order to address those things that have been troubling them. At the Ending Stage, you will be looking forward to what healthy habits and ways of being can be harnessed and utilized in the future. Examples of inner and external resources can be found in Figure 6.2. It is important to bear in mind that identifying resources is not about 'looking on the bright side' (Joyce and Sills, 2014) or solving a problem. It is about finding ways that the client can support themselves moving forward. The key questions you will be asking your client will be:

- What has helped you manage what you're going through so far?
- What do you imagine might help you with these problems in the future?
- What has gotten in your way of addressing these issues as you have gone along?
- What unhealthy patterns have you previously tended to fall into that have tripped you up before?

Examples of inner resources	Examples of external resources
Identifying and naming feelings	Contact with supportive friends
Taking time to reflect	Being involved in community activities
Resilience	Listening to music
Reframing problems to consider other perspectives	Structuring the day or week
Holding hope	Sleep
Being courageous	Diet & physical exercise
Remembering strengths	Breathing exercises

FIGURE 6.2   *Resources*

Future planning may also include thinking about referral options. This may be referral to another therapist or counselling and psychotherapy service, or to other sources of help. Elton-Wilson (1996: 1) views therapists as 'secondary to the life pattern of an individual client's psychological development' believing that, 'to achieve transformation, one client may use the services of a variety of professional helpers, as well as drawing upon the support of external resources'. Therefore, it might be useful to explore alternatives to being in therapy with you, which may be liberating to clients (Elton-Wilson, 1996). De Young (2015: 170) argues that what is important is not helping our clients develop complete autonomy but rather 'how individuals open themselves to mutually empowering relationships that extend outward in networks of respect and empowerment'. In other words, and to return to a fundamental point discussed in Chapter 1, as social creatures we survive and thrive *in relationship*. Certainly, the research investigating the development and influence of resilience, for example, highlights the importance not only of personality traits and factors external to the individual, but also networks, communities and systems (Seaman et al., 2014). Any future planning for life after therapy should consider seriously how healthy relationships – found in multiple contexts including counselling and psychotherapy, the workplace, community, family and friends – provide support, build resilience and help us to reach our potential.

Case example: Tonya

Tonya sought therapy from a community counselling service after the death of her mother and was offered 26 sessions with Elodie. Tonya had taken responsibility for managing and organizing her mother's estate and funeral arrangements following her death. These activities had kept Tonya busy at the time but several months after the funeral she began feeling less and less able to cope. She went back to work, but felt disengaged and unmotivated, often calling in sick. She had started taking sleeping pills at night when she felt at her worst, which helped her to 'block out her feelngs'. She had withdrawn from her friends and other family members and stopped attending her singing group because singing reminded her of her mother. Elodie recognized that Tonya's usual mechanisms for support – friends, family and singing – had been neglected and Tonya had begun engaging in unhelpful coping strategies, such as taking time off work and sleeping pills. However, she recognized that Tonya had been brave in reaching out and seeking help from a therapist, which spoke to her inner courage, and that when Tonya was not consumed by grief, she was a well-organized and resourceful woman, capable of personally managing her mother's estate, funeral arrangements and wake as well as working full time. As they approached the final month of their working therapy contract, Elodie wanted to work collaboratively with Tonya to identify what she had found helpful inside and outside therapy, as well as identifying those things that been unhelpful and unsupportive, so that Tonya could plan for her future. Tonya shared that she had found talking to someone about her mother helpful. She had found that surprising, as she had previously thought that she should remove herself from any activities that left her thinking about her to avoid getting upset. This realization had led her more recently to confide more in a close friend and encourage more conversations about her mother with family. She thought she would like to return to the singing group before she ended therapy with Elodie so that she had a chance to talk to Elodie about it afterwards. Tonya wanted to stop taking sleeping pills and so visiting her GP for advice on lowering the dose became another goal for her future beyond therapy. Recently she had recognized that the structure of working life, with its opportunities to talk to other people every day, while often effortful, was helping her feel stronger and more able to cope and so she had stopped taking days off sick.

Skills needed to close the work and say goodbye

How strange, the change, from major to minor

Every time we say goodbye. (Cole Porter, 1944)

Ending the work with your client is significant in many ways. It involves change, separation and loss. When therapy has been helpful and you have worked well together, the ending will mean your client is saying goodbye to someone who has come to mean something very important to them (De Young, 2015). A client's success in addressing their issues comes at the price of losing the relationship with you. As an active participant in the process, you will also likely be emotionally moved, challenged and changed. Equally, 'managing change usually involves confronting a loss of self, or at least the loss of elements that made up parts of what we used to be in terms of attitudes, habits and/or deep-seated values about ourselves or others' (Bager-Charleson, 2010: 147). Therefore, in ending their therapy, clients will potentially be saying goodbye to a part of themselves. Endings and separation can represent many things to our clients as well as to ourselves, stirring up memories (consciously or unconsciously) of previous endings including death and losses, and potentially confronting us with our 'aloneness'. The Ending Stage, and the final session or final few sessions, can therefore trigger feelings of fear, anger, sadness, helplessness, guilt, resentment, panic, or betrayal to name but a few. As such, endings can often be avoided in all sorts of ways by the client, therapist or both through some form of collusion.

However, Elton-Wilson (1996: 97) argues that it can be counterproductive to *assume* links between the ending of therapy and the client's previous endings and losses, and urges therapists to explore with clients the meaning and importance *they* place on the ending of therapy with you. To hold these multiple possibilities simultaneously – that ending is painful and/or triggering *and* that ending may be avoided *and* that ending may not as yet feel important to the client – requires 'maintaining a delicate balance between avoidance of the painful previous experiences of loss … and too premature a focus on the existential truths of termination.'

However, when endings are acknowledged and worked with, and any associated discomfort or pain has been identified and named, these feelings have more chance of being processed. Some of these feelings may be directly related to what hasn't happened, but was hoped for, in the therapy. As Elton-Wilson (1996: 104) writes, 'However beneficial the therapeutic engagement has been, there are likely to be disappointments and dissatisfactions. The freedom to voice these feelings may in itself be a reparative emotional experience.' Actively working with an 'ending stage' also makes space for more positive feelings and experiences related to the ending and the work itself (such as gratitude, compassion, courage, pride or empowerment and excitement about the future). It also offers an opportunity for a new experience of ending – this may be particularly important for clients who have been starved of supportive and constructive relationships in their lives and/or have had painful experiences of endings in the past. De Young (2015) uses the phrase 'letting the story tell itself out' as a key aspect of ending the therapeutic work. That is, in having provided a space for your client to share their narrative through your thoughtful attention to them, they have been able to make meaning of their experience and ultimately find 'resolution'. Another way of thinking of this is in finding 'closure' – an acceptance for what has been and a capacity to move forward to something new. Below we discuss two key considerations in closing the work: when to end and types of ending.

When to end?

While in an ideal world, the ending of the therapeutic work will be planned and prepared for, endings may also be unplanned and each type of ending requires attention to different aspects of the work and your relationship. We discuss types of ending in more detail below, but let's begin by thinking about how you and your client will decide to bring the work to an end when you are able to plan for your ending.

A natural end to the work happens when the issues your client has brought and goals they hoped to reach have been addressed and met. Sometimes this is relatively straightforward to identify – for example, a client presenting with low mood and trouble sleeping reporting a sustained period of feeling well and sleeping easily, or a client who suffers with panic attacks before public speaking having given several presentations and each time managed their anxiety well. However, sometimes resolution, closure and change may not be easy to name. That does not mean change hasn't happened. As De Young writes:

> The change may be as hard to name as what happens within us as a last series of chords brings to an end the complex themes and variations of a powerful piece of music, but we know, we feel, that all that matters most in this story has been aired, and there is resolution. (De Young, 2015: 161)

In an open-ended contract – that is, a contract where no time limit is placed on the work at its commencement – it is important to involve the client in decisions about when to end. This approach is one of respect and dignity for the human being sitting opposite you and promotes a commitment towards equality and anti-oppressive practice. In this way, involving the client in making decisions about when to end therapy can be empowering. It speaks to the client's ownership of their personal and psychological development, it encourages the client to take responsibility for the work they want to undertake or having courageously undertaken, and it may help them to ask for what they most want and need.

Many therapists will initiate regular reviews of their work with a client in order to ensure that the ending of therapy occurs at a time that is both collaborative and meaningful for the client (Etherington and Bridges, 2011). As discussed in Chapter 5, reviews provide an opportunity to assess progress and what is working well between you. When you and your client are deciding when to end, your review questions may have a particular focus. The following questions may help guide your reflections on when to end:

- Have the client's original goals been met?
- How would additional time be used and what would you focus on?
- Is there a sense that all the exploration the two of you can do together has been done?
- If the client is facing new issues, or has a new set of goals, are these within your areas of competence or is an onward referral needed?
- How motivated to be in therapy is the client?
- Do either of you feel it would be useful to take a break, or to end therapy?
- If an ending seems appropriate, how much time do you both feel you need together to end well?

Let's look at how a client, Bill, and his therapist, Yewande, consider when to end Bill's therapy. Bill referred himself to therapy because of problems in his marriage to Ava who had been having an affair. Bill and Ava had been married for eight years and had no children. Bill had been aware that over the past few years, following a promotion, he had been devoting more and more of his time to his job. However, as Ava was also career driven, he had assumed that the lack of time they spent together was because they had both been consumed by their jobs. He knew they had grown further apart and that they seemed to be leading separate lives but had not appreciated how deep their problems lay. Bill had felt shocked and betrayed by Ava's affair and sought therapy to help him come to terms with what had happened, the current state of their marriage and to figure out what he wanted in his future. As they approach the end of their contract, Yewande begins their session by inviting Bill to think with her about when they should end the work.

Yewande: Bill, I'd like to start today's session by considering how much time we have left. I'm aware that we originally contracted to work for four months – that means that as from today, we have four more sessions remaining. Does that feel like the right place to end our work to you?

Bill: Four more sessions? Hmm … OK, well, I feel like we've covered a lot of ground … I've processed a lot of how I've been feeling. Generally I feel a bit better, like stronger, in myself … the shock of it all has subsided anyway.

Yewande: I know that one of the things you wanted to get out of therapy was to come to terms with what happened in your marriage. It sounds like you've started to do that?

Bill: Yeah for sure. Its not like I don't have any feelings about what happened, but I understand much better how things started to go wrong. Coming here has helped to get everything 'out'.

Yewande: And what about the other hopes you had for therapy – to figure out what you want next? Over the last few sessions in particular, I've heard you really devote some thinking time to that …

Bill: Yep, that's true. Feeling a bit stronger has helped me think a bit straighter! I love Ava. I think I want this to work, I want us to get through this, but right now I think I need some space … and I want us to stop arguing and start talking. I've decided to temporarily move out of the house – give us both a 'breather'. It feels sad, but also like the right thing to do.

Yewande: OK – you've made some decisions about what you want in your immediate future – I can hear that hasn't been easy for you. It's sad to move out, even temporarily, but it's also a positive decision, in that it might give you both the space you need to talk properly.

Bill: Yeah …

Yewande: So, if we return for a moment to my first question – does another four sessions feel like the right place to end our work … what are your thoughts?

Bill: I think so … I'm guessing I'd like to use those sessions to talk about how I'm feeling having moved out! I've also been wondering if Ava and I might benefit from couple's therapy – it's just a thought. Perhaps … would it be possible to take a break from therapy and maybe come back if I need to?

Yewande: Yes Bill, for sure. My door is always open and you have my contact details. Couples therapy could be a really productive next step for you both … but for now, with four sessions in mind – shall we focus on how you're feeling about moving out as you suggest?

In this segment, Yewande attempts to work collaboratively with Bill to consider when to end their work. She focuses on whether his original goals have been met and assesses what his plans are for his future. It can be important at this stage to hear from clients what they plan to do without their therapy with you – this might be about planning to access a different service or type of professional (e.g. Bill's thoughts about seeing a couple's therapist) or it may be about how they will use the time they would normally be attending therapy. For example, one of my (Megan's) clients had revived her love of running during the course of her therapy and found it had a significant impact on her sense of wellbeing. She decided that, after ending our work, in the hour she would normally come to see me she would go for a run and continue to protect the space each week as a time to invest in herself. Supporting clients to consider what life will be like post therapy can galvanize them to acknowledge the ending itself, identify and express the feelings they have around it, and potentially promote positive and creative thinking about their future.

Reflection point

Considering an ending

Consider Yewande and Bill's conversation around when to end therapy. What else might Yewande have needed to talk about with Bill in order to establish when to end? How might you have verablized this thinking with Bill? If you were Bill's therapist, would you have agreed that it was the right time to end?

Many practice settings will define the length of time you and your client will work for. This is commonly known as 'time-limited' therapy but might more usefully be thought of as 'time-conscious' therapy (Elton-Wilson, 1996). For example, within the NHS or in many low-cost, community counselling services contracts are frequently offered on a basis of between 6 and 12 sessions. These time frames will be predetermined from the outset and it won't be feasible for your client (or you) to negotiate differently. This often facilitates closer attention to the aims and progress of therapy, as when time is focused in such a way attention to change may be particularly acute (Elton-Wilson, 1996). However, such contracts can also be experienced as restrictive, and clients (and therapists) may feel pressurized to 'get better quick' or be disappointed when goals have not been reached within the time allocated. When a time frame or ending date is non-negotiable, being prepared for the ending from the beginning may help address some of these kinds of issues and manage expectations. Preparation can be facilitated by review points in time-conscious work, just as with open-ended work; however, the review will have a more specific focus with an end-date in sight.

Types of ending
All therapists have experienced, and will experience, 'good' and 'bad' endings with their clients. Attachment theory, and current neuroscientific research, can help explain the various responses we have to saying goodbye and what makes an ending feel 'good' or 'bad' (see Schore, 2000; Wallin, 2007; Holmes, 2009; Porges, 2011). Attachment theory, first proposed by John Bowlby (1907–1990) and developed

extensively by Mary Ainsworth (1913–1999) and Mary Main (b.1943), is a psychological model attempting to describe the dynamics of interpersonal relationships and the mechanisms by which we seek and maintain our relationships. It posits that we are innately driven to attach and to find proximity with some clearly defined individual who is conceived as better able to cope with the world by offering protection and affect regulation. 'Attachment behaviour' is about maintaining proximity to that individual and helps us to do this. We develop deep and enduring emotional bonds with our primary attachment figures (our primary caregivers usually) who are internalized as 'inner working models' of security, such that, 'our first relationships of attachment provide the original blueprint of the mind' (Wallin, 2007: 84). Our subsequent 'attachment style' may be described, broadly, as 'secure', or 'insecure'.

From this perspective, our attachment style is seen as determining how we enter into and engage in our relationships with others, as well as how we manage the ending of our relationships. Marmarosh (2017) calls our attention to the ways in which secure, and two types of insecure (known as 'preoccupied' and 'dismissive') attachment styles shape the ways in which we might manage endings in therapy.

We attach securely when our primary caregivers have been consistently reliable, which has allowed us to explore and play with confidence. Importantly, in secure attachments, we have learnt the general rule that when our primary caregiver leaves, they will return. That means that those with a secure attachment style tend to cope better with loss, have a greater capacity for intimate engagement and so, unsurprisingly, tend to cope better with the ending of therapy (Holmes, 2009). 'Secure' clients can appreciate what has worked well and not worked so well and can regulate their various emotions around the ending (Marmarosh, 2017).

When our primary caregivers are less reliable, we develop insecure attachments. This happens for a whole host of reasons such as having parents under a lot of stress, having lots of children, or having mental or physical health problems, for example. An insecure-preoccupied attachment style develops in response to a primary caregiver experienced as inconsistently available, sometimes absent and sometimes 'too much'. The general rule learnt here is that the primary caregiver might abandon us, or conversely overwhelm us emotionally, and so insecure-preoccupied clients struggle to tolerate separations and losses because of the uncertainty that comes with them. They might engage in 'protest behaviours' around endings, such as missing sessions, re-engaging with old issues, overt or sometimes passive expressions of anger or anxiety (Marmarosh, 2017), or struggling to let go of therapy and finding ways to delay or avoid the end (e.g. discovering new issues).

An insecure-dismissive attachment style develops in response to learning that expressions of emotion will not be responded to. Needs and emotions may even be seen as things that might result in a caregiver withdrawing or abandoning us, and so these clients cope by deactivating their distress and defending themselves against feelings such as longing or sadness by pushing these feelings aside and bypassing them completely. These clients seem highly self-sufficient; however, their true thoughts and feelings about the ending of therapy have been side-stepped so as to avoid feeling vulnerable or experiencing any kind of dependency on another person (Marmarosh, 2017). They are likely to appear unaffected by the ending or deny its importance but begin to emotionally withdraw or even prematurely end therapy.

Let's consider how this might look in practice, first with Akari, a client with a predominantly insecure-preoccupied attachment style, and then with Callum, a client with a predominantly insecure-dismissive attachment style. Akari and Callum share the same therapist – Nina.

> *Nina:* I've been thinking about the fact that we are ending, and I'm wondering about how you are feeling and thinking about that Akari?
>
> *Akari:* I've really, really liked working with you Nina. I've been feeling anxious to be honest. I don't think I'm ready to end yet – how will I cope?
>
> *Nina:* I've enjoyed working with you too Akari. And, I can really hear how difficult the thought of ending therapy is for you – you're feeling anxious and worried, as though you think you won't be able to cope on your own.
>
> *Akari:* I can't! I feel like all my old problems are just resurfacing, I've been feeling depressed again, I've been ruminating on my break-up with my ex-boyfriend again … I've been thinking lately, perhaps now isn't the best time to end? It feels as though there is still so much I need to work on.
>
> *Nina:* You're really worried about coping well. For you, it feels like the time isn't right. And yet, we're not able to have more sessions – we have to work with what the service offers and the contract we agreed.
>
> *Akari:* I really hate goodbyes …
>
> *Nina:* It might be helpful if we focused on that Akari … perhaps we can use the time we have left to really support you with the feelings you have about ending? Can you tell me more about what you hate about goodbyes?

Akari expresses her struggle in tolerating the imminent separation with Nina, which has begun to manifest as anxiety ('I've been feeling anxious to be honest'). She shares her worry about how she will cope with the uncertainty of managing alone and in response to her worry, seeks to delay the ending of therapy ('perhaps now isn't the best time to end? It feels as though there is still so much I need to work on'). Nina responds by acknowledging the importance of their relationship ('I've enjoyed working with you too Akari') and the feelings Akari is sharing ('you're feeling anxious and worried, as though you think you won't be able to cope on your own'), and in doing so respects Akari and her style of ending. However, Nina maintains the boundaries of their contract and looks to help Akari regulate her feelings in a more manageable way. Now let's consider Nina's ending with Callum.

> *Nina:* I've been thinking about the fact that we are ending, and I'm wondering about how you are feeling and thinking about that Callum?
>
> *Callum:* I haven't really thought much about it to be honest. I've always known we have a set number of sessions after all … what's there to think about?
>
> *Nina:* Goodbyes can mean different things to different people. I'm interested to know what saying goodbye here might mean to you?
>
> *Callum:* I don't tend to dwell much on goodbyes. It's been great to come here, I've made plenty of positive changes! But if I'm really honest, I'm half out the

door already! Things are going fine now … I'm wondering if we even need
to keep meeting?

Nina: It's really great to hear you in such high spirits Callum, and I'm pleased that
coming here has been a positive experience. However, it still feels important
to me that we continue to meet for our sessions right up to the last one we
have planned – this is still your space.

Callum, unlike Akari, has not engaged with any thoughts or feelings about ending therapy ('I haven't really thought much about it to be honest') and has neatly side-stepped
them and moved away from any interpersonal contact with Nina that might leave him
feeling vulnerable ('I'm half out the door already!'). He denies the significance of the
ending ('I don't tend to dwell on goodbyes') and begins to withdraw his energy from
the process by suggesting they end prematurely. Nina appreciates Callum's style of ending therapy, while simultaneously gently inviting him to consider this in more depth
('Goodbyes can mean different things to different people …'). She also maintains the
boundaries of the work, but in a different way to her work with Akari – this time Nina
encourages Callum to attend their remaining sessions and reminds him that the space
is his. This respects the possibility that, out of his awareness, Callum has thoughts and
feelings about their work that are as yet unacknowledged.

Reflection point

Endings in practice

Consider the way in which Akari and Callum thought and felt about their respective
endings with Nina, and imagine that you were their therapist:

- What internal responses do you have to Akari? What internal responses do
  you have to Callum?
- Do you feel and think differently about these two clients?
- How do you imagine the rest of the session might go with each of them?
- What might be important to do in preparation for your last session with each
  of them?

Marmarosh (2017) argues that it is precisely because endings arouse such powerful responses and behaviours that they can be an important opportunity to provide a
new experience of saying goodbye and to teach our clients how to manage, or learn to
'self-regulate', painful and challenging emotions and thoughts. Marmarosh (2017) also
draws our attention to the subjective experiences of both people in the room – client
and therapist – in thinking about attachment style and endings in therapy. Essentially
this speaks to the 'intersubjective matrix' determining the interpersonal process of saying
goodbye (a '2-person philosophy'; see Chapter 1) – that is, it is important to look out

for the ways in which the different attachment styles of your clients may influence the way they choose to end their therapy with you, and it is *also* important to consider your own attachment style in terms of how you view and experience the ending. In other words, considering your client's attachment style really only gives you half the picture. A therapist with an insecure-preoccupied attachment style, for example, may be particularly sensitive to endings and experience anxiety in the face of saying goodbye. This may lead to an over-emphasis on the positive aspects of therapy, or conversely the pain and sadness of ending (Marmarosh, 2017). A therapist with an insecure-dismissive attachment style may minimize the importance of the therapy relationship to their client, and in avoiding their own feelings and thoughts miss the fact that their clients have their own thoughts and feelings about ending (Marmarosh, 2017). So, if we do not carefully reflect on our own process with regard to endings in therapy, we may make assumptions or fail to spot the meaning and importance our client is placing on the relationship and the goodbye. As Joyce and Sills (2014: 177) write, 'We need to ensure that our own patterns of modifying contact around ending do not get in the way of our client doing what she needs to do.'

Reflection point

How do you say goodbye?

Reflect on how you manage endings and goodbyes, considering the following questions:

- Is there a familiar way in which you say goodbye?
- What might influence the way you engage in saying goodbye?
- Are there particular endings in your life you feel regretful about, or conversely, you remember fondly?

Endings may be planned as a result of a pre-specified time frame on the contract, or because of a shared decision between therapist and client in an open-ended contract to close the work. In the former, endings can sometimes feel forced upon the client (and therapist) and may not always feel optimal or timely. In these circumstances it is important to allow enough space to express and process the whole range of feelings, however difficult, and to acknowledge what feels unresolved or disappointing as well as what has been achieved. Importantly, when an ending date has been set, it should usually be adhered to even when new (or old) issues and problems arise (Joyce and Sills, 2014). Endings may also be unplanned – clients may leave unexpectedly, or seem to 'disappear', or they may express the desire to leave prematurely. Wherever there is the possibility to talk this through with a client, it is important to try. You will need to consider with them what is happening for them that is affecting their decision and be open-minded and alert to the possibility that they may be avoiding something or struggling in their

relationship with you. It can be difficult for us, as therapists, when clients leave prematurely, unexpectedly or seem to disappear. We can be left with feelings of shock, worry
for them, confusion and sometimes inadequacy. These are important experiences to talk
through and make sense of in supervision.

Some tips for ending include:

- **Plan your ending from the beginning**. As Elliot and Williams (2003: 37) write,
  the therapy relationship 'is probably the only close relationship a person enters into
  with the clear aim that it should end.' Given how significant endings can be it is not
  surprising that it is unhelpful, possibly even damaging, for a client if you bring an
  ending to the work which appears out of the blue. The ending date may be a natural
  part of agreeing the working therapy contract, or it may be that you discuss the fact
  of ending at each review point if you are working with an open-ended or long-term
  contract. Planning your ending also involves considering how much time you may
  need to say goodbye – this is not an activity unique to the final session but may need
  several sessions to process well.
- **Explore with clients the meaning and importance they attribute to
  ending**. This may involve exploration of other endings – as we have discussed, an
  ending in therapy can stir up memories of previous goodbyes. It is important to
  respect the client's pace and accept that you may have different thoughts, ideas and
  feelings about the ending. It may be appropriate to congruently share those with
  your client, but it is also important for you to understand any differences, or choices
  (both 'in' and 'out' of awareness) the client ultimately makes about their ending
  with you.
- **Remain mindful of the centrality of your relationship**. The relationship you
  have built with your client is at the heart of your work. It is this relationship that has
  enabled any change, growth and healing to occur. It is also what will facilitate safe
  expression of any negative feelings and thoughts about the work or the progress your
  client may not feel they have made. In preparing for your ending, you need to
  consider the kind of relationship you have developed together, as well as how you are
  both, respectively, approaching the end.
- **Look to facilitate a range of thoughts and feelings**. As discussed previously, at
  the Ending Stage, your client may share their respect for the process, appreciation
  for you as their therapist, pride in their achievements, as well as hope for their future.
  Some clients may respond positively to being reminded of where they started from
  and compare this to where they are now. Noting the progress that they have made
  can help to build confidence in their own resourcefulness. Other clients may experience their therapy very differently. They may simultaneously (or alternatively) feel
  disheartened about what hasn't changed, frustrated with the process or angry with
  you. It can be challenging for us as therapists when clients bring this kind of negativ-
  ity into the room. However, allowing your client space to engage with and communicate their experiences of therapy and feelings about the ending is vital to support
  true self-expression. This does not mean you should collude with negative and
  destructive patterns or expect to be diminished in the process. Rather, it is about

understanding that endings can evoke a range of emotions and thoughts in all of us, for many reasons.

- **Involve clients in the decision to end wherever feasible**. This can be empowering and facilitates personal responsibility. In this way, clients may be able to take pride in what they have achieved and feel more engaged as authors of their own lives moving forward.
- **Prepare yourself**. We have previously discussed the two-person nature of therapeutic work, and the fact that you will have your own feelings, thoughts and ideas about each ending with your client. Allowing yourself time to reflect on how you are approaching the ending will help you to become aware of any biases or preferences you may have personally and separate this from what your client needs to do. It also models to your client, implicitly, self-compassion and self-care. Through the course of your work as a counsellor or psychotherapist, you can expect to experience a variety of endings with your clients – some will feel 'good' other won't. Draw on the support available to you in supervision to help you navigate this process.

Summary

This chapter looks at the final stage in the therapeutic process, in which you both work with and build on the connection you and your client have developed in order to end well together. Important ideas inherent in this process are those of active reflection and review. In this chapter we outlined a model proposed by Carroll and Gilbert (2011) to guide you and your client through these tasks. In order to facilitate your client's transition to the next stage of their lives (be it in or out of therapy), we have looked at the importance of identifying your client's resources for the purpose of future planning. Finally, we consider the significant, and sometimes challenging, task of saying goodbye and closing the work. We highlighted two areas for particular thought and reflection – when to end and types of ending – and drew attention again to a key concept underlying the therapeutic relationship, that is a '2-person philosophy'. With this in mind, we have suggested that an examination of your clients' different relational styles that influence their different 'goodbyes' would not be complete without also looking at your own subjective experience around endings and closing the work with your client.

Further resources

- Bager-Charleson, S. (2010) *Reflective Practice in Counselling and Psychotherapy*. London: SAGE.
- Carroll, M. and Gilbert, M. (2011) *On Being a Supervisee: Creating Learning Partnerships*. Ealing, London: Vukani Publishing.
- Wallin, D.J. (2007) *Attachment in Psychotherapy*. New York: Guilford Press.

Online resources

Visit https://study.sagepub.com/staffordandbond4e to watch:

Video 6.1   Resilience

Video 6.2   Ending the Counselling Relationship

Video 6.3   Ending Counselling

7

Working in Practice

Common Issues, Competency and Self-Care

Chapter contents

This chapter covers:

- Information about common presenting issues
- Challenging situations
- Therapist competency
- Therapist self-care
- Further resources

Introduction

Used adroitly, counselling and psychotherapy skills can be immensely enabling to clients by offering them opportunities to explore issues that are causing concern and find ways to a better future. They present the therapist with powerful tools for engaging with complex issues, and as such these skills can be both personally and professionally rewarding to learn. However, the potency of the skills can sometimes also expose us all to areas of human pain and difficulty we feel ill equipped to manage. It often feels like, and sometimes is, taking a step into the unknown and so the work of a therapist can feel highly demanding.

The issues raised by clients can be demanding in other ways too. Often, they will be raising issues for which they have been unable to find adequate support and help from their own network of social support. This may indicate that these are the types of issues for which help is not obviously or easily available. Equally, clients may bring material into the room which is challenging to work with because of our own previous or existing personal issues. Our aim in writing this chapter is to provide some additional basic information that we hope will be of immediate assistance as you step into the unknown to meet your client in his or her own experience. We have indicated some additional resources that we have found helpful in our work. We begin by looking at some common presenting issues clients bring and include some situations that therapists commonly find challenging to work with. We then turn our attention to discussing therapists' competency and the importance of self-care.

Common presenting issues

It is not, of course, possible to attempt to write a truly comprehensive account of all the issues that clients may bring into therapy – a potentially infinite list. It is important to hold in mind that, even if it was possible to list every problem a client has ever presented in therapy, the way a problem is experienced is unique to each individual and the various possibilities of experience are therefore limitless, even if the events or issues are common. It is our job, as therapists, to hear the idiosyncratic threads of experience that weave together each client's particular story. However, it is equally useful to hold in mind that we also share similar experiences of particular events or issues. Understanding this can enable us, as therapists, to be sensitive and alert to these common responses – for example, understanding that feelings of shock and denial in the immediate aftermath of loss are arguably to be expected. This is when our shared experiences of being human can act like flexible guidelines that, if we hold to lightly, can help us navigate the nuanced, complex and rich subjective narrative of another.

What we include here is not therefore an exhaustive list of client issues. Rather, we hope to provide some information on some of the typical issues clients present when they begin therapy to give the reader (particularly those readers about to begin, or currently in training) a sense of what they may expect to hear about and work with in practice. We present here a basic introduction to, and overview of, each issue in order to help you plan your work with a new client, and encourage you to access the resources provided at the end of this chapter to further your learning, and find support to work with these. We include:

- Coping with life changes
- Bereavement
- Depression
- Anxiety
- Suicidal feelings and self-harm
- Trauma

Coping with life changes

Facing and struggling with life changes is one of the most common issues presented in counselling and psychotherapy. Equally, we have often found that life changes will precipitate other issues and difficulties. Life is a continual sequence of changes, many of which are minor or incremental and may pass virtually unnoticed. Others, however, may be tougher because of their scale or significance. Typical of the latter are the 'life stage' changes – for example, negotiating adolescence, developing adult relationships, having – or not having – children, retirement. Other significant changes might be in social or economic status, often related to health or occupation, or involving a change of community or location, perhaps due to moving employment or home. There is a growing body of research about the impact of change and the ways changes can be negotiated successfully (Sugarman, 2001).

Our experience and research studies suggest that:

- People respond very differently to seemingly similar levels of change in their lives. As a consequence, they experience different levels of difficulty, often for no immediately apparent reason. Listening to each person's unique experience is fundamental to helping them through.
- The same person may respond very differently to similar levels of change at different times in their lives.
- Unexpected changes or the simultaneous occurrence of several major changes complicates the process of integrating and coping with change.
- Positive changes can be as problematic as negative ones. This is so counterintuitive that some people feel disorientated, sometimes to the point of doubting their sanity, when they experience emotional difficulties in handling positive changes such as winning a large prize, falling in love, the birth of a long-awaited child, or a promotion.
- Being supported in a respectful and informed way through problematic transitions is beneficial and speeds up the transition process.

One model representing the transition process that has stood the test of time, and in our experience provides useful background information for both therapists and clients, was developed by Hopson (1981). We have adapted this model in Figure 7.1.

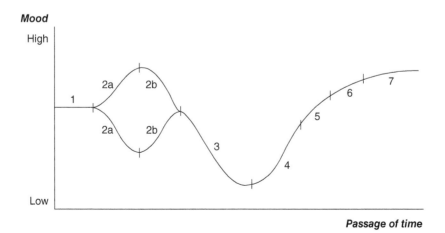

FIGURE 7.1   *Model representing the transition process (after Hopson, 1981)*

In the Hopson (1981) model, mood is represented on the vertical axis as 'low' to 'high', and the passage of time is represented on the horizontal axis. The numbers dotted through the middle represent different phases of mood following change and transition. It is probably more accurate and helpful to regard each of the moments identified on the graph as phases rather than strictly sequential points that follow each other in order. The lived experience of the phases is often messier and more confused than the diagram suggests. Phases may blur into each other, run concurrently for a while or reappear periodically within a general progression through the process. The seven phases involve:

1. **Disbelief.** A time when the change seems unreal and unbelievable so that the emotional and cognitive responses are muted. The dominant experience is one of shock.
2. **Emotional reaction.** Feelings surge and there is a period of elation or despair (point 2a) followed by these strong feelings being countered by their opposite (point 2b). For example, delight at success might be dampened by doubts about being able to cope; sadness at failure might be tempered by relief at being under less pressure to succeed.
3. **Self-doubt.** During this phase the reality of what is happening begins to penetrate but the person concerned may be questioning how or whether they can respond. This phase is often associated with periods of anxiety, anger and apathy, sometimes with mood changes of disorientating rapidity. People may experience themselves as depressed. You will need your reflective skills and methods for exploration to help someone through these first three stages.
4. **Emerging sense of new reality.** During this phase there is movement from a focus on the past, evident in the earlier phases, to letting go in order to focus on the present. Sadness and anger may be experienced where the letting go involves a sense of loss or injustice over the changes taking place. Strategies for reframing and introducing different perspectives become particularly relevant at this phase.
5. **Exploring the new situation.** The previous phase marks a first step towards accepting the new situation. This phase is concerned with exploring and testing new possibilities; this may include focusing on goals and constructing action plans.
6. **Searching for meaning.** Making sense of the changes and their causes is an important part of coming to terms with any major transition. It can be a time of transformative learning and consolidation.
7. **Integration.** This is the point of acceptance and a sense of ease with the new situation. It marks the end of the transition.

Bereavement

Bereavement is perhaps the most psychologically distressing and painful change to be negotiated. Grief is often considered a response to someone we love dying. It can also be a response to the loss of something else in our life that had a special significance to us (a job, home, pet, etc.). The very use of the term 'bereavement' is one way of marking the significance of the loss and the difficulty of what someone may be facing. Counselling and psychotherapy may be particularly helpful for those of us living in societies where there are few or no traditions to support mourning, or a lack of understanding (or underestimation) about the impact of death and loss. Worden's classic text (2010) on grief counselling suggests four tasks that need to be accomplished during the grieving process. These tasks complement the process of responding to transitions. The tasks are:

- To accept the reality of the loss
- To work through the pain and the grief
- To adjust to an environment in which the deceased is missing
- To find an enduring connection with the deceased while embarking on a new life

There are many different approaches to the tasks or stages of grief, with more contemporary thinking in the field acknowledging the process as a potentially jumbled and chaotic one, filled with a vast array of sometimes seemingly conflicting emotions such as shock, anger, guilt, loneliness, relief, sadness, denial and fear. These feelings can be confusing, unsettling and even debilitating. However, as Reeves (2018: 248) writes, 'we can move backwards and forwards between different stages, but the direction of travel may still be a healing one'. Worden's ideas and observations can be useful to think about in terms of the aims you might consider when working with a client who is experiencing a bereavement. Equally, the 'Continuing Bonds' model (see Klass and Steffen, 2018) is a useful framework for understanding the task of grieving as finding new attachments to the deceased and redefining our own personal relationship to them. This attachment, or bond, is seen as a continuing one. This challenges theories which assert that the task of grieving is to 'let go' of the bond with the deceased in order to accept the loss. In our experience, grieving is an intensely personal and subjective experience. Ultimately, it is important to provide a space in which the individual client can talk through their own experience of loss and grief in an accepting, empathic and respectful environment. It is also important to remember that grief responses can be influenced by many different things (Cruse Bereavement Care, 2012). For example, the grieving process can be complicated by ambivalent feelings about the deceased, or by multiple bereavements occurring either simultaneously or in quick succession. Sudden or unexpected deaths create particular difficulties in the acceptance of the reality of the loss. Bereavement by suicide is perhaps one of the most traumatic because of the legacy of guilt arising from 'if only … had done more' and the implied hostility or indifference of the deceased's feelings towards the survivors.

Depression

According to WHO (2017) depression is the leading cause of ill health and disability worldwide. The Mental Health Foundation (2012) report that between 4 and 10 per cent of people in England will experience depression in their lifetime. 'Depression' and 'feeling depressed' have become part of our everyday language and we commonly use these words to describe a low mood which can range from 'feeling down' to something much deeper. It is worth checking with clients who describe themselves as 'depressed' what this means to them (e.g. how often they feel this way and the severity of their experience) and whether they have received a formal diagnosis. To receive a diagnosis, an individual is assessed by a medical professional as meeting certain criteria. For example, the Diagnostic and Statistical Manual for Mental Disorders (American Psychiatric Association, 2013) edition 5 (DSM 5) provides a comprehensive classification and diagnostic tool for mental health formulation of this kind. Criteria relate to particular symptoms experienced over a defined period of time. Symptoms of depression include (but are not limited to) such things as depressed mood, markedly diminished interest or pleasure in usual activities, changes in appetite and sleep, fatigue, feelings of worthlessness and an excessive or inappropriate sense of guilt.

Diagnostic systems, such as the DSM 5, have the advantage of providing a clinical framework and common interdisciplinary language to work with individuals experiencing significant psychological distress. For some clients, medical concepts can be valuable in aiding the provision of necessary medication or normalizing the experiences they are having (Boyle, 2007). However, blind adherence to such systems runs the risk of missing important cultural and socioeconomic contextual issues (Boyle, 2007). Symptoms of depression require consideration of the complex interplay between class, gender and employment and acknowledgment of the potential sociopolitical biases in the construction of the DSM (Pilgrim, 2000; Boyle, 2007). Additionally, a simple dichotomy of 'sick' and 'well' may reduce human experience to a pathology, neglecting large areas of our knowledge and understanding of what it means to be human. As previously referenced in Chapter 4, the recent contributions of Johnstone and Boyle (2018) have contributed to this debate substantially, providing an alternative to functional psychiatric diagnosis and highlighting problems of medicalization and psychiatric diagnosis, which may be viewed as obscuring the multiple levels of meaning in mental distress. In our view it is important to try to balance these arguments in the service of the client.

The experience of depression varies considerably in intensity. At its most severe, it may lead to someone lying inert in the foetal position for days, completely indifferent to whether they live or die, or perhaps more typically, to someone experiencing a combination of high levels of anguish and anxiety in conjunction with extreme lethargy.

One of the characteristics of depression is a profound sense of helplessness. This has direct implications for using counselling and psychotherapy skills. Depressed people often feel overwhelmed and confused by their problems. Even when their difficulties are broken down into more manageable components, they may require assistance in deciding which aspect of the problem to tackle first. This is precisely the kind of situation for which focusing can be a really helpful skill.

Many of the standard texts that focus on helping people with depression tend to be written rather impersonally within the medical style of writing. A refreshingly accessible account, and one that is useful in helping people with depression has been written by Rowe (2003), who views depression as a way of someone protecting themselves from pain and fear. Reeves (2018) highlights the importance of taking a holistic approach to working with an individual with depression, due to the social and physical factors involved, not just the psychological ones. It is also particularly important to assess and remain alert to the risk of suicide and self-harm when working with clients who are depressed, as they are strongly associated with depression. We discuss them below.

Anxiety

As Reeves (2018) argues, anxiety is one of the most difficult issues to define – it means so many different things to different people. Returning for a moment to the use of a traditional diagnostic system highlights some of the complexity of working with a client who describes themselves as 'anxious': the number of anxiety disorders listed in the DSM 5, for example, exceeds ten, including generalized anxiety disorder, separation anxiety disorder, specific phobia, social anxiety disorder and panic disorder. However, anxiety disorders are some of the most prevalent of the mental health disorders, affecting up to 33.7 per cent of the population during their lifetime (Bandelow and Michaelis, 2015). Anxiety disorders are also highly comorbid with other disorders. Mixed anxiety and depression is the most common mental disorder in Britain, with 7.8 per cent of people meeting criteria for diagnosis (Mental Health Foundation, 2012). Bandelow and Michaelis (2015: 327) argue that 'anxiety is a characteristic feature of our modern times … the prevalence of anxiety disorders has increased due to certain political, societal, economical, or environmental changes.'

As with the other presenting issues we have been describing, it is important to understand what anxiety and 'being anxious' mean to the individual client you are working with. Often clients will report some of the following experiences: excessive worry, feeling 'on edge', sleep disturbance, distress, trouble concentrating, accelerated heart rate and fear of losing control. Sometimes anxiety will be linked to a feeling of panic, or even panic attacks – these are physiological symptoms that can be so overwhelming as to feel life threatening, such as pounding heart, difficulty breathing normally, nausea, dizziness and chest pain. Certain techniques may be employed to manage the symptoms of anxiety and some clients may opt for these strategies and not wish to look more closely at the underlying problems (Reeves, 2018). These include relaxation techniques, mindfulness, self-help books, particular breathing exercises and medication. Because anxiety includes a set of physiological responses which can supersede our normal functioning, it is important to attend to them before attempting deeper exploration of the client's issues. That's because when we are highly anxious and physiologically aroused, it can be difficult to take in new information or receive another person's care, empathy or attunement.

We now turn our attention to presenting issues and situations that therapists commonly find challenging to work with. These include suicidal feelings and self-harm, and trauma. These are issues which we feel usually require specific, tailored training in addition to standard counselling and psychotherapy training.

Suicidal feelings and self-harm

Anyone placed under sufficient pressure and deprived of adequate support can reach their breaking point and may contemplate suicide. Suicidal thoughts are one of the symptoms of depression and may be temporal. Counselling and psychotherapy skills can be particularly appropriate both for providing essential support and for exploring a number of issues that may be helpful to the person concerned.

It is first important to understand the difference between suicidal *intent* and suicidal *ideation*. Suicidal intent is the intention to commit suicide, including planning how to do it. Suicidal ideation occurs when you wish were dead or that you could die, but you don't have any plans to commit suicide. That is not to say that these concepts are clear cut. For example, it is not unusual to find that a client has no deliberate and considered intention to die, but rather that life seems so intolerable that they are willing to gamble with death. With some people, it helps to regard suicidal intent as a signal that they cannot continue life as they are living it and that something new – a perspective, a relational experience, the introduction of hope – is required to effect significant changes. When assessing a client's suicidal thoughts and their intentions, it is important to evaluate the possible protective factors that may act to prevent planning or action. These are things which make it less likely that individuals will consider, attempt or die by suicide, such as the client's sense of connectedness to others (family, friends, community) – for example, 'I could never do that to my parents'.

When you are working with either suicidal intent or ideation, the first barrier to be overcome is the cultural taboo on talking about suicide. It is as though there is a belief that talking about it will increase the likelihood of someone implementing their self-destructive tendencies. The opposite is more likely to be the case. Someone who is unable to find appropriate support or to voice their sense of desperation is much more vulnerable to suicide.

One of the major tasks in helping someone who is feeling suicidal is to start to understand what the prospect of suicide represents. It may be an escape route to oblivion from an intolerable situation. If this is the case, the priority is to explore whether and how the intolerable can be made more tolerable. It may be envisaged as a means of communicating something that matters deeply to the client – for example, an indirect way of making a protest or expressing anger. An effective way of moving forward with the client is to explore the sources of these feelings. This exploration provides a basis for considering alternative and constructive ways of expressing those feelings and addressing the distress.

One of the ways to empower someone who is feeling suicidal is to help him or her identify the pressures that are making suicide a possible option. Typically, the problems will have reached the point where they are overwhelming and, when viewed together, form an insuperable barrier to any sense of hope for the future. A great deal of useful information and practical guidance can be found in a book based on the experience of Eldrid (1988) as the Director of the Samaritans in London, an international befriending service.

Self-harm is 'self-poisoning or injury, irrespective of the apparent purpose of the act … [and] an expression of personal distress, not an illness' (National Institute for Health and Care Excellence, 2004). Self-harm is a coping strategy to deal with overwhelming feelings such as anger, pain or very low self-esteem and, as Reeves (2018: 258) puts it, 'a means of living rather than dying.' It is therefore important to understand that self-harm is not necessarily an indicator of suicidal thoughts, although it is correlated with risk of suicide. Both self-harm and suicide require therapists to be cognizant of the client's values and beliefs about their acts, or thoughts of harm, as well as the legal and ethical parameters of working with clients who present with these issues.

There seems to be no way of sharing in the suicidal person's burdens, or those of an individual who is self-harming, without leaving the therapist weighed down and typically with a heightened sense of responsibility. Access to adequate support from someone experienced in working with suicidal and self-harming people is essential for anyone undertaking this type of work. We would also like to draw your attention to the importance of self-care, discussed later on in this chapter.

Trauma

Trauma has received a great deal of attention in recent years, due in part, to the increasing and now substantial body of research and neuroscientific findings in this field of study. Such findings have informed our understanding of the central role of brain functioning in how traumatic experiences and memories are processed neurologically, physiologically and psychologically. For professionals working in counselling and psychotherapy, these findings have had particular importance to our work, as they strongly support the contention that we are hardwired to relate, demonstrating human brain development as 'experience-dependent' and affect dysregulation as impeding the structural growth of neuroanatomical structures known to be responsible for our emotional and social lives.

Trauma is an event of repetitious experience 'that overwhelms people's existing coping mechanisms' (van der Kolk, 1996: 279) and 'fear in its most primal form' (Gerhardt, 2004: 134). Trauma does not arise solely from extreme experiences or result in post-traumatic stress disorder (PTSD). It may be viewed on a continuum, with 'milder' or periodic trauma at one end and intense, sustained trauma and possibly PTSD at the other (Gerhardt, 2004). PTSD is a specific clinical diagnosis, with a correlating set of criteria. Symptoms include (but are not limited to), reliving the event through experiences known as 'flashbacks' or nightmares, avoidance behaviours, negative changes in beliefs and the way you think about yourself, and 'hyper' or 'hypo' arousal (high physiological alertness such as panic or hypervigilance, or emotional numbness, emptiness or freezing up).

In traumatized individuals, abnormal psychophysiological responses have overridden normal, adaptive responses to threat to some degree, and ordinary systems of arousal, attention, perception, memory and emotional responses have been jeopardized (Herman, 1992; van der Kolk, 1996). Working with a client who has experienced a trauma can involve listening to material which may be shocking, distressing or painful. Therapists can experience anger, fear and panic, as well as physical and emotional burnout – sometimes referred to as 'vicarious trauma' – as they attend to their traumatized clients. We recommend the following authors as providing accessible introductions to the rich and evolving literature in this area: Rothschild (2004), Gerhardt (2004) and Cozolino (2016). However, we wish to highlight that, much like working with suicide and self-harm, theoretical understanding is not sufficient to equip you to work with this issue and we cannot overstate the importance of self-care, training and supervision in working with trauma safely and ethically.

Finding further information on presenting issues

Responding to the potential range of problems for which people seek help is a daunting challenge for any therapist. The internet, of course, makes obtaining information considerably easier. For example, if you search for 'bullying' or 'domestic violence' you will have rapid access to a range of good and highly informative web pages. The same is true of many other topics. However, the quality of the information available on the internet is very variable. It is not always easy to distinguish between good and poor information, especially if you have no previous knowledge or experience of a subject. In this situation, it is often best to restrict yourself to information that has been provided by a reputable charity or agency, rather than sources that appear to be merely personal opinion. Having access to other people more experienced in helping with the specific issue raised by your client is invaluable in making sense of any source of information.

In some cases, your clients may already be very knowledgeable about the issue that concerns them. Using counselling and psychotherapy skills is more than just being well informed. It is about developing the skills that will help you to support someone through a process leading towards a constructive outcome.

As already discussed, it is not possible within the scope of the current text to discuss every issue presented in counselling and psychotherapy. There are an abundant and diverse range of issues that you may face as a counsellor and psychotherapist and it will be important to make an honest and thorough assessment of your competency to work with each new client that you meet (see Chapter 4 and below for further discussion). Some other issues that clients may present with are listed below, with a short description of each, together with a useful and reliable website link to help you begin the process of resourcing yourself with information and knowledge needed to work with some of these issues, or know where and how to refer a client onwards for specialist help. Many of the issues listed require input from a professional with expertise and experience in the given area, and/or specialist services to be worked with effectively and ethically.

- **Addictions**. Addiction takes many forms. It may be addiction to nicotine, alcohol, or other legal and illegal substances, or to a particular behaviour such as work, gambling or pornography. Addiction means not having control over doing, taking or using something to the point where it could be harmful to you. See: www.addaction.org.uk
- **Domestic violence**. Domestic violence is abuse, physical, emotional or sexual, in relationships – couple relationships, between family members or involving carers. The abuse may be a single incident or pattern of incidents, and will involve controlling, coercive, threatening, degrading and/or violent behaviour. See: www.nationaldomesticviolencehelpline.org.uk
- **Eating disorders**. Eating disorders involve having an unhealthy attitude to food, which can take over your life to the point of making you ill. They include anorexia nervosa, bulimia, binge eating disorder and 'other specified feeding or eating disorder'. See: www.nhs.uk/conditions/eating-disorders
- **Issues related to gender identity**. Any issues that arise as a result of questioning conventional gender expectations, and/or having a strong identification with

another gender and discomfort with one's own assigned gender and sex, including wanting to develop a body that is congruent with gender feelings. See: http://gids. nhs.uk/evidence-base

- **Psychosexual issues**. These include sexual problems, such as problems in arousal or satisfaction, that are psychological in origin rather than physiological. See: www. relate.org.uk/relationship-help/help-sex
- **Psychosis**. This is a mental health diagnosis that causes people to perceive and interpret things differently from other people, such as sights, sounds, smells and physical sensations. Often this will include hallucinations or delusions. See: www. nhs.uk/conditions/psychosis

Competency

In Chapter 4, we discussed the need to consider your level of competency as part of a thorough assessment process in the Beginning Stage of your work. Here we elaborate on this concept further with the aim of helping you to consider your own personal and professional capacity for working with the clients you encounter.

A therapist's competency refers to the way in which a therapist has been able to integrate knowledge, skills, values and attitudes into their therapeutic practice (BACP, 2018). In Figure 7.2 we have included some of the key elements of the kind of knowledge, skills, values and attitudes that are commonly considered central to working as a therapist. For an example of a full and comprehensive competency framework, we recommend you access the SCoPEd framework (SCoPEd, 2019).

Your limitations as a therapist will be determined by your level of training and experience. Assessing these 'limits of competency' involves a thorough examination of your own knowledge, skills, values and attitudes with an open, honest and non-defensive attitude. As a therapist, you will of course be striving towards helping your clients with a range of issues. However, we all need to ensure that this intention doesn't drive on ahead of what we are truly capable of offering. Being effective in your role is not only about learning a set of skills, or a particular theory, but also relies on your capacity for knowing your own personal and professional limits and learning edges. This speaks to your ability to take personal and professional responsibility and is an ethical issue which may ultimately prevent you from causing undue harm.

It is important to see a therapist's competency as a process (a continual acquisition of competencies), rather than an outcome (McLeod, 2009). This means competency is forever evolving, and that in choosing to train and work as a therapist you are making a commitment to continued professional (and personal) development (CPD). As discussed in Chapter 4, there will also be times in your life when working with particular issues that clients bring, or working through your own personal issues, re-shapes your competency and your limits. Being able to say, 'I am not ready to …', or 'Right now, at this point in my life, I don't have the capacity to …' is not something to be ashamed of or feel criticized about. On the contrary, it may be an honest and ethically sound judgement which speaks to your level of professionalism. Supervision provides an excellent space within which to discuss these issues.

Knowledge:	Skills:	Values and attitudes:
• Theoretical knowledge related to a specific modality (e.g. person-centred) • Area knowledge related to a presenting issue (e.g. addiction) • Ethical and legal understanding related to the context and client you are working with (e.g. Equality Act) • Knowledge of the setting, including policies and contract arrangements • Knowledge of assessment and onward referral procedures	• Ability to build good rapport • Attending • Communicating • Active listening • Ability to use techniques appropriately • Reflection and reflexivity • Capacity to give and receive feedback • Observation • Agreeing a working therapy contract • Ability to hold multiple perspectives simultaneously • Ability to sit with uncertainty	• Integrity • Respect • Openness and non-defensiveness • Belief in equality and anti-oppressive practice • An interest in understanding others • Compassion • Commitment to developing self-awareness • Curiosity • An interest in ongoing learning • Willingness to honestly reflect on personal and professional limits

FIGURE 7.2 *Therapists' competency*

Reflection point

Assessing your current level of competency

1. Consider the points listed in Figure 7.2 and review what you have learnt as you have read this book.
   - What areas do you feel most competent in?
   - Which areas do you want to learn more about?

2. Some questions to help you think through your level of competency with each new client include:
   - Do I feel able to work with this client's presenting issues at the present time?
   - What additional knowledge or experience might I need to acquire to work with this client?
   - Do I feel cognizant of the ethical and legal issues involved in working with this client?
   - How will I use supervision to enhance my understanding of this client and the way in which we take the work forward?

3. Some more general questions to ask yourself about your current level of competency:
   - Can I describe some of the key elements of the approach I take to working therapeutically?

> ○ Do I feel able to sit with uncertainty and difficult emotion without feeling destabilized?
>
> ○ Can I engage in giving and receiving feedback non-defensively?
>
> ○ How would I define the values that underpin the way I work?

Self-care

What is self-care?

Self-care is considered imperative in our profession. It is the ability to adequately meet your psychological, emotional and physical needs by intentionally and actively cultivating attitudes and engaging in activities that support you to do this. Porter (1995: 247) describes therapists' self-care as a 'proactive ethical approach', noting, 'therapist well-being is positively related to the client's therapeutic outcome'. The SCoPEd framework (SCoPEd, 2019) describes the 'ability to monitor and evaluate fitness to practise, and maintain personal, psychological and physical health' as a key component in therapist competency.

Training and working as therapists puts us at the heart of what it means to be human. As well as experiencing and witnessing some of the most inspirational aspects of humanity – our ability to love, to show courage, to inspire hope, to take risks, and to change and adapt – we are at the coalface of demands of everyday life, difficulties, pain and suffering. We must learn to take care of ourselves as we endeavour to help others. Self-care also builds resilience. Therapists who are able to attend to their own psychological, emotional and physical health are often better able to cope with everyday stressors and reduce the likelihood of burnout and feeling emotionally drained. Conversely, therapists who are unable to, or do not, attend to their own wellbeing place themselves at risk of impaired professional functioning (Barnett et al., 2007). That is to say, self-care enables us to work safely and optimally because when our own needs are well met, we are better able to assist others in meeting theirs. Furthermore, as Norcross and Guy (2007) argue, we must practise what we preach! Therapist self-care has an important modelling quality for our clients whom we are hoping, through therapy, will develop greater self-awareness, self-compassion and resilience.

Despite the importance that is placed on self-care in the counselling and psychotherapy professions, we have observed time and again how difficult many of us (trainees and qualified therapists alike) find it to make a commitment to. Self-care is often equated with self-indulgence and, because it requires therapists to take moments or periods of time in which they put themselves first, it can be associated with being selfish and behaving in ways that disregard others. Self-care, as we have described above, is in fact the antithesis of disregard. It is an essential component of caring for others. Another common response that we hear in response to the practice of self-care relates to time, specifically not having enough of it. When therapists feel they are already stretched with the demands of work, family and domestic life, and personal issues, self-care frequently drops to the bottom of the priority list. Again, we want to highlight its importance as an integrated part of professional practice. We encourage you to view it as a part of the work, rather than an optional added extra. You are already aware that working as a therapist is more than the time (sessions) you spend with your clients. Think about self-care in the same way you think about other aspects of your work such as ensuring you are on time to see your clients, or making time to write up your session notes, or putting aside days for additional training, or reading this book!

However, we acknowledge that for many, self-care may not be automatic, come naturally or feel easy. It may be important to discuss your feelings and views about your own self-care with your supervisor. It can also be useful to remember this: self-care is a discipline. It can take time to learn, refine, practise and observe.

We think of self-care activities as those that directly relate to professional practice and those that indirectly relate to professional practice, but nonetheless are just as important to your psychological, emotional and physical needs, sitting at the interface of the personal and professional you. The former includes such things as supervision, personal therapy, time with peers and colleagues, reflective practice and training. These are pre-defined activities we would expect all trainees and qualified therapists to participate in at different times. The latter are undefined activities that are informed by personal preference and we have included some examples in the reflection point box below. We would suggest that in any given working week you aim to be able to tick off an activity from each of the two lists.

Reflection point

Applied self-care

Which activities from the two lists below can you 'tick off' as having completed this week?

Directly related professional activities that support my self-care

- Supervision   ☐
- Peer and colleague support (e.g. discussion)   ☐
- Personal therapy   ☐
- Reflective practice (e.g. journaling)   ☐
- Training and CPD   ☐

Indirectly related, personal activities that support my self-care

- Meditation   ☐
- Watching a film   ☐
- Going to a gym class   ☐
- Getting a massage   ☐

- Going for a walk ☐
- Taking 20 minutes to have (and enjoy!) a coffee ☐
- Meeting a good friend for dinner ☐
- Setting boundaries with friends or family ☐
- Reading (not a counselling or psychotherapy book!) ☐
- Other/alternatives: ☐

....

....

....

How to cope when you are feeling overwhelmed or out of control

We live in a culture that is favourably disposed to success, stamina and enthusiasm. It can be risky to talk about personal failure, difficulty or misery. In some settings and cultures, talking about personal difficulties involves such a loss of face and personal status that the deterrents to doing so are almost insurmountable. However, personal distress is not easily contained and people do take the risk of disclosing deeply personal and painful matters, almost regardless of the consequences when they are sufficiently overwhelmed. All defences may be swept aside if the forces building up against them are sufficiently powerful. Learning and using counselling and psychotherapy skills often connects thera-pists to their own personal pain, past and present, and can carry the risk of picking up and shouldering the client's distress and torments. This can lead to feeling overwhelmed and out of control.

In response, therapists can inadvertently react in ways that can compound the difficul-ties their client, and they, are experiencing – for example, panicking and acting in ways that increase the sense of chaos or emergency for the client; rushing to involve others regardless of the client's wishes or confidentiality; or collapsing into a personal sense of inadequacy and thus compounding the client's hopelessness. In these moments, key principles behind what you do can be forgotten, but it can be helpful to remind yourself of the following points.

- Emotional expression is cathartic, instils hope and establishes a sense of universality (Yalom, 1995). Feelings can be released and worked through and, when you communicate to your client a sense of positive purpose to your encounter, you instil the belief that change is possible. Clients begin to see they are not alone in having problems or personally inadequate in having been unable to resolve them.
- Listening is powerful. Listening 'actively' is enabling because it allows others to have an impact on you at a time when they are feeling powerless, it acknowledges *them* as well as their experiences, and it affords them respect. Most importantly, it allows them to listen to themselves saying things that might be impossible to voice elsewhere.

- Recognizing the feelings elicited in you as a potentially valuable source of information about how the client is feeling can help you to gain insight into their inner world, and re-connect you to the sense of empathy, acceptance and genuineness essential for effective work. It will also be easier to work with your own discomfort if you are adequately supported and know that you will be able to attend to your own unresolved feelings and issues with a trusted colleague, peer or supervisor.

Familiarity with counselling and psychotherapy theory and practice will greatly help to give you confidence. Our hope is that the function of the skills model we have described in this book is to bring an added sense of order and containment to what are often initially frightening, complex and painful situations. It is also helpful to have some on the spot tips for coping and managing challenging and demanding situations.

- Sit in a centred position, become aware of your chair supporting you and feel the ground under your feet.
- Raise your voice slightly; this will boost your energy and confidence.
- Try to slow your breath – this helps to reduce anxiety.
- Roll your shoulders back a little – this will give your chest and lungs more space to breathe.
- Acknowledge the 'rationale' of what the client is telling you so that you focus on understanding his or her experience.
- Let go of the pressure to be clever, and allow yourself time to respond.
- Remind yourself that clients are responsible for their actions and their lives – not you.

Summary

The way in which each client will experience their particular problems will be unique to them and the various possibilities of experience are endless. However, we also share in the experience of what it means to be human, and this can enable us, as therapists, to work with common issues as they arise in practice. In this chapter we have provided a basic introduction and overview to some of the typical issues clients present when they begin therapy to give you a sense of what you may expect to work with in practice. In addition, we discussed therapist competency and limits of competency as a process of continual acquisition. This can be supported through therapist self-care which we considered as an ethical imperative and a key component in therapist competency. We invite all our readers to consider their own self-care in their future work with clients as an important discipline and integrated aspect of their work.

   In the next chapter we present a case study which draws on the skills model presented in this book, as well as the additional information regarding applied practice in this chapter.

Further resources

- There are a number of organizations and useful websites that can provide you with information about some of the presenting issues we have discussed. They include:
  - www.mind.org.uk
  - www.cruse.org.uk
  - www.samaritans.org
  - www.somatictraumatherapy.com

- For more information about therapists' competency, practice and training, see SCoPEd (Scope of Practice and Education) (SCoPEd, 2019), for example, www.bacp.co.uk/about-us/advancing-the-profession/scoped
- For one of the most helpful sources of up-to-date information on bereavement, see www.cruse.org.uk/

Online resources

Visit https://study.sagepub.com/staffordandbond4e to watch:

Video 7.1   Suicidal Intent – Scenario

Video 7.2   Suicidal Intent – Discussion

Video 7.3   Supervision and Feeling Stuck – Scenario

Video 7.4   Supervision and Feeling Stuck – Discussion

Video 7.5   Supervision and Emotional Wellbeing – Scenario

Video 7.6   Supervision and Emotional Wellbeing – Discussion

8

Case Study

Introduction

All the case examples presented so far have been used to illustrate specific aspects of our stage model approach to using counselling and psychotherapy skills. In this chapter we propose to demonstrate how work with a client moves between the stages. We want to capture some of the difficulties and challenges faced by anyone who is attempting to use this structure. In real life, therapy does not typically conform to the neat and linear progression of conceptual or theoretical models. Therapists need to assess and review which skills, interventions and direction would be appropriate in the moment, and this is largely informed and shaped by the issues the client brings and how they present in the room.

The example we have chosen is that of a typical client presenting to a community service. It is fictitious but draws upon genuine experiences we have had as therapists and trainers. It is intended to be a realistic account of how counselling and psychotherapy skills can be used effectively We certainly believe that no one, especially someone who is in training, or newly trained, should provide therapy without adequate personal and professional support, so we have included examples of how good supervision can enhance the work.

The case study

Background of the therapist

Sunita is 44 years old and has been qualified as a therapist for ten years. She describes her approach to working therapeutically as taking her lead from the client and paying particular attention to the quality of the relationship that develops. She believes that these are the essential elements of successful counselling and psychotherapy. Sunita initially trained as a therapist after she received bereavement counselling following the death of a close friend. She found therapy supportive, transformative and influential in her subsequent self-development in ways she had not expected. This experience aroused her interest in training herself, which was heightened when her younger sister was diagnosed with depression. She witnessed how difficult her sister found it to cope, as well as the painful impact it had on loved ones around her. Sunita works part time for the service and receives supervision from Leo, a qualified therapist and supervisor.

Setting and referral

The low-cost, community counselling service within which Sunita works is located in a busy, multicultural urban town. Clients will usually self-refer, having been recommended by their GP or having discovered the service online. The service offers up to 12 sessions for each client. There is a large team of therapists, including qualified and experienced practitioners as well as trainees, who are all supported by a team of supervisors. Clients present with a wide range of issues and levels of mental ill health. Qualified therapists, such as Sunita, conduct their own assessments of new clients, and supervisors conduct initial assessments on behalf of trainees.

Neal, a new client to the service, was referred to Sunita. Before their first in-person session, Sunita had a brief telephone call with Neal in order to introduce herself and the service, and to gain some information about his referral in advance of their first meeting. Sunita made the following notes during their call.

Date: 05/11/2019

Client initials: N.B.

Client's age: 24 years

Brief account of client's presenting issue: Neal presented with symptoms of depression and anxiety to his GP two weeks ago. He has been prescribed anti-depressants and recommended to seek help from the service. He describes 'very low mood' and 'no energy', lack of interest in usual activities and problems sleeping. At work he feels isolated, finds it hard to concentrate and becomes easily irritable. He feels 'anxious about life', experiencing recurring, worrying thoughts.

Level of risk (if applicable): Some days he feels so lonely and depressed he has not wanted to get out of bed and thinks it would be better for everyone if he wasn't around any more: 'my bleakest moments'. These thoughts are infrequent and he has never made plans to end his life. He says, 'I could never do that to my parents.' He has a few close friends, but contact is minimal as they are away at university. Neal appears to present with suicidal ideation, but no suicidal intent.

Pre-session preparation

After her call with Neal, Sunita made a request to the service administrative staff to schedule an initial session with Neal for the following week. In preparation for her first session with Neal, Sunita made some reflective notes for her own records, using the 'Checklist and worksheet for preparation and management of the first session' (see Chapter 4):

- **What features of this client's story have I been struck by?** Sunita was particularly struck by Neal's feelings of loneliness. She remembers a time in her early twenties when, just like Neal, her loneliness could feel debilitating. This was a very emotionally painful time for her, and she feels moved by what Neal shared. Her sister had also described her feelings of loneliness and depression to Sunita, which left her feeling unable to cope and physically diminished.
- **Is there specific information I need to clarify with them?** Sunita wants to ask Neal how often he feels depressed and anxious, the severity of this experience and the effectiveness of his antidepressants. Sunita also wants to re-assess Neal's level of risk and to continually re-appraise this throughout their work. She makes a note to obtain a clear understanding of Neal's expectations and hopes for their 12 sessions.
- **How have I been reflecting on this client? What expectations do I have of them?** How have I been feeling about meeting them? Sunita was aware that aspects of Neal's story resonated strongly with her. She felt she needed to be careful not to over-identify with Neal and stay cognizant of her 'listening filters'. She aimed to make space for him to explore his own unique experiences. She was expecting to meet a young man with little energy in a depressed state of mind. She was keen to work with Neal; however, she was also feeling daunted by his suicidal ideation – these are feelings and thoughts she noted down to take to supervision.

Reflection point

Consideration of the client so far

Imagine that Neal has been referred to you. Use the same preparation questions that Sunita used above to consider working with Neal. Are your answers the same or different from Sunita's?

The Beginning Stage (sessions 1 to 3)

Initial session

Neal arrives for his first session with Sunita half an hour early, and as Sunita passes through the waiting room on her way to the administrative office, she notices him waiting and looking nervously at the floor, his knee bobbing up and down and his hands clasped firmly in front of him. His face looks pale against his dark hair, which falls uneasily across his face and he's dressed in a faded black t-shirt and dark jeans, all of which seem shapeless, falling off his very slight frame. Sunita thinks this has the effect of leaving him looking fragile, somewhat uncared for and a little awkward.

At 5pm, their appointed time, Sunita appears at the open doorway of her therapy room and smiles warmly at Neal, who smiles encouragingly but shyly back at her. She welcomes him into her room, noting again the nervousness in his smile and shallow breathing. She imagines his arriving early might also indicate something of how he is feeling about coming into therapy. Knowing that the first session can evoke anxious feelings for any client, Sunita tries to demonstrate that she is 'with' Neal by attending, non-verbally, through a warm, soft tone of voice, relaxed body language and open, kind eye gaze.

She begins the session by welcoming Neal, introducing herself and acknowledging the possibility for anxiety around the first session in an attempt to put Neal at ease and start to build a good rapport: 'The first session can seem quite a daunting prospect. Often clients don't quite know what to expect and that can lead to feeling anxious … that's quite normal.' She provides information about the service, discusses confidentiality and sets the boundaries for the session (see Chapter 4). Sunita then uses the skill of focusing to establish Neal's reasons for seeking therapy.

Sunita:	So, Neal, when we spoke on the phone you said you had been to see your GP because of how you had been feeling. Is that a good place for us to start?	← *Helps Neal to begin the process of sharing something about himself*
Neal:	Yeah. I'm struggling, emotionally.	
Sunita:	Struggling emotionally. Can you tell me a little about that – what does that involve, for you?	← *Restating; use of an open question; helps Neal find a place to start*
Neal:	[*Speaks very softly and slowly*] I've had days, back-to-back where I just felt awful, like really low – emotionally, y'know? I drag myself into work and after work I just want to go home – I don't want to see anyone, don't want to do anything. When I'm at work I'm really slow … I find it hard to concentrate on anything.	
Sunita:	[*Matches the soft tone of Neal's voice*] So struggling emotionally means you've been feeling really low – depressed, would that be the right word Neal? [*Neal nods yes*] Emotionally low, depressed, unable to focus.	← *Attending non-verbally – attuning to the volume and quality of Neal's voice; re-stating and paraphrasing with an open question which seeks to check out with Neal the language she is using ('depression')*
Neal:	[*Nods again yes, then looks away*] Yes. Work is so difficult – sometimes I just don't want to be there.	

Sunita:	[*Mindful of Neal's lack of eye contact, Sunita aims to keep a gentle, non-intrusive feel to her own eye contact*] What I'm hearing is that your feelings are having quite a negative impact on your working life. Are there other areas of your life that have also become difficult for you?	← ***Uses a short summary; begins the process of assessment by looking at how Neal's issues are affecting his life***

Underneath his troubles at work, Sunita learns that since 'dropping out' of university two years ago, Neal has had 'on-off' periods of depressed mood with bouts of anxiety. He drinks alcohol frequently and used to put his low moods down to having a hangover. He recognized more recently that his moods and state of mind indicated something deeper. When Sunita asks him what has prompted him to seek help, Neal describes a panic attack one morning on his way into work: 'I was waiting for the bus just thinking, dreading going into work. The thought of sitting at my desk … the dreariness, the loneliness. My heart just sunk like a boulder into my stomach. The more I thought it, the more out of control I felt. My head was spinning … I couldn't breathe. Later, when I had recovered, I realized that reaction just wasn't right – it's no way to live, but my anxiety had completely gotten the better of me. That was happening a lot – feeling so bad about myself.'

He describes feeling 'incompetent' and 'incapable' at university. He felt unmotivated and he began to skip lectures. He was arguing a lot of the time with his boyfriend, Roland, at around the same point he discovered he had failed the academic year and expressed some bitterness towards Roland, as well as his lecturers, blaming them for not being supportive. He admits to 'pushing Roland away' when he feels depressed or anxious. After university, Neal moved back home with his parents and got an administrative job which was intended to be temporary, but two years later he was still there. Neal describes himself as a 'failure'.

Neal:	I've messed everything up – uni, my relationship with Roland … I'm in a job I hate and I'm living back at home [*hunches his shoulders*]. I feel this pressure to make everything right, better, but I don't know what to do …	
Sunita:	I noticed you tense your shoulders there, as you said 'pressure' [*Neal nods and sighs*]. You're tense and you feel stuck.	← ***Paraphrasing; empathy; acceptance; observing body language***
Neal:	Yes [*looks down at his feet and then away out of the window. There's a pause*]. I feel trapped. Sometimes I sit in my room on my own … those are my worst moments, my bleakest moments.	
Sunita:	Tell me about those moments Neal – when things feel bleak for you. How dark do they get for you?	← ***Gently explores the assessment she made on the telephone of 'suicidal ideation, but not intent'***

Neal: I just feel so alone. Once or twice I've
           thought I just don't want to exist … it's
           not that I want to die, just somehow not
           be around any more. I'm not going to do
           anything … I just wish I wasn't *in my* life.

Sunita: 'Not wanting to exist' speaks to just how   ←   *Empathy; acknowledges Neal's despa-*
           bad things feel, how lonely you can feel,   *ration and sits with painful feelings*
           how much you want to escape how   *without feeling destabilized herself*
           things are right now.

Sunita goes on to make the same assessment of risk as she had previously – suicidal
ideation, but no intent. She goes on to establish that Neal is very keen to do 'whatever
it takes' to address his issues and seems motivated to be in therapy. Neal shares that he
continues to drink alcohol frequently, and reluctantly admits that this probably doesn't
help, but his social life – when he does have enough energy to go out – tends to centre
around the pub. Neal says that he used to enjoy cycling and was also part of a creative
writing group a few years ago, but hasn't felt confident or inspired to do either in the last
year. Sunita wonders to herself to what extent the heavy drinking and lack of engagement in hobbies he used to enjoy may be undermining the possibility of change. She
makes a mental note to herself to look out for opportunities to explore this with him.

Sessions 2 and 3

Sunita begins to feel that she and Neal have started to establish a good therapeutic alliance. She feels they have a good rapport and is hopeful they will continue to develop a
good relational bond. They have collaborated well in working on the goals Neal wanted
to achieve and have a mutual understanding of the tasks of the work. Sunita feels she has
made a comprehensive assessment and she and Neal have a mutual, agreed understanding of their 'working therapy contract'.

    In the two sessions that follow, Sunita is keen to build on her sense of their growing rela-
tional bond, with the intention of creating an environment that engages Neal fully in the
therapeutic process; and in which he feels understood, accepted and able to reflect honestly.

    Neal arrives for their next session looking dishevelled and tired. He says he slept
poorly and that this is an ongoing problem. He was kept awake at night by racing
thoughts and worries about being in a 'dead-end job' as well as his relationship with
Roland ('I know I'm not making enough time for him. I know I can be dismissive,
almost rude.'). He also felt ashamed of himself for still living at home while so many of
his friends were at university 'doing what everyone is supposed to do.'

Sunita: You've named a number of powerful   ←   *Restating; empathically focusing spe-*
           sounding emotions, Neal: worry, guilt,   *cifically on Neal's individual, unique*
           shame … so strong they keep you from   *experience*
           sleeping.

Neal: Yeah … it happens a lot. I'm so tired
           [*becomes tearful*].

Sunita:	It sounds almost relentless. You're tired … exhausted even.	← *Using paraphrasing to empathize*
Neal:	[*Begins to cry and rubs his eyes*] Yes, yes. I really am … [*A silence falls*]	← *Sunita listens to the silence. She sits with the silence for a little while which allows him space to cry. She senses Neal reflecting on the feelings he has named and she reflects back to him*
Sunita:	[*Neal's tears dry and he sighs deeply*] I'm wondering, what's going on for you in this moment?	← *Sunita takes her cue to interrupt the silence with thought and respect, demonstrating she is attending to him and still 'with him'*
Neal:	I'm tired physically, but I'm also so tired of feeling this way. Tired of my own thoughts … I guess, if I'm honest, it's been good to start therapy and everything, but … well, it seems to stir up a lot. Look at me, I'm crying! [*Another big sigh*] After our session last time, I started to feel … well, a bit disheartened. I thought therapy was supposed to make you feel better, not worse! Is this really going to 'fix' anything? [*with irritation in his voice*]	

Sunita is aware that on entering therapy, facing significant issues and painful problems (perhaps for the first time) can leave clients feeling vulnerable and anguished, and that these painful feelings need to be worked through as part of the process towards healing and change. However, she is also alert to how Neal's feelings about being in therapy may be impacting their developing therapeutic alliance. She attempts to work with understanding, respect and acceptance for how Neal is feeling, rather than panicking or getting defensive of the process. She offers Neal some hope for moving forward: 'These are difficult issues to face. It's taken courage on your part to seek help.'

Following session 3, Sunita feels reasonably satisfied that most of the aims of the Beginning Stage have been met. She feels they are establishing a therapeutic alliance; however, she remains aware of Neal's sense of being 'disheartened' by the process of therapy. She has made a reasonable assessment of the key issues and her own potential to work with Neal and their 'working therapy contract' is in place. She feels she and Neal can now turn their attention to deeper exploration of where Neal finds himself and what is troubling him and considers that, as they move to session 4, they will be moving into the Middle Stage of their work together.

Supervision of the Beginning Stage

In supervision with Leo, Sunita presents her reflections on Neal, their relationship and her own internal responses (see Chapter 3, 'Listening to your internal responses and self-reflection' as a guide) as they have formed over sessions 1 to 3. Leo and Sunita agree that it remains important to attend to the relationship Sunita and Neal are forming, particularly in light of Neal's irritation in therapy regarding his progress. However, they agree the therapeutic alliance is 'good enough' at this stage to move the work towards the aims of the Middle Stage.

Sunita shares her sense of resonance with Neal, in terms of the loneliness she has felt in her own life and her sister's experience with depression. They explore this further, concluding that Sunita has worked through these experiences sufficiently well and is able to separate out her own material from Neal's material. Her hope is to use her own experiences to deepen her empathy as the 'wounded healer'.

Leo suggests to Sunita that she does some reading around suicidal ideation in order to support her work with Neal and address some of her own anxiety in working with this issue – an area in which she feels limited in terms of her previous experience.

The Middle Stage (sessions 4 to 9)

Sessions 4 and 5

Sunita looks to focusing the following sessions on deepening her connection with Neal, and their exploration of his issues. Neal reports that his sleep is improving and puts this down to a mixture of his antidepressant medication and being able to talk to Sunita.

Sunita and Neal look back on his last few years. Neal starts to recognize that he began feeling anxious as soon as he began university. He knew he had made the wrong decision about the course he enrolled on because, feeling pressure to go to university like all his friends, he made a 'snap decision'. When he started to feel like he couldn't cope with the demands of his course, he put it down to being 'stupid, not good enough'. He socialized a lot but described 'a fairly empty existence – drinking too much, never really getting to know people'. When he was drunk, he would argue with Roland but never remember what had happened the next day.

In one session Neal tells Sunita about a recent 'heated' argument he and Roland had, when Roland asked Neal to go a friend's birthday party with him and Neal felt 'too anxious and depressed to face it'. Sunita listens out for what may be hidden underneath what Neal shares, sensing there are other emotions and thoughts Neal has not yet explored.

Neal:	Roland just didn't get it. And then, when he realized I really meant it – I really wasn't going to go – he started shouting: 'It's like you *want* to be depressed, like you *want* to have a job you hate. Where are you going with this? Where are you going Neal?' [*Neal's face flushes and tears spring to his eyes*]
Sunita:	You really couldn't bear to go … and his words really impacted you. ← ***Paraphrasing; acceptance***

Neal:	They felt like a slap in the face! I felt so … so *angry* with him.	
Sunita:	As if you had been literally struck. You felt angry.	← *Paraphrasing; restating*
Neal:	Yes! [*Neal looks up to the ceiling and clenches his fists*] [*There is a pause. Neal looks down to his lap as his upper body slouches and he puts his head in his hands*]	
Sunita:	And now Neal? How are you feeling? I'm sensing something more going on for you …	← *Advanced empathy; exploration through an open question; testing a hypothesis (there is more going on for Neal)*
Neal:	He made me feel like … like this small [*indicates a small gap between his forefinger and thumb, his eyes are closed and his breathing quickens*].	
Sunita:	So, you felt angry … and unimportant and embarrassed …	← *Paraphrasing; advanced empathy – noting the thoughts and feelings underneath Neal's hand gesture and body language*
Neal:	[*Opens his eyes and looks up, speaks softly*] Yep.	
Sunita:	It sounds really painful, Neal. This argument with Roland really triggered a lot of difficult emotions …	← *Empathy; acceptance; depth of relational experiencing*
	[*There is a minute or so of silence. Sunita notices how moved she feels, and how deep the connection between them was as he looked up at her. She notes that Neal's breathing calms*]	← *Allows the silence to provide a space for Neal to ground himself, before exploring further what she senses at an advanced empathic level; focusing to help Neal attend to deeper levels of meaning in his experience*
	I'm wondering about what might be underneath your embarrassment? I thought I could hear some anxiety in your voice … something fearful, would that be right?	
Neal:	[*Reflective pause, sighs again*] To be honest I am afraid. His accusations just hit 'the hard spot'. The things I worry about all the time – I have no plan, I don't know where I'm going and I'm terrified I'm never going to get 'unstuck'.	

As Sunita facilitated Neal to uncover his previously unexpressed fears, Neal becomes more in touch with other emotions, such as his sense of helplessness and defeat, as well as self-critical thoughts that compromised his self-esteem and eroded his confidence. In moments of 'self-defeat', at home alone or on occasional social events with work, he ends up drinking too much alcohol and waking up feeling 'groggy, emotionally low and agitated'. He feels even less inclined to see people or go cycling, and notices his diet is unhealthy. Sunita decides to offer a challenge, 'I'm wondering about how much you drink Neal … I can hear that at one level it serves a purpose because it stops you *feeling*, it stops you hurting … but only for a short while. I'm also thinking – does it sabotage your chances for change?' Neal responds, 'Yeah … but it's what everyone does at my age isn't it? It could be worse … I mean, I've got mates who are out every night. And besides, what do I do if I'm out with work colleagues – that's a really heavy drinking scene so I go along with it. What else can I do?'

Reflection point

Using challenge in the Middle Stage

Consider what you learnt in Chapter 5 about how and when to challenge clients, as well as how Neal might, at this stage, be resisting change.

- Do you agree with Sunita, that challenging Neal's drinking was important and appropriate?
- What other ways might Sunita have considered addressing this issue?
- What do you notice about Neal's response to Sunita? Can you recognize any of the following in his responses?
  - *Rationalizing*
  - *Dismissing*
  - *Delaying*
  - *Externalizing*

Supervision during the Middle Stage

In supervision Sunita is keen to examine her relationship with Neal and her attempt to challenge him. She feels they have developed a significant and meaningful relational bond in a relatively short space of time. She feels her challenge was a risk, and yet one worth taking; however, she feels frustrated by his response. Leo and Sunita think together about whether this is an aspect of her genuine experiencing that Sunita could find a way to share with Neal.

Sunita also recognizes that as she works with Neal, she is opening herself up to a deep sense of connection and some of her past wounds. She feels highly engaged in the work, and at the same time this is leaving her feeling vulnerable at times. Leo inquires into her self-care regimen. Sunita admits that aside from directly related systems of support for her therapy work – supervision, peer support and a recent seminar she attended on suicide and risk – she has not been engaging in time for herself. Leo observes the parallels between Sunita's lack of self-care, and Neal's lack of self-care (this is often referred to as a 'parallel process' – that is, when a therapist recreates, or parallels, the client's problems or material in some way) and suggests that it could be really important for Sunita to model good self-care to her client.

Sunita and Leo also note that the following session will be the sixth – the review session. At this point they will have six sessions remaining, and Sunita would like to begin preparing for their ending at around session 9 in order that the ending doesn't appear out of the blue as well as trying to ensure there is some time to process any difficult feelings that arise from it.

Sessions 6 to 9

In session 6 of their work, Sunita and Neal review Neal's progress and what has been working well between them. Neal shares that he feels at ease with Sunita, often feeling relief after their sessions. This matches Sunita's sense of their relationship. Compared to when he started, Neal says he feels 'slightly better' within himself – he has noticed that he has fewer 'really bad days' and even though he continues to worry about his future and his relationship with Roland, he no longer experiences any panic or thoughts of death, and hasn't been kept awake so much at night by racing thoughts.

Neal begins to 'reframe' his university experience, realizing that not getting on in the course may have reflected the fact that he hadn't enjoyed it, rather than his 'incompetency'. This reframing is important because it enhances Neal's sense of personal responsibility and agency. However, it is painful to see that he allowed the thought of being a failure to dominate his actions since leaving university.

Neal acknowledges that his drinking wasn't helpful and wants to set himself a new goal: to stop drinking alcohol in the week. Sunita explores with him ways in which he could support himself to do that and Neal recognizes that he may need an alternative activity. Reflecting on this is a task he takes away with him at the end of the review session.

Over the next few sessions Neal continues to talk about Roland and shares how much he means to him. Organizing his thoughts and understanding his feelings with Sunita helps him open up to Roland more authentically. He arrives for one session feeling really positive about a day out cycling they have spent together. It was the first time, in a long while, that they really enjoyed doing something together, as well the first time Neal has been out on his bicycle for months. He notices the positive effect cycling has had on his physical wellbeing and he has felt a 'little lift' in his mood. He has kept to his commitment to give up alcohol in the week – he hasn't found this easy, but admits to feeling more energized and alert during the day time.

Neal continues to worry about his job and home situations, which still affect his mood. He continues to feel 'stuck', 'embarrassed' and despairing with frequent thoughts of a 'grim and oppressive future'. Sunita chooses to self-disclose something of her own experience with the intention of creating a sense of hope that change is possible, and provide comfort and encouragement to Neal in his sense of isolation and shame.

Sunita:	There have been times in my life when I have also felt alone with my problems and completely lacking in hope for the future. Is this something of how you are feeling, Neal?	← ***Empathic, genuine self-disclosure –*** *Sunita is careful to restrict what she shares to something she has a reasonable level of self-awareness of*
Neal:	Have you? [*looks surprised, but pleased*] Well yes, I do feel kind of like that … like nothing will ever change.	
Sunita:	Yes, I understand. Back then, I lost sight of the fact that change is possible. I'm sharing this with you, Neal, to show you that things can turn around.	← ***Offers hope; is transparent in her intention behind her intervention***
Neal:	I do feel sometimes like I've lost hope, like change is unimaginable … [*reflective pause*], but now I'm thinking about it, small things have already started changing – like me giving up drinking and how about going for that cycle ride the other day with Roland?	

The end of the Middle Stage and the transition to the Ending Stage is to some extent dictated by the 12-week contract Sunita and Neal are working with, determined by the service. However, Sunita also recognizes that through a good therapeutic alliance, her work with Neal has facilitated him to focus on and explore his issues, experience a sense of emotional release and understand himself more. He has started to make important steps towards managing his feelings, and is less impacted by depression and anxiety. She feels they can now turn their attention towards reflecting on that process and thinking about his future. Knowing that endings in therapy can represent many things to different clients Sunita wants to ensure that they have some time to explore the meaning and importance Neal may be attributing to the ending, and so she feels that reminding Neal of the time frame is important around session 9.

When the ending is discussed in session 9, Neal says that he feels the end of the contract has come around 'too quickly'. He recognizes that he feels some anxiety resurfacing as he thinks about ending and worries about whether he will cope in the absence of therapy. Though he acknowledges feeling he is managing much better than when they began, he believes there is more he wants to talk about. He describes feeling some anger that Sunita can not extend their sessions. Sunita suggests they use their final three sessions to explore these feelings, review what Neal has achieved and consider some post-therapy plans.

The Ending Stage (sessions 10 to 12)

Sessions 10 to 12

In the final three sessions, Sunita wants to encourage and support Neal to look back and review their work together, and his personal journey up to this point, with a purposeful focus on the changes he has made and the things that have been helpful, and those things that haven't changed or have been unhelpful. She is mindful of Neal's fears around ending therapy too soon and wants to address these with him. She feels he may be helped in this respect by identifying his resources and strengths.

As Neal reviews his sessions from the beginning, he recalls recognizing in his first session how his anxiety and low moods had left him feeling defensive about not doing well on his university course and his decision to leave, and how he had blamed his lecturers and Roland for not helping him more. Sunita and Neal can see how feeling 'disheartened' after the first few sessions of therapy, while at one level understandable, was a further manifestation of his defensiveness. Neal can now see how this general attitude had contributed to feeling stuck, because he attributed the agency and vitality he needed to move forward to factors outside of himself.

As he reflects further on the feelings he has been struggling with over the past few years, he has begun to see that some of the other decisions he made were rooted in his low self-esteem and poor self-concept ('I'm a failure'). This included choosing to work in his current job role: 'I thought it was all I was good for.' Neal has been able to reframe his current situation, from 'being in a dead-end job' in which he felt unmotivated and unsettled, and that he responded to with passivity and apathy, to one in which he understands that he has choices. This has enhanced his sense of autonomy and resilience.

Neal has considered his relationship with Roland and his tendency to push him away when he felt emotional. This had been a difficult dynamic to admit to, but Neal feels that he is starting to see how he contributed to their relationship problems.

Neal:	I don't like it if he sees me feeling really down, depressed … or when I'm all anxious over something. I guess … I'm kind of embarrassed [*looks away and out of the window*].	
Sunita:	Underneath you're feeling embarrassed. That sounds similar to how you described feeling ashamed before … what do you think Neal?	← *Paraphrasing, hypothesis testing, open question; advanced empathy*
Neal:	Well, yeah [*big sigh*]. I do feel ashamed. I look pathetic.	
Sunita:	'Pathetic'?	← *Restating; gentle challenge of Neal's self-concept*
Neal:	Yeah … I guess 'pathetic' is a bit harsh on myself … I just feel so, so … *over*-sensitive, weak …	

Sunita:	What I'm hearing is that when you are emotional in front of Roland you feel vulnerable.	← *Paraphrasing; empathic*
Neal:	Yes, exactly. And that's difficult, y'know? So, I push him away, like I'll start a fight or something. I guess I do that so he won't see me vulnerable? But then of course, he leaves and I'm alone! And I know that I've made him feel awful too …	
Sunita:	[*Pauses*] What you have just said, Neal, reminds me of one of our early sessions when you were irritated that therapy had stirred things up for you and didn't seem to be helpful. And then again, more recently, when you expressed some anger with me because I'm not able to extend the length of our contract. On those occasions I noticed I felt a little pushed away by you too.	← *Uses immediacy to focus on the here-and-now therapeutic relationship and help Neal think about possible relational patterns; demonstrates genuineness*
Neal:	You did?	
Sunita:	I'm wondering if we can make a bit more sense of this by thinking about those moments between us in therapy?	← *Transparent about her intentions behind using immediacy*
Neal:	[*Neal nods encouragingly*] I do remember … if I'm honest, I think I was pushing you away! Same thing. I guess I was feeling that vulnerability again.	
Sunita:	What's it like to be vulnerable here, with me?	← *Continues to use immediacy to explore Neal's feelings in therapy; uses an open question*
Neal:	Scary … exposing … it's like, on the one hand I want your help, like I wanted you to extend our sessions, and then on the other – well, I know this sounds like a contradiction, but don't want you to see that I need help. Like with Roland, I've felt like I always need to look 'strong'.	
Sunita:	That sounds like a lot to ask of yourself, to always look strong.	← *Gentle challenge*
Neal:	Yeah … yeah … I can see that. Now I'm realizing that Roland doesn't actually need me to be either.	

Reflection point

Reflective practice

Consider Carroll and Gilbert's (2011) Six Levels of Reflection model outlined in Chapter 6. Which levels of reflection do you notice Neal has been engaged in as he looks back and reviews his work with Sunita?

1. Zero reflection
2. Empathic reflection
3. Relational reflection
4. Systemic reflection
5. Self-reflection
6. Transcendental reflection

Do you consider that Neal's reflections have helped him reach a point of 'transformative learning'?

Sunita suggests to Neal that they explicitly evaluate what they both consider his resources and strengths to be and acknowledge the work he has done in therapy. This will help him think about moving forward post therapy and identify behaviours and ways of coping that would help (as well as those that would hinder) his continued progress. At the top of Neal's list of 'dated and unhelpful coping strategies' are: 'drinking too much, too often; not getting any exercise and withdrawing socially. Even though it feels like an effort to see people sometimes and I even get anxious about it, afterwards I usually feel a bit better in myself if I'm honest.' Neal wants to write out the following list of his inner and external resources.

Resources identified by Neal

External resources:

- Relationship with Roland
- Supportive parents
- Cycling
- Getting enough sleep

Inner resources:

- Being reflective
- Being honest with myself about my part in my problems, e.g. drinking too much alcohol
- Actively seeking help and being courageous

As they consider Neal's next steps, Neal develops some new goals for himself. These relate to activities and approaches he has recognized through his work with Sunita that have helped him with his feelings of depression and anxiety. He describes some of these as 'taking the edge off … they don't solve the problem, but they help'. His new goals include spending more time with Roland and being alert to the times when his emotions overwhelm him in such a way that he feels the urge to push back. He recognizes that his relationships – with Roland, with his parents and his friends – are sources of support. He resolves to visit one of his friends at university before the end of term and think about how his ability to 'actively seek help and be courageous' can be used to reach out to loved ones. He also wants to return to his creative writing course, an activity he used to enjoy and has the benefit of socializing with like-minded people.

Identifying his resources and planning for his future help remind Neal of his personal authority and power. This helps to ground him as he and Sunita discuss his anxieties about ending this therapy with her. They begin to talk about what the ending of therapy means to Neal.

Neal:	The thing is, the last 'ending' I can remember was leaving university … it was pretty awful. Finding out I'd failed the year – I couldn't bear to tell my friends or anyone I knew … [*voice drops to a whisper*] so … I just left. Didn't tell anyone the real reason …	
Sunita:	[*Attunes to Neal by dropping the volume of her voice a little*] Your voice became very quiet as you said that Neal … I'm wondering what's going on for you?	← *Observes the volume of Neal's voice, not just his words; open question to explore what is underneath the words he is sharing*
Neal:	I feel such regret – never saying goodbye to my mates.	
Sunita:	Regret.	← *Re-stating*
Neil	Yeah, regret. And sad. Sadness … I feel sorry. It seemed like everything went downhill after that too.	
Sunita:	Tell me about the regret and the sadness.	← *Giving a directive to open up exploration*
Neil:	I wish I'd done things differently … I should have just been honest – at least with those mates I was close to. I could have said goodbye then. Properly. Maybe we could've stayed in touch.	

Sunita:	What would saying a 'proper goodbye' ←	*Open question to explore the meaning*

Sunita: What would saying a 'proper goodbye' ← look like for you?

Open question to explore the meaning Neal attributes to endings; focusing; restating ('proper goodbye')

Neil: Um, well. Like I said, honest, like 'I haven't done so well this year, I've got to have a re-think about what I'm doing next.' Chance to say, y'know, 'It's been good hanging out with you, I want to stay friends', that sort of thing.

Neal and Sunita continue to explore Neal's feelings about endings and goodbyes. Neal shares his anxiety that, as with the ending of university life he found things started to go 'downhill', he is afraid that on leaving therapy things will 'get worse again'. He is still living at home and still working in a job he doesn't like and admits to some disappointment that this hasn't changed. Equally, he feels energized and proud of what he has achieved and can recognize his own strengths – the things that will continue to help him on leaving therapy. He concludes that he now knows what he can do to help himself in the future, in particular allowing people, like Roland, into his emotional and relational world.

Supervision of the Ending Stage

Sunita and Leo reflect on Sunita's experience of her work and ending with Neal. She feels he has made reasonable progress through their work, noting that he has worked towards his original goal (wanting to manage his feelings of depression and anxiety) well. She too, admits to some disappointment that he hasn't changed jobs or moved out, but also wonders if her expectations of what could be achieved in 12 sessions were a little ambitious.

Reflecting on their relationship, Sunita is curious and interested in her sense of vulnerability part way through the work, which emerged in response to feeling better connected and closer to Neal. She can now see that this preceded Neal's vulnerability when he shared his emotions and reached out relationally. This experience deepened Sunita's learning about how her internal responses may reflect what is happening for her client. In addition, she feels that their therapeutic alliance, as well as their mutual willingness to reflect and engage with ending, resulted in a 'good' ending and a sense of closure, which are important learnings for her future work.

She considers her own personal response to ending with Neal. Sunita is aware that her personal bereavement has always played a role in the way she says goodbye to people, including how she feels saying goodbye to her clients. Additionally, Neal's presentation reminds her of her sister's depression and this has been evocative for Sunita, often stirring memories of previous pains. She has been encouraged by Neal's motivation to be in therapy, reminded of the courage it takes to be a client, and stimulated by his hard work and openness to reflect. She feels sad to end their work and a sense of reward for what has been achieved.

Summary

This case study provides glimpses of counselling and psychotherapy skills in action. The therapist, working in a formal counselling setting, used the stage model together with supervision, her knowledge of depression and anxiety, and her capacity for reflection, to inform her use of skills.

9

Success in Practice: Using Your Learning

Something important

Is about to happen (…)

It takes courage to enjoy it

The hardcore and the gentle (Björk, 1993)

Our experience of using counselling and psychotherapy skills in a great variety of settings, and with a diverse range of issues, suggests that this skills model integrates methods and approaches that are invaluable in the therapeutic endeavour, aiding you to:

- understand clients' views and experiences rather than merely directing them towards a course of action
- demonstrate your acceptance and respect for them as fellow human beings
- enable healing, growth and personal change through relationship
- help your client discover and learn new ways of being (cognitively, emotionally, behaviourally and interpersonally) that serve them well
- hold sometimes divergent, subjective views about a problem in an open and non-defensive way
- work collaboratively with your clients, bringing together their experiences, ideas and inner knowledge, with your own
- work holistically with your clients' emotions, behaviours, cognitions and physiological experiences
- understand your clients within the contexts (social, economic, political and cultural) in which they live.

The specific issues and problems to which this model can be applied successfully are enormously varied. Characteristically, successful therapists are both technically and relationally competent but, perhaps most importantly, are constantly open to, and striving for, new learning about themselves, based on their experiences of using the skills in practice as well as their interactions with their clients.

If you are learning counselling and psychotherapy skills for the first time, our hope is that you will enhance your learning opportunities by following the suggestions in this book. Some of the techniques may initially seem artificial and strange, but as you become more confident of their impact you will be better placed to evaluate their relevance to your work and to adapt them to your preferred style. In our experience, the pace and focus of learning does change as you become more experienced. As your proficiency and familiarity with these skills grows, so will your confidence.

The optimum standard to be achieved in acquiring and using these skills is one of 'good enough'. An obsessive desire to seek perfection or to conform exactly to the model and guidance we have provided would be to miss the point of this book and destine you and your clients to disappointment. Techniques cannot be understood or implemented independently of the relationship you construct with your client, and no two relationships will be exactly the same. Maximizing the help offered by counselling and psychotherapy skills requires simultaneous attention both to the intervention and to the relationship. Over-emphasizing technique will focus attention on the act of communicating and may obscure a sense of the client as a person and the relationship you are forming. Equally, you need to remain mindful of the purposeful nature of the encounter to ensure you are using the most appropriate technique. The constant challenge within therapy is being attentive to both technique and relationship. Both need to be balanced and held in the forefront of the therapist's awareness. Sometimes these two aspects will seem to be in harmony and at other times in creative tension. This represents both the artistry and the discipline of using counselling and psychotherapy skills.

The good enough therapist is sufficiently competent to be able to:

- take account of the existing quality of the relationship and work towards enhancing it
- identify the phase or stage reached in the therapeutic relationship
- understand the skills appropriate to the particular stage of the work, selecting creatively from these and using them in ways that are compatible with the therapist as a person
- understand and listen to the impact of the skills in practice so that they can be used productively, and the therapist can appreciate when they are having unexpected or unhelpful effects
- constantly adapt and respond to the communications from the client
- evaluate strengths and weaknesses in the use of these skills with any particular client and support their evaluation with reasons.

The minimum aim of any training experience should be to take the trainee to a basic level of competence. Attaining this basic level is both the first step in the learning process and also the point from which the therapist becomes well placed to acquire further experience. During the early stages of acquiring unfamiliar counselling and psychotherapy skills, implementing them will probably seem and feel awkward. You might wonder, 'Am I doing this right?' and 'Am I doing this at the right time?' or 'in the right circumstances?' The beginner's focus is not unsurprisingly on making progress towards becoming an effective 'doer'. The experience of learning is well represented by the learning cycle described in Chapter 1 in terms of progression through four phases from 'unconscious incompetence' to 'unconscious competence'. At this latter stage the focus is on the learner's internal process.

Attaining a level of proficiency is an expansive process and can be represented by Kolb's (1984) four-stage learning from experience model originally presented in Chapter 1.

1. **Experiencing or doing**. A skill or technique is appropriately timed and adequately implemented at a 'good enough' level of competence.
2. **Reviewing and reflecting**. The therapist observes the response that is evoked cognitively, emotionally and bodily. This type of experiencing is sometimes referred to as a 'felt sense' (Gendlin, 2003). It is characteristic of experiential learning about working in relationship with clients.
3. **Learning and drawing conclusions**. Carefully considering 'What went well?', 'What was unexpected?' and 'What went badly?' and seeking the explanations for each evaluation by asking 'Why?'.
4. **Applying and experimenting**: Skills are refined. Specific experiences of 'doing' are reinforced or adjusted in accordance with the therapist's reflections and evaluations. And so the cycle is renewed with the next instance of using the revised practice. The successful practitioner will continue to engage with this learning cycle so that the practice of counselling and psychotherapy skills becomes a stimulus for further learning. Gradually the use of these skills becomes integrated seamlessly into the 'person' of the practitioner, maturing and changing as the practitioner develops both personally and professionally.

The rewards and challenges of learning about and using counselling and psychotherapy skills is that there is no finite body of knowledge and skills to acquire. Developing these skills has the potential for ongoing personal and professional fulfilment, self-realization and interest.

What matters to clients?

It is important not to become too precious about the nuances and subtleties of these skills. Clients do not come into therapy looking for a particular technique to be applied on them. The come into therapy for a relational experience. Theory and skills may be absorbing for the therapist but it is worth remembering that when used well they become invisible to the client. Like the pianist from Chapter 2, all the hard, technical work that goes into learning the first scale to a performance of a concerto, is transformed into something that appears effortless and flowing to an audience.

From the clients' perspective, what seems to matter is often much more fundamental and basic. It is their sense and experience of:

- you as a person and your personal qualities, including your trustworthiness
- your ability to relate to them, especially the quality of your listening and the attention that you give both to them and to what they tell you

- the level of safety that you provide that allows them to be vulnerable and to experiment with new possibilities – clients are often looking for the personal equivalent of a safe harbour in a storm or an anchor in a running sea.

Don't take our word for this. Ask your clients! You may be as surprised as we have been by their answers. You may be astounded by the examples of wisdom and knowledge that are offered to you by your clients, as well as surprised at some of the misunderstandings that might have otherwise gone unmentioned.

Clients' views are important. It is the work with our clients that justifies the investment of time and resources in acquiring and using counselling and psychotherapy skills. Our clients' views are probably the best possible foundation on which to build our development as therapists.

Closing thoughts

As I (Megan) write the final few pages of this book, I am simultaneously coming to another end of an academic year (2018/2019) and saying goodbye to my cohort of students – trainees on a psychotherapy training course. These are students who, next year, will begin working with clients in practice for the first time. As we said our goodbyes on the last day of teaching, and considered their transition to the next phase of their training journey, these students bravely shared their feelings through poems, literature, the sharing of gifts and their own words about the ending of one year and the beginning of the next. I was reminded of the resilience, courage, passion and *com*passion, integrity, humility and commitment I had witnessed through the teaching year – qualities that they will need to take with them into their respective therapy rooms as they begin to apply their learning with their own clients. As you consider training and working with your own clients, perhaps for the first time, or perhaps with renewed interest, I would like to share a quote from the following poem with you, with special thanks to Brad McCaw one of my students who shared this with his training group on our final day:

Awaken your spirit to adventure;

Hold nothing back, learn to find ease in risk;

Soon you will be home in a new rhythm,

For your soul senses the world that awaits you. (O'Donohue, 2008)

Glossary

2-person philosophy   A theory that espouses the inseparable nature of interpersonal relating, and of individuals as participating in a matrix of subjective experiences which shape and co-create our relational world. See also 'relational turn'.

Acceptance   Valuing and affirming others because they are human.

Active listening   Listening with purpose and communicating that you have listened.

Anti-oppressive practice   An approach highlighting social, economic, cultural, racial and gendered oppression and inequalities; focusing on creating an environment which is based on egalitarian and inclusive values, free of discrimination and prejudice.

Anxiety   A feeling of unease, worry and fear manifesting in troubled or disturbing patterns of thought, feelings and physiological functioning.

Bereavement   A period of mourning and grief following a loss.

British Association for Counselling and Psychotherapy (BACP)   Registered charity, limited company and professional association for members of the counselling professions in the UK.

Confidentiality   A commitment that limits access or places restrictions on personal information by way of protecting a client.

Depression   A mood disorder which involves a persistent feeling of deep sadness, negatively affecting thoughts, feelings and behaviour.

Directives   Giving a 'directive' involves the therapist openly directing the client to do something or directing the therapeutic process in some way.

Drama Triangle   A model for thinking about the interpersonal conflicts that clients experience, that may be re-enacted in the therapy room.

Empathy   An attitude and way of being that involves striving to sense your client's world from their perspective, and to be open, sensitive and aware of their experiences.

Equality Act   A legal framework intended to protect the rights of individuals and promote equality of opportunity for everyone. Nine 'protected characteristics' are listed under the Equality Act 2010.

Genuineness   How real we are as people in response to, and in relationship with, our clients.

'Good enough'   A Winnicottian concept originally emphasizing that the mother (seen as the primary caregiver) need only be 'good enough' and does not need to be perfect (Winnicott, 1971).

Immediacy   Focusing on the 'here and now' of the therapy, specifically how the therapist is feeling about the client, about the therapy relationship, or about themselves in relation to the client.

Intersubjective matrix   A concept pertaining to the psychological relationship between people, and the interaction of the subjective experiences of all parties. This matrix contains these different subjectivities highlighting their influence on the interpersonal experience between individuals.

Listening filters   Those things that interfere with our ability to listen, such that some pieces of information are attended to more than others, while other pieces of information are inadvertently 'blocked'. These include culture, personal history and present issues.

Open-ended contract   A contract between therapist and client, where no time limit is placed on the work at its commencement.

Parallel process   A process in which the therapist recreates, or parallels, the client's problems or material in some form, in their own life.

Phenomenological method   A method of inquiry that attempts to gradually eliminate bias, assumptions and interpretations so that we can fully attend to the information we are presented with.

Post-traumatic stress disorder   A diagnosis of an anxiety disorder caused by very stressful, frightening or distressing events.

Presenting issue   The initial and explicit issue(s) a client brings to therapy.

Protective factors   Factors which make it less likely that individuals will consider, attempt or die by suicide.

Psychosis   A diagnosis in which an individual has sensory experiences of things that do not exist and/or beliefs with no basis in reality.

Reflective practice   An examination of our experience and practices, and their component parts.

Reflexivity   A deeper level of reflective practice involving an appreciation for what we perceive, how and when we interact with what we perceive and the meanings we draw out of a given experience, as influenced by our subjective standpoint.

Relational bond   The experience of a positive emotional bond between therapist and client, including things like the degree of trust, respect and sense of affinity between them.

Relational turn   A movement in the fields of counselling and psychotherapy towards viewing human beings as fundamentally connected, experiencing each other in a co-created field of relating. See also '2-person philosophy'.

Risk factors   Factors that indicate a client is at risk of suicide or self-harm.

Self-disclosure   Therapist self-disclosure refers to the therapist actively and explicitly disclosing to their client something personal from his or her own experience.

Self-harm   A behavioural expression of distress involving self-poisoning or injury.

Suicidal ideation   A wish not to exist, to be dead or to die but without any plans to commit suicide.

Suicidal intent   The intent to commit suicide, with clear plans to do so.

Supervision   A regular and protected space for therapists to reflect on their work with their clients, with the intention of supporting and facilitating in-depth learning to develop skills and competencies required in the work, and ultimately to ensure the welfare of and best service for the client.

Therapeutic alliance   A concept that describes the quality and strength of the relationship between therapist and client, and degree of collaboration that exists between them. Commonly understood as being defined by goals, tasks and bonds. Also referred to as 'working alliance'.

Therapeutic tasks   The things that will happen in therapy including in-therapy behaviours and processes.

Therapeutic goals   The aims or purpose of the therapeutic work, what can be achieved and what the outcome(s) might look like.

Therapist competency   The therapist's ability to work with clients skillfully, creatively, ethically and knowledgeably, developing over time and with experience.

Time-conscious therapy   An approach to the therapeutic work which aims to be flexible and individualized to the client, while working within a structured, stage-based contract, or series of contracts.

United Kingdom Council for Psychotherapy (UKCP)   Registered charity, limited company and professional association for psychotherapists and psychotherapeutic counsellors in the UK.

Working therapy contract   A specific commitment from both therapist and client to a clearly defined course of action.

Wounded healer   A Jungian archetype. The concept suggests that we can use our own wounds in the service of our clients as they increase our capacity for, and experience of, empathy and humanness (Jung et al., 1982).

References

Adams, L. (n.d.) Learning a new skill is easier said than done. Available at www.gordon training.com/free-workplace-articles/learning-a-new-skill-is-easier-said-than-done, accessed on 5 July 2019.

Adler, H.M. (2002) The sociophysiology of caring in the doctor–patient relationship, *Journal of General Internal Medicine*, 17, 11: 883–90.

American Psychiatric Association (2013) *Diagnostic and Statistical Manual of Mental Disorders* (5th edition). Arlington, VA: American Psychiatric Association.

Bager-Charleson, S. (2010) *Reflective Practice in Counselling and Psychotherapy*. London: SAGE.

Bandelow, B. and Michaelis, S. (2015) Epidemiology of anxiety disorders in the 21st century, *Dialogues Clin Neurosci*, 17, 3: 327–35.

Barnett, J.E., Baker, E.K., Elman, N.S. and Schoener, G.R. (2007) In pursuit of wellness: the self-care imperative, *Professional Psychology: Research and Practice*, 38, 6: 603–12.

Björk & Hooper, N. (1993) *Big Time Sensuality* [from the album Debut]. One Little Indian Records.

Bond, T. (2015) *Standards and Ethics for Counselling in Action* (4th edition). London: SAGE.

Bordin, E.S. (1979) The generalizability of the psychoanalytic concept of the working alliance, *Psychotherapy: Theory, Research & Practice*, 16, 3: 252–60.

Boyle, M. (2007) The problem with diagnosis, *The Psychologist*, 20, 5: 290–92.

British Association for Counselling and Psychotherapy (BACP) (2016) *Clinical Reflections for Practice: Equality, Diversity and Inclusion within the Counselling Professions*. Leicestershire: BACP.

Buber, M. (1958) *I and Thou* (R.G. Smith, trans.). New York: Charles Scribner and Sons. (Original work published 1923.)

Cacioppo, J.T., Hughes, M.E., Waite, L.J., Hawkley, L.C. and Thisted, R.A. (2006) Loneliness as a specific risk factor for depressive symptoms: cross-sectional and longi-tudinal analyses, *Psychology and Aging*, 21, 1: 140–51.

Carroll, M. and Gilbert, M. (2011) *On Being a Supervisee: Creating Learning Partnerships*. Ealing, London: Vukani Publishing.

Christiansen, E. and Jensen, B.F. (2007) Risk of repetition of suicide attempt, suicide or all deaths after an episode of attempted suicide: a register-based survival analysis, *Australian & New Zealand Journal of Psychiatry*, 41: 257–65.

Chughani, H., Behen, M., Muzik, O., Juhasz, C., Nagy, F. and Chughani, D. (2001) Local brain functional activity following early deprivation: a study of post-institutionalised Romanian orphans, *Neuroimage* 14: 1290–1301.

Clarkson, P. (1995) *The Therapeutic Relationship*. London: Whurr Publishers.

Cooper, M. (2008) *Essential Research Findings in Counselling and Psychotherapy: The Facts are Friendly*. London: SAGE.

Cozolino, L. (2016) *Why Therapy Works*. New York: W.W. Norton & Company.

Cruse Breavement Care (2012) *About Grief*. Available at www.cruse.org.uk/get-help/about-grief, accessed on 22nd July 2019.

Daines, B., Gask, L. and Usherwood, T. (2007) *Medical and Psychiatric Issues for Counsellors* (2nd edition). London: SAGE.

De Young, P.A. (2015) *Relational Psychotherapy. A Primer* (2nd edition). New York: Routledge.

Dryden, W. and Feltham, C. (2006) *Brief Counselling: A Practical Guide for Beginning Practitioners* (2nd edition). Milton Keynes: Open University Press.

Egan, G. (2006) *The Skilled Helper: A Problem-Management and Opportunity-Development Approach to Helping* (International edition). Belmont, CA: Cengage Learning.

Eldrid, D. (1988) *Caring for the Suicidal*. London: Constable.

Elliot, M. and Williams, D. (2003) The client experience of counselling and psychotherapy, *Counselling Psychology Review*, 18, 1.

Elliot, R., Bohart, A.C., Watson, J.C. and Murphy, D. (2018) Therapist empathy and client outcome: an updated meta-analysis, *Psychotherapy*, 55, 4: 399–410.

Elton-Wilson, J. (1996) *Time-Conscious Counselling and Psychotherapy*. Chichester: Wiley.

Ericcson, K.A. Charness, N., Feltovich, P.J. and Hoffman, R.R. (eds) (2006) *The Cambridge Handbook of Expertise and Expert Performance*. Cambridge: Cambridge University Press.

Etherington, K. and Bridges, N. (2011) Narrative case study research: on endings and six session reviews, *Counselling and Psychotherapy Research*, 11, 1: 11–22.

Evans, K. (1994) Healing shame: a gestalt perspective, *Transactional Analysis Journal*, 24, 2: 1023–108.

Flückiger, C., Del Re, A.C., Wampold, B.E. and Horvath, A.O. (2018) The alliance in adult psychotherapy: a meta-analytic synthesis, *Psychotherapy*, 55, 4: 316–40.

Flückiger, C., Del Re, A.C, Wamplod, B.E. and Horvath, A.O. (2019) Alliance in adult psychotherapy, in J.C. Norcross and M.J. Lambert (eds), *Psychotherapy Relationships that Work. Volume 1: Evidence-based Therapist Contributions* (3rd edition) (pp. 24–78). New York: Oxford University Press.

GDPR (2018) European Union General Data Protection Regulation. Available at: https://ec.europa.eu/commission/priorities/justice-and-fundamental-rights/data-protection/2018-reform-eu-data-protection-rules_en

Gelso, C.J., Kivlighan, D.M. and Markin, R.D. (2018) The real relationship and its role in psychotherapy outcome: a meta-analysis, *Psychotherapy*, 55, 4: 434–44.

Gendlin, E.T. (2003) *Focusing: How to Open up Your Deeper Feelings and Intuition*. London: Vintage/Ebury.

Gerhardt, S. (2004) *Why Love Matters*. Brunner-Routledge: East Sussex.

Gerhardt, S. (2015) Why Love Matters. *How Affection Shapes a Baby's Brain* (2nd edition). Hove: Routledge.

Gilmore, S.K. (1973) *The Counsellor-in-Training*. Englewood Cliffs, NJ: Prentice-Hall.

Hawton, K., Zahl, D. and Weatherall, R. (2003) Suicide following deliberate self-harm: long-term follow-up of patients who presented to a general hospital, *The British Journal of Psychiatry*, 182: 537–42.

Herman, J. (1992) *Trauma and Recovery: The Aftermath of Violence – From Domestic Abuse to Political Terror*. New York: Basic Books.

Hill, C.E. (2004) *Helping Skills: Facilitating, Exploration, Insight, and Action* (2nd edition). Washington, DC: American Psychological Association.

Hill, C.E. and Knox, S. (2001) Self-disclosure, *Psychotherapy*, 38, 4: 413–17.

Hill, C.E., Thompson, B.J. and Landany, N. (2003) Therapist use of silence in therapy: a survey, *Journal of Clinical Psychology*, 59, 4: 513–24.

HM Government (2019) *Cross-Government Suicide Prevention Workplan*. Available at https://assets.publishing.service.gov.uk/government/uploads/system/uploads/attachment_data/file/772210/national-suicide-prevention-strategy-workplan.pdf, accessed on 11 October 2019.

Holmes, J. (2009) *Exploring in Security: Towards an Attachment Informed Psychoanalytic Psychotherapy*. New York: Routledge.

Holt-Lunstad, J., Smith, T.B., Baker, M. and Harris, T. (2015) Loneliness and social isolation as risk factors for mortality: a meta-analytic review, *Perspectives on Psychological Science*, 10, 2: 227–37.

Hopson, B. (1981) Response to the papers by Schlossberg, Brammer and Abrego, *Counselling Psychologist*, 9: 36–9.

Hycner, R. and Jacobs, L. (1995) *The Healing Relationship in Gestalt Psychotherapy*. Gouldsboro, ME: The Gestalt Journal Press Inc.

James, B.D., Wilson, R.S., Barnes, L.L. and Bennett, D.A. (2011) Late-life social activity and cognitive decline in old age, *Journal of the International Neuropsychological Society*, 17, 6: 998–1005.

Johnstone, L. and Boyle, M. with Cromby, J., Dillon, J., Harper, D., Kinderman, P., Longden, E., Pilgrim, D. and Read, J. (2018) *The Power Threat Meaning Framework: Towards the Identification of Patterns in Emotional Distress, Unusual Experiences and Troubled or Troubling Behaviour, as an Alternative to Functional Psychiatric Diagnosis*. Leicester: British Psychological Society.

Joyce, P. and Sills, C. (2014) *Skills in Gestalt Counselling and Psychotherapy*. London: SAGE.

Jung, C., Adler, G. and Hull, R.F.C. (1982) *The Collected Works of Carl Jung. Volume 16: Practice of Psychotherapy*. New Jersey: Princeton University Press.

Karpman, S.B. (1968) Fairy tales and script drama analysis, *Transactional Analysis Bulletin*, 7, 26: 39–43.

Kasper, L., Hill, C.E. and Kivlighan, D.M. (2008) Therapist immediacy in brief psychotherapy: case study I, *Psychotherapy Theory, Research, Practice, Training*, 45, 3: 281–97.

Klass, D. and Steffen, E.M. (eds) (2018) *Continuing Bonds in Bereavement*. New York: Routledge.

Kohut, H. (1984) *How Does Analysis Cure?* Chicago: University of Chicago Press.

Kolb, D. (1984) *Experiential Learning*. Englewood Cliffs, New Jersey: Prentice Hall.

Landany, N., Hill, C.E., Thompson, B.J. and O'Brien, K.M. (2004) Therapist perspectives on using silence in therapy: a qualitative study, *Counselling and Psychotherapy Research*, 4, 1: 80–9.

Larkin, C., Di Blasi, Z., Arensman, E. (2014) Risk factors for repetition of self-harm: a systematic review of prospective hospital-based studies, *PLOS One*, 9, 1: 1–13. Available at: www.plosone.org

Leijssen, M. (2006) Validation of the body in psychotherapy, *Journal of Humanistic Psychology*, 46, 2: 126–46.

Lister Ford, C. (2002) *Skills in Transactional Analysis Counselling and Psychotherapy*. London: SAGE.

Luft, J. and Ingham, H. (1955) The Johari window, a graphic model of interpersonal awareness. *Proceedings of the Western Training Laboratory in Group Development*. Los Angeles: University of California.

Lyons-Ruth, K. (1999) The two-person unconscious: intersubjective dialogue, enactive relational representation, and the emergence of new forms of relational organization, *Psychoanalytic Inquiry*, 19: 576–617.

Mandal, M.K. and Ambady, N. (2004) Laterality of facial expressions of emotion: universal and culture-specific influences, *Behavioural Neurology*, 15: 23–34.

Marmarosh, C.L. (2017) Fostering engagement during termination: applying attachment theory and research, *Psychotherapy*, 54, 1: 4–9.

McLeod, J. (2009) *An Introduction to Counselling* (4th edition). Maidenhead: Open University Press.

Mearns, D. and Cooper, M. (2018) *Working at Relational Depth* (2nd edition). London: SAGE.

Mearns, D. and Dryden, W. (eds) (1990) *Experiences of Counselling in Action*. London: SAGE.

Mearns, D. and Thorne, B. (1988) *Person-Centred Counselling in Action*. London: SAGE.

Mearns, D. and Thorne, B. (2007) *Person-Centred Counselling in Action* (3rd edition). London: SAGE.

Mental Health Foundation (2012) *Mental Health Statistics: The Most Common Mental Health Problems*. Available at www.mentalhealth.org.uk/statistics/mental-health-statistics-most-common-mental-health-problems, accessed on 22 July 2019.

Miller, S., Hubble, M. and Duncan, B. (2005) *The Secrets of Supershrinks: Pathways to Clinical Excellence*. Psychotherapy Networker. Available at: https://www.scottdmiller.com/wp-content/uploads/2014/06/Supershrinks-Free-Report-1.pdf (accessed 20 January 2020).

Miller, S.D., Duncan, B.L., Brown, J., Sorrell, R. and Chalk, M.B. (2006) Using formal client feedback to improve retention and outcome: making ongoing, real-time assessment feasible, *Journal of Brief Therapy*, 5, 1: 5–22.

Murphy, D. and Cramer, D. (2014) Mutuality of Rogers' therapeutic conditions and treatment progress in the first three psychotherapy sessions, *Psychotherapy Research*, 24, 6: 651–61.

National Institute for Health and Care Excellence (NICE) (2004) *Self-Harm: The Short-Term Physical and Psychological Management and Secondary Prevention of Self-Harm in Primary and Secondary Care*. Clinical Guideline 16. London: NICE.

Nelson-Jones, R. (2008) *Introduction to Counselling Skills* (3rd edition). London: SAGE.

Norcross, J.C. and Guy, J.D. (2007) *Leaving it at the Office: A Guide to Psychotherapist Self-care*. New York: Guilford.

Norcross, J. and Hill, C. (2004) Empirically supported therapy relationships, *The Clinical Psychologist*, 17, 3: 19–24.

Norcross, J.C. and Lambert, M.J. (2019) Evidence-based psychotherapy relationship: the third task force, in J.C. Norcross and M.J. Lambert (eds), *Psychotherapy Relationships that Work. Volume 1: Evidence-based Therapist Contributions* (3rd edition) (pp. 1–23). New York: Oxford University Press.

Norcross, J. and Wampold, B.E. (2010) What works for whom: tailoring psychotherapy to the person, *Journal of Clinical Psychology*, 67, 2: 127–32.

O'Donohue, J. (2008) *To Bless This Space between Us: A Book of Blessings*. Doubleday: New York.

Office for National Statistics (ONS) (2017) Suicide by occupation, England: 2011 to 2015. Analysis of deaths from suicide in different occupational groups for people aged 20 to 64 years, based on deaths registered in England between 2011 and 2015. Available at: www.ons.gov.uk/releases/suicidesbyoccupationengland2011to2015, accessed on 16 July 2019.

Oldfield, S. (1983) *The Counselling Relationship: A Study of the Client's Experience*. London: Routledge and Paul.

Palmer, S. and McMahon, G. (eds) (1997) *Client Assessment*. London: SAGE.

Pilgrim, D. (2000) Psychiatric diagnosis: more questions than answers, *The Psychologist*, 13: 302–5.

Porges, S.A. (2011) *The Polyvagal Theory: Neurophysiological Foundations of Emotions, Attachment, Communication, and Self-Regulation*. New York: W.W. Norton & Company.

Porter, C. (1944) *Ev'ry Time We Say Goodbye*. London: Chappell & Company.

Porter, N. (1995) Therapist self-care: a proactive ethical approach, in E.J. Rave and C.C. Larsen (eds) *Ethical Decision Making in Therapy: Feminist Perspectives* (pp. 247–66). New York: Guilford Press.

Reeves, A. (2018) *An Introduction to Counselling and Psychotherapy: From Theory to Practice* (2nd edition). London: SAGE.

Rogers, C. (1957) The necessary and sufficient conditions of therapeutic personality change, *Journal of Consulting Psychology*, 21, 2: 95–103.

Rogers, C.R. (1980) *A Way of Being*. New York: Houghton Mifflin. (Original work published 1961.)

Rogers, C.R. (2004) *On Becoming a Person*. London: Constable & Robinson.

Rothschild, B. (2004) Applying the brakes. Available at www.somatictraumatherapy.com/applying-the-brakes, accessed on 31 July 2019.

Rowe, D. (2003) *Depression: The Way out of Your Prison*. London: Taylor & Francis.

Safran, J.D. and Muran, J.C. (2000) *Negotiating the Therapeutic Alliance: A Relational Treatment Guide*. New York: Guilford Press.

Scaer, R. (2005) *The Trauma Spectrum: Hidden Wounds and Human Resiliency*. New York: W.W. Norton.

Schon, D.A. (1983) *The Reflective Practitioner*. New York: Basic Books.

Schore, A. (2000) Attachment and the regulation of the right brain, *Attachment & Human Development*, 2, 1: 23–47.

Schore, A.N. (2003) *Affect Regulation and the Repair of the Self*. New York: W.W. Norton.

Schore, A.N. (2011) Effects of a secure attachment relationship on right brain development, affect regulation, and infant mental health, *Infant Mental Health Journal*, 22, 1–2: 7–66.

Schore, J.R. and Schore, A.N. (2007) Modern attachment theory: the central role of affect regulation in development and treatment, *Clinical Social Work Journal*, 36, 1: 9–20.

SCoPEd (Scope of Practice and Education) (2019) Available at: www.bacp.co.uk/about-us/advancing-the-profession/scoped/, accessed on 16 July 2019.

Seaman, P., McNeice, V., Yates, G. and McLean, J. (2014) *Resilience for Public Health: Supporting Transformation in People and Communities*. Glasgow: Glasgow Centre for Population Health.

Sharpley, C.F. and Sagris, A. (1995) When does counsellor forward lean influence client-perceived rapport? *British Journal of Guidance and Counselling*, 23, 387–94.

Sharpley, C.F., Jeffrey, A.M. and McMah, T. (2006) Counsellor facial expression and client-perceived rapport, *Counselling Psychology Quarterly*, 19, 4: 343–56.

Siegal, D.J. (2007) *The Mindful Brain: Reflection and Attunement in the Cultivation of Well-Being*. New York: W.W. Norton.

The Slits (1980) *In the Beginning There Was Rhythm / Where There's a Will There's a Way* [Single]. Rough Trade Records and Y Records.

Spinelli, E. (2005) *The Interpreted World: An Introduction to Phenomenological Psychology* (2nd edition). London: SAGE.

Stern, D.N. (2004) *The Present Moment in Psychotherapy and Everyday Life*. New York: W.W. Norton & Company Inc.

Stewart, I. (2007) *Transactional Analysis Counselling in Action* (3rd edition). London: SAGE.

Stolorow, R.D., Atwood, G.E. and Orange, D. (2002) *Worlds of Experience. Interweaving Philosophical and Clinical Dimensions in Psychoanalysis*. New York: Basic Books.

Sugarman, L. (2001) *Life-Span Development: Frameworks, Accounts and Strategies*. Hove: Psychology Press.

Tears for Fears (1985) *Everybody Wants to Rule the World* [from the album *Songs from the Big Chair*]. Phonogram.

Tipper, C.M., Signorini, G. and Grafton, S.T. (2015) Body language in the brain: constructing meaning from expressive movement, *Frontiers in Human Neuroscience*, 9: 450.

Tolan, J. (2017) *Skills in Person-Centred Counselling and Psychotherapy*. London: SAGE.

Truax, C.B. and Carkhuff, R.R. (1967) *Towards Effective Counselling and Psychotherapy Training and Practice*. Chicago, IL: Aldine.

Valtorta, N.K., Kanaan, M., Gilbody, S., Ronzi, S. and Hanratty B. (2016) Loneliness and social isolation as risk factors for coronary heart disease and stroke: systematic review and meta-analysis of longitudinal observational studies, *Heart*, 102: 1009–16.

Van der Kolk, B. (1996) Trauma and memory, in B. van der Kolk, A. McFarlane and L. Weiseath, L. (eds) *Traumatic Stress. The Effects of Overwhelming Experience on Mind, Body and Society* (pp. 279–302). New York: Guilford Press.

Van Rijn, B. (2015) *Assessment and Care Formulation in Counselling and Psychotherapy*. London: SAGE.

Wallin, D.J. (2007) *Attachment in Psychotherapy*. New York: Guilford Press.

Winnicott, D.W. (1971) *Playing and Reality*. London: Tavistock Publications Ltd.

Woodfox, A. (2019) *Solitary*. Melbourne: The Text Publishing Company.

Worden, J.W. (2010) *Grief Counselling and Grief Therapy: A Handbook for the Mental Health Practitioner* (4th edition). London: Routledge.

World Health Organization (WHO) (2017) *Depression: Let's Talk*. Available at www.who.int/mental_health/management/depression/en, accessed on 22 July 2019.

Yalom, I. (1989) *Love's Executioner and Other Tales of Psychotherapy*. London: Penguin Books.

Yalom, I. (1995) *The Theory and Practice of Group Psychotherapy*. New York: Basic Books.

Yalom, I. (2002) *The Gift of Therapy*. New York: Harper Collins. On prest fuga. Et odis aut accusdant voluptatum eos illamusandam se nullectur aut evellab orrum, imolupt

Zachary, L. (2002) *The Mentor's Guide: Facilitating Effective Learning Relationships*. San Francisco, CA: Jossey-Bass.

Index

CPSIA information can be obtained
at www.ICGtesting.com
Printed in the USA
BVHW010423180720
583891BV00015B/359